Silver Burdett & Ginn

SCIENCE

Chapter 13 pp. 306–307. Material courtesy of the U.S. Space Camp, Huntsville, Alabama; p. 307; © 1987 Young Astronaut™ Council. All rights reserved.

Chapter 14 pp. 336–337. Based on an article by Sharon Begley with Patricia King, "The Deadliest Kind of Cold" in *Newsweek*, March 9, 1987, and an article by C. Eugene Emery, Jr., "Surviving Underwater" in the *Providence Sunday Journal,* January 25, 1987. Reprinted courtesy of Newsweek Magazine and by permission of the Providence Journal Company. Copyright © 1987.

Chapter 15 pp. 358–359. Based on information in MACMILLAN ILLUSTRATED ALMANAC FOR KIDS, by Ann Elwood, Carol Orsag, and Sydney Solomon. New York, Macmillan Publishing Company, 1981, p. 84–88, 367, 368, 388, 389. Copyright © 1981. Information on Midori printed courtesy of I.C.M. Artists, Ltd.

Contents

The Adventure of Science

What Is Science?

Why can't a perpetual motion machine be built? How does the giving off of an odor like rotting flesh help the rafflesia (rə flē′ zhē ə) plant to survive? How are lava tubes formed? How does cancer harm healthy cells?

Science is a way of asking and answering questions like these. Science can be divided into four areas. One area of science involves living things. A second area studies matter and energy. The earth and outer space are studied in a third area of science. The fourth area includes the study of the human body. Into which area of science would you place each of the photos shown here?

B

What Will You Learn in Science?

Scientists try to understand how and why things happen the way they do. The process all scientists use to do this is called the scientific method. In using the scientific method, scientists form a hypothesis about something they observe. The hypothesis is a statement that explains an event. Then the scientists test their hypothesis. Scientists often test hypotheses with experiments. They gather and analyze data, and draw conclusions.

In science class you will learn to use the scientific method. For example, this boy and girl wanted to know which balloon rocket would travel faster — one made with a round balloon or one made with a long balloon. They found that the long balloon travels faster. How could you use the scientific method to understand why this happened? What hypothesis can you make? How could you test your hypothesis?

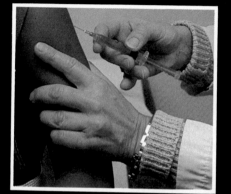

How Is Science Important in My Life?

In history, certain important events stand out because they are turning points. These turning points changed the way people live. Many turning points involve scientific discoveries or inventions. The invention of the light bulb is one such turning point. The discovery of penicillin is another. Some people might say that a recent turning point is the discovery of interferon. Find out about interferon. How might it affect your life? What other new discoveries or inventions might be turning points?

An Egg-Citing Discovery

Try to solve this science problem. Imagine that you are a scientist in the year 3000. You are exploring a deserted island off the west coast of North America. You are on an expedition to learn more about the people who lived there hundreds of years earlier. You know that the people were forced to leave the island because of constant lava floods from volcanoes on the island. However, you know nothing else about this civilization of the distant past.

You and the other scientists are excited about the discovery of a small egg-shaped object. The object was left unchanged in volcanic ash. Where did the object come from? Was it ever alive? What evidence does the egg provide about the people? What conclusions can you draw about the people, using only this small object?

The Mystery of the Dinosaurs' Last Days

Suppose you could step into a time machine and go back in history to find the answer to a single question. What question would spark your imagination enough to take you on such a journey? For many people that question is, What really did happen to the dinosaurs?

Some scientists try to answer this question every day. The time machine these scientists use is the layers of rock beneath their feet. The story of the dinosaurs is written there. While they know the dinosaurs became extinct, the mystery of <u>how</u> they became extinct is still unsolved.

Why is it so difficult to determine what caused the disappearance of the dinosaurs? One reason is that understanding something that happened millions of years ago requires finding indirect evidence. It is difficult to find and understand clues that have been hidden for so long.

Scientists have proposed a number of hypotheses to explain the disappearance of the dinosaurs. Some are shown here. In order for any hypothesis about the disappearance of the dinosaurs to be accepted, it must explain a number of facts. For example, many scientists believe that all the dinosaurs, along with many other plants and animals, disappeared around the same time. Also, scientists believe that the disappearance of dinosaurs occurred both on land and in the sea.

Determining why the dinosaurs disappeared is like putting together a puzzle. In 1977 a new piece to the puzzle was found accidentally. A scientist named Walter Alvarez was studying the layers of rock in the hills of Italy. Something unusual caught his eye. One layer contained thousands of tiny fossils. The layer on top of the first layer looked like dull red clay. There were no fossils in this layer. On top of the clay layer was another layer of rock that contained more fossils. To everyone's surprise, these fossils were completely different from the fossils in the first layer.

The clay sparked Dr. Alvarez's curiosity. It came from around the time that many dinosaurs and other living things became extinct. Could this clay contain a clue to their disappearance?

Dr. Alvarez sent a sample of the clay to a laboratory at the University of California to be analyzed. He was astounded at the results. The clay contained large amounts of iridium, a rare metal found only in small amounts on the earth. Where could the iridium have come from?

Working with his father, geologist Luis Alvarez, Walter formed a hypothesis. Objects in space, such as asteroids and comets, contain large amounts of iridium. Suppose a large object from space collided with the earth during the time the dinosaurs were alive. Rock dust and iridium particles would have been thrown into the atmosphere and would have blocked the sun's light. Why did the scientists think this could have caused animals and plants to become extinct?

The scientists began to search for evidence to support their hypothesis. The scientists went to other parts of the world. They studied rock layers from the time of the dinosaur's extinction. At all the locations, they found high levels of iridium in the clay. How do these facts support their hypothesis?

Not all scientists agree with Alvarez's hypothesis. Some scientists argue that there are many unanswered questions. They want to know where the crater formed by the collision can be found. They ask why some dinosaur fossils in Alaska indicate that dinosaurs there did not die when others in the world did. Finally, they ask how any plants and animals survived such a disaster.

What really happened to the dinosaurs? Scientists are getting closer to solving the puzzle. That makes this an exciting time. But more evidence still needs to be gathered. What do you think about Dr. Alvarez's hypothesis?

UNIT ONE

Investigating Our Living World

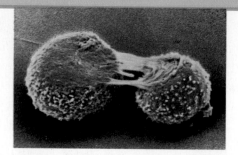

Chapter 1—Living Things Living things are made up of one or more cells. New cells are formed by cell division, shown here. In this chapter you will find out how cells function as the basic units of life.

Chapter 3—Animal Adaptations This Rocky Mountain bighorn sheep feels at home on narrow rocky ledges and steep slippery slopes. Chapter 3 presents ways that animals are adapted to living in different environments.

Chapter 2 — Plant Growth and Responses

An unsuspecting fly is about to become a meal for this plant. Many plants make their food, but the Venus's-flytrap is adapted to catching its food. Plants grow and respond to their environment in different ways.

Chapter 4 — Climate and Life

These coral polyps, found in the Red Sea, open only at night. In Chapter 4 you will learn about different regions of the earth — each inhabited by only certain kinds of plants and animals.

1

CHAPTER 1
Living Things

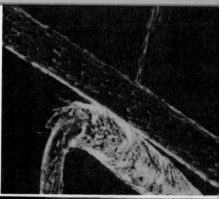

When you hear the words *living things,* what comes to your mind? Do you think of dogs? Cats? Horses? Flowers? Trees? All of these things are large enough for humans to see easily. But there are uncounted numbers of living things just barely large enough for us to see with the unaided eye. The details of their structure are beyond the range of the human eye. Still more living things are too small to be seen except with a hand lens or microscope. These living things are part of an unseen world. We are going to explore this "unseen" world in this chapter.

Mosquito sucking up blood

Imagine that it is summertime. A mosquito has just landed on your arm, and you are about to swat it. This stinging crea-creature is fairly small. From what you can see, its six legs look almost smooth. Its stinger looks thinner than a strand of hair.

Come a little closer. With the help of a hand lens, you can see the mosquito piercing your skin with its stinger. You can see the mosquito's body filling up with blood. A mosquito can suck up its own weight in blood and still fly.

Move a little closer. You can see the mosquito much better now. You are using a special kind of microscope that can magnify objects hundreds of times. You have a good view of the mosquito's legs. As you can now see, the legs are not completely smooth. They are covered with tiny scale-like structures. The insect's head has little clumps of "hair." And look at that stinger! Now it looks really deadly. It has a pair of sharp needlelike parts that can pierce skin. Look at the sharp spines along the sides of the point of the stinger.

Mosquito on human skin

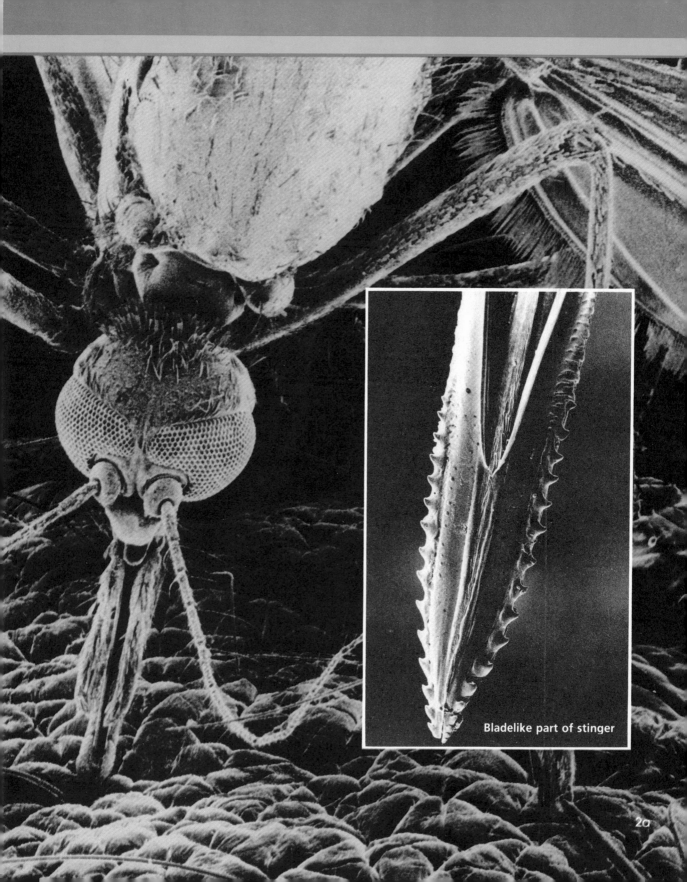

Bladelike part of stinger

2a

The arrow points to a tiny mite riding on a mosquito.

2b

Has a tiny creature landed on the mosquito's body? Come in for a closer look. You are aided by a microscope that can magnify objects thousands of times. You can see that there is a tiny mite clinging to the hairs on the mosquito's body. A white arrow points to the mite. This tiny living thing does not harm the mosquito. It is just hitching a ride!

Can there be any living things smaller than a mite? Do you think these tiny creatures could be clinging to the mite's body? Sure enough, there are organisms living in and on the body of the mite. These organisms are called bacteria (bak tir' ē ə). One of these tiny organisms is shown on this page.

2c

Can there be anything in or on the bacterium? The photographs on this page show tiny things called viruses (vī′ rəs əz) that are in bacteria. The viruses multiply inside the bacteria. In time, the viruses cause the bacteria to burst.

How small are viruses? About 700,000 viruses lined up side by side could fit across the width of this page.

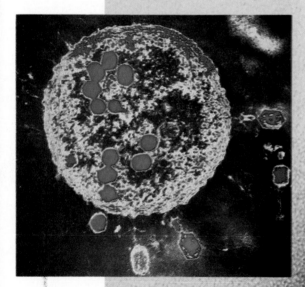

2d

You have just looked at photographs of very small, thin things. Some things you see every day are "thin." How thin are they? How can they be measured? Use a metric ruler to measure the thickness of the following thin objects: the cover of this book, a dime, a paper clip, a sheet of notebook paper, and a bristle of a paintbrush. Decide on a method for taking these measurements. You may wish to use several of the objects to find the thickness of a single object. Write your method down on a sheet of paper. Take the measurements. Compare your results with those of other students in your class.

In this chapter you will learn about some of the smallest living things known to scientists. You will find out how living things are alike and how they are different. You will also learn how living things differ from nonliving things.

Living and Nonliving

How do living things differ from nonliving things?

Triggerfish

Ant

What living things do you see in these pictures? How can you tell whether something is living or nonliving? All living things carry out certain activities called life processes. These life processes distinguish living things from nonliving things.

What are these life processes? First, living things grow. In the spring, for example, new plants grow from seeds in the soil. New leaves grow on trees, and trees also grow in size. If you have ever had a puppy or a kitten, you have seen your pet grow bigger. How much have you grown since last year? Nonliving things, like rocks and sand, do not grow the way living things grow.

Second, living things can respond to the world around them. For example, plants may respond to

Ghost crab

Canada geese

sunlight by growing toward it. Flowers may open in the morning and close at night. A frog will jump if you try to catch it. If you see a car coming, you will step back onto the sidewalk instead of trying to cross the street. Nonliving things do not respond in these ways.

Third, living things can produce more living things like themselves. This process is called reproduction. Different living things reproduce in different ways. Some plants produce seeds that grow into new plants. Other plants, like mushrooms, reproduce from seedlike parts called spores. Still other plants grow directly from a parent plant. New strawberry plants grow in this way. The young of some animals are born alive. Examples are bear cubs, deer fawns, and baby rabbits. Canada geese lay eggs from which the baby geese hatch. Young lizards, such as the one shown in the picture, also hatch from eggs. Nonliving things cannot produce more of themselves.

Finally, living things need energy. They need energy to grow, to respond, and to reproduce. Where do living things get this energy? You get your energy from food. All living things need food to get energy to carry out their life processes.

Jack rabbit

Horned lizard

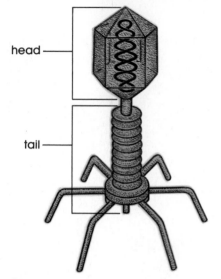

head

tail

Structure of a virus

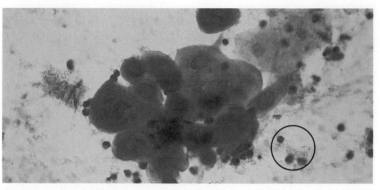

Photomicrograph of a virus (circled)

Scientists have a special name for living things. A living thing is called an **organism** (ôr′gə niz əm). Birds and trees are organisms, but feathers and bark are not. Feathers and bark are only parts of organisms. They cannot live on their own.

All organisms are alike in that they carry out the life processes that were mentioned earlier. All organisms are alike in another way. They are all made of cells. A **cell** is the smallest living part of an organism. Many organisms, such as the plants and animals that you know, are made of millions of cells. The cells of plants and animals are alike in some ways, but very different in other ways.

Some things that reproduce seem to be neither living nor nonliving, nor are they made of cells. These things are called **viruses** (vī′rəs es). Perhaps you have been sick and been told that you had a virus. By itself a virus is not a living thing. Yet it can do some of the same things that a living thing can do. A virus can produce more of its own kind, and it uses energy. But a virus cannot do these things on its own. A virus uses the energy of a living cell to reproduce. Hundreds of viruses may form inside a cell. The cell may even explode. This is how viruses spread to other cells. Although a virus is not a living cell, it does seem to be a complex chemical link between living and nonliving things.

For Lesson Questions, turn to page 384.

Animal Cells

What are the parts of an animal cell?

Almost all animal cells are alike in certain ways. Most animal cells have a nucleus (nü′klē əs). The **nucleus** is a round body inside the cell. It controls the cell's activities. Find the nucleus in the picture of the cheek cell.

Now look at the drawing. Notice that the nucleus is surrounded by a membrane called the nuclear membrane (nü′klē ər mem′brān). The nucleus contains threadlike structures called **chromosomes** (krō′mə sōmz). How many chromosomes are there in the nucleus shown in the drawing? It is known that the cell's genes are on the chromosomes. The **genes** are the tiny units that control most of the cell's activities. Since the genes are in the nucleus, the nucleus is referred to as the cell's control center.

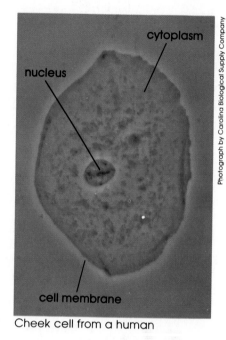

Cheek cell from a human

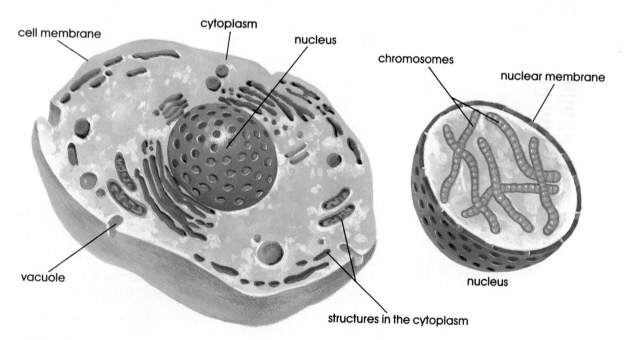

Animal cell

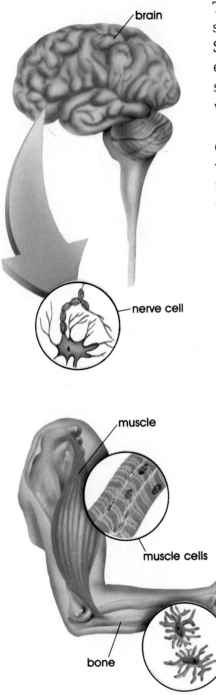

CELLS FROM THE BODY

brain

nerve cell

muscle

muscle cells

bone

bone cells

Animal cells have a jellylike material called the **cytoplasm** (sī′tə plaz əm) that surrounds the nucleus. The cytoplasm has many small structures in it. These structures carry out activities that keep the cell alive. Some carry out chemical reactions that release energy for cell activities. Some destroy disease-causing substances that get into the cell. Others provide pathways for the movement of materials within the cell.

Sometimes, small clear regions can be seen in the cytoplasm. Such regions are actually structures called **vacuoles** (vak′yu̇ ōlz). In some vacuoles, the clear fluid inside contains stored food for the cell. Other vacuoles hold waste materials.

All animal cells are surrounded by a **cell membrane.** The cell membrane helps to control the movement of materials into and out of the cell. The cell membrane is somewhat like a fence around a house. Nothing can enter or leave the cell without going through the cell membrane. Just as some things cannot get past a fence, some materials are too large to pass through the cell membrane. Find the cytoplasm, vacuoles, and cell membrane of the cell in the drawing on page 7.

There are many kinds of animal cells. Different kinds of cells may have different shapes. Some different kinds of cells found in the body are shown here. Compare these cells. How are all of these cells alike? How are they different?

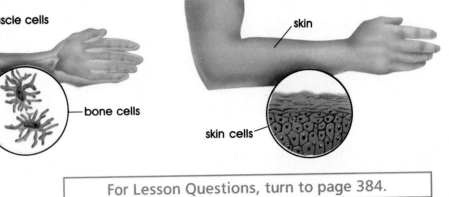

skin

skin cells

8

For Lesson Questions, turn to page 384.

What do cheek cells look like? Activity

Materials medicine dropper / water / microscope slide / flat toothpick / iodine solution / coverslip / microscope

Procedure

A. Use a medicine dropper to put a drop of water on a microscope slide.

B. Collect some cheek cells. Gently rub the inside of your cheek with the large end of a flat toothpick.

C. Roll the large end of the toothpick in the water on the slide. Add a drop of iodine solution to the water. *Caution Iodine will stain and can be harmful if swallowed.* Place a coverslip over the water. Gently tap the coverslip to get rid of the air bubbles under it.

    1. What will the iodine do to the cells?

D. Observe the cheek cells under the low power of the microscope.

    2. Draw a few of the cells.

E. Observe the cheek cells under high power. Focus on one cell and identify the cell parts.

    3. Make a drawing of the cell. Label the cell parts you identified.

Conclusion

1. What do cheek cells look like?
2. What differences did you see when observing the cells under low and high power?
3. When making your observations, how could you tell an air bubble from a cheek cell?

Using science ideas

Observe other materials, such as tissue paper and salt grains, under the microscope. How do those materials compare in appearance with cells?

Plant Cells

How do plant cells differ from animal cells?

Plant cells, like animal cells, have a nucleus, cytoplasm, and a cell membrane. However, plant cells differ from animal cells in an important way. Outside the cell membrane, plant cells have a thick wall called the **cell wall.** Find the cell wall in the drawing below.

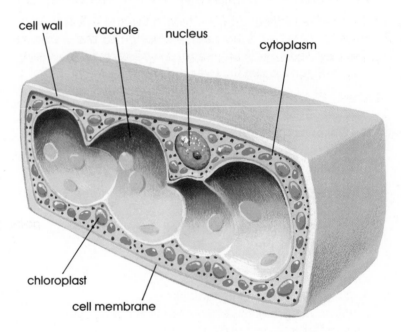

cell wall   vacuole   nucleus   cytoplasm

chloroplast

cell membrane

Plant cell

The cell wall and the cell membrane are different. The cell membrane is very thin and is a living part of the cell. The cell wall is thick and is a nonliving part of the cell. The cell wall gives shape and strength to the plant cell. Why do plants need cells with strong walls?

In addition to a cell wall, some plant cells have other structures not found in animal cells. These structures are called **chloroplasts** (klôr'ə plasts).

Chloroplasts are little bundles of **chlorophyll** (klôr′ə fil), the green coloring matter in plants. Those plant parts that contain cells with chloroplasts appear green. Leaves, for example, contain chloroplasts. Plant cells make their own food in the chloroplasts. There the chlorophyll traps energy from sunlight. This energy is used to make food from carbon dioxide and water. A plant cell may contain many chloroplasts. You can see chloroplasts in the picture showing cells from a water plant.

Plant cells also contain vacuoles. However, the vacuoles in plant cells are often larger than those in animal cells. A single vacuole may take up most of the space in a plant cell, pushing the nucleus to one side.

You learned that animal cells have different shapes. Plant cells also have different shapes. The shape of a cell is often related to the cell's function. Some kinds of plant cells are shown here. How are all of these cells alike? How are they different?

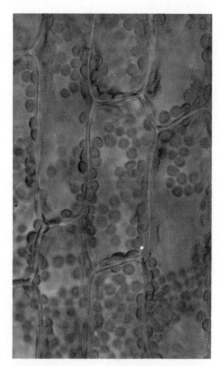

Cells from a water plant

CELLS FROM PLANT PARTS

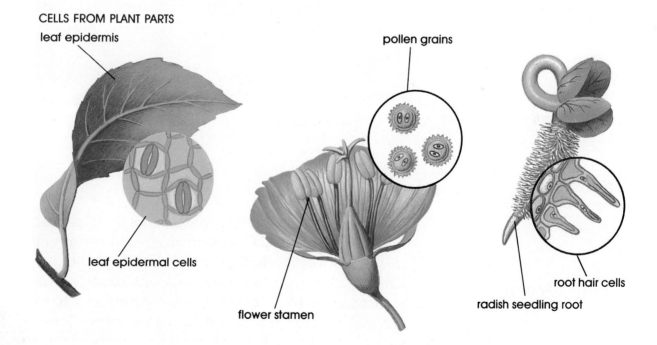

leaf epidermis

leaf epidermal cells

pollen grains

flower stamen

root hair cells

radish seedling root

11

Now look at the pictures. These pictures were taken through a microscope. Some of the pictures show animal cells and some show plant cells. Which cell parts listed in the table can you identify? Which pictures show plant cells?

Cell part	Found in animal cells	Found in plant cells
Nucleus	Yes	Yes
Cytoplasm	Yes	Yes
Cell membrane	Yes	Yes
Cell wall	No	Yes
Chloroplasts	No	In some
Vacuoles	Yes	Yes

For Lesson Questions, turn to page 384.

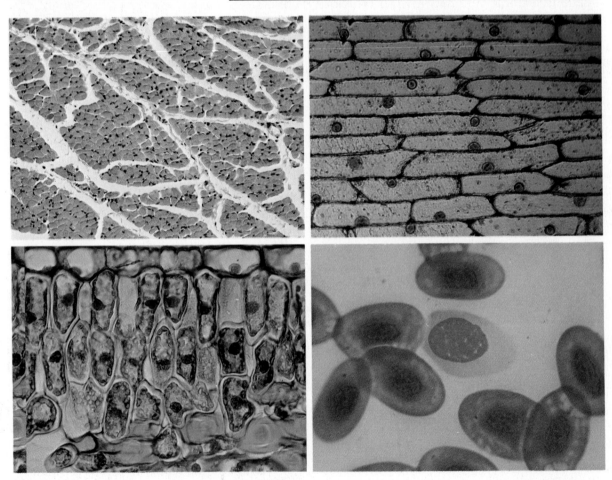

Activity

What do onion cells look like?

Materials   medicine dropper / water / microscope slide / piece of onion / tweezers / iodine solution / coverslip / microscope

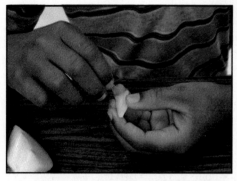

Procedure
A. Put a drop of water in the center of a slide.

B. Bend a piece of onion back so that it breaks in two. Slowly pull the two halves apart. A thin layer of tissue will peel off. With tweezers or your fingers, remove a piece of the tissue.
   1. Why is a thin layer of tissue used?

C. Float the onion tissue in the drop of water. The tissue must lie flat. Add a drop of iodine to the water. **Caution** *Iodine will stain and can be harmful if swallowed.* Place a coverslip over the tissue.

D. Observe the tissue under the low power of the microscope.
   2. Draw several of the cells you see.

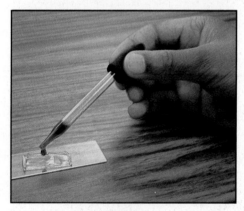

E. Observe the tissue under high power. Focus on one cell and identify the cell parts.
   3. Make a drawing of the cell. Label the cell parts you identified.

Conclusion
1. What do onion cells look like?
2. List the cell parts you observed. What is the function of each part?

Using science ideas
Observe cells from a lettuce leaf, a tomato skin, and other plant parts. Compare these observations with those for onion cells.

How Cells Reproduce

Most plants and animals are made of many cells. Your body is made of trillions of cells. But cells can become damaged or worn out. For example, each day you rub off thousands of skin cells as you wash. How does your body replace the cells that it loses?

New cells are formed by cell division. During cell division, one cell divides into two new cells. This process is called **mitosis** (mī tō′sis). The drawings and pictures show how a cell divides into two cells during mitosis. Refer to them as you read about each stage of mitosis.

1. As mitosis begins, the nuclear membrane starts to break apart. The cell's chromosomes get thicker at this time and can now be seen with a microscope. Each chromosome has made a copy of itself. Therefore, each chromosome is now actually two identical chromosomes that are attached.

2. The chromosomes line up in the center of the cell. A web or network of fibers appears to be connected to the chromosomes.

3. The pairs of identical chromosomes separate. One member of each pair moves to one end of the cell. The other member moves to the opposite end of the cell. There are now two groups of identical chromosomes at opposite ends of the cell.

4. A nuclear membrane forms around each group of chromosomes. A cell membrane develops down the middle of the cell. In this final stage of mitosis, two new identical cells are formed.

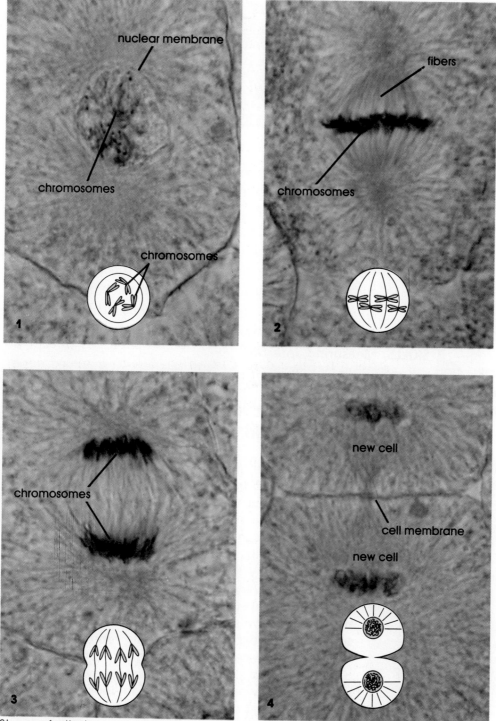

nuclear membrane

chromosomes

chromosomes

1

fibers

chromosomes

2

chromosomes

3

new cell

cell membrane

new cell

4

Stages of mitosis

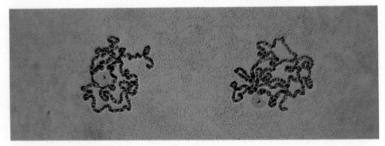
Fruit fly chromosomes

Perhaps you are wondering why the chromosomes made copies of themselves. Remember that the chromosomes contain the cell's genes. The genes control the cell's activities. During mitosis, each cell gets a complete set of chromosomes. Therefore, each cell gets a complete set of genes. If the chromosomes didn't make copies of themselves, each cell would be missing some genes. Then the cells probably would not be able to function properly.

SKILLS: Measuring, Inferring

Finding Out

What would happen if your old cells did not die?

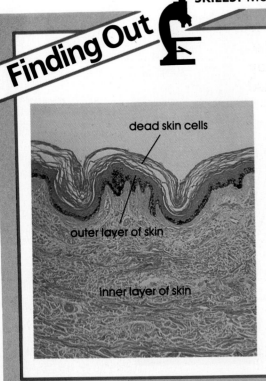
dead skin cells

outer layer of skin

inner layer of skin

It is estimated that the body of the average person is made of 100 trillion (100,000,000,000,000) cells. Scientists believe that each second, millions of the old cells die. Of course, new cells are constantly forming through the process of mitosis. Compared with some other body cells, skin cells reproduce rapidly. They reproduce every 10 hours. Suppose that none of your old skin cells ever died. Also suppose that one million (1,000,000) of your skin cells reproduce in 10 hours. How many new skin cells would be formed? Now suppose that each of those cells reproduce. How many new skin cells would there be 10 hours later? How many new skin cells would you have after 100 hours? Predict what your body might look like. Why is it important that old cells die?

For Lesson Questions, turn to page 384.

Single Cells

What kinds of organisms exist as single cells?

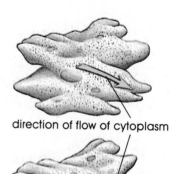

direction of flow of cytoplasm

Some organisms are made of just a single cell. A single-celled organism is called a **protist** (prō′tist). A microscope is usually needed to see protists. Most protists live in water or in moist places. The protists can be separated into three groups — animallike protists, plantlike protists, and bacteria (bak tir′ē ə).

The animallike protists are called **protozoans** (prō tə zō′ənz). Protozoans do not have chloroplasts, so they cannot make their own food. Protozoans are usually classified by the way they move.

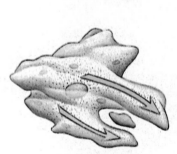

Some protozoans, like the amoebas (ə mē′bəz) shown here, move with a flowing motion. Their cytoplasm is constantly moving. The flowing cytoplasm presses against the cell membrane at a certain place. The drawings show how the shape of the amoeba changes as the membrane bulges outward. These protozoans flow along in the direction of the bulge, much like flowing syrup. They eat other protists by flowing around and over them. Once one of these other protists is surrounded, it is taken into the cell.

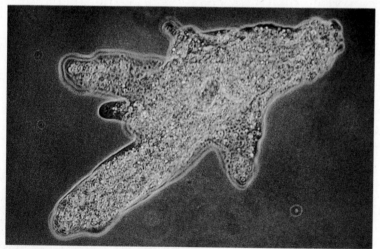

Amoeba

Some protozoans have tiny hairlike structures covering the cell. A paramecium (par ə mē′shē əm), like those in the picture, is an example of a protist with such hairs. The hairs move back and forth like tiny oars and help this protist to spin through the water. This is how a paramecium moves in search of food.

Some protozoans have a taillike structure near one end of the cell. These protozoans move through the water by whipping this taillike structure in a circular motion. A euglena (yü glē′nə) is an example of a protozoan that moves in this way. Euglenas are unusual in that they take in food and also have chloroplasts to make their own food.

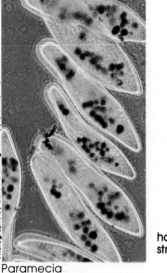

hairlike structures

Paramecia

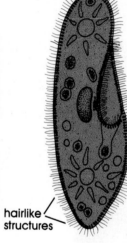

taillike structure

Euglena

A second group of protists are the plantlike protists. The plantlike protists have cell walls and chloroplasts. These protists make their own food. Most plantlike protists, such as diatoms (dī′ə tomz), float in the ocean. These protists are food for many other living things in the ocean. Organisms that eat the plantlike protists may in turn be food for other organisms. So all organisms in the ocean depend directly or indirectly on the plantlike protists for food.

Diatoms

The simplest protists are the **bacteria.** Bacteria differ in some ways from the plantlike protists and the protozoans. A bacterial cell is surrounded by a cell wall, but there is no nucleus inside the cell. Most bacteria do not contain chlorophyll, so they cannot make their own food. Most bacteria are smaller than the protozoans and the plantlike protists. Several hundred bacteria could fit inside one large protozoan.

Scientists classify bacteria according to shape. As you can see in the drawing, cocci (kok′sī) are round, bacilli (bə sil′ī) are rod-shaped, and spirilla (spī ril′ə) are spiral-shaped.

Bacteria are found almost everywhere. They live in water, in soil, and in the air. Some types of bacteria cause substances to decay. For example, when plants and animals die, bacteria break down the bodies into simpler materials. These materials enrich the soil, making it suitable for new growth. Some bacteria help to change milk into cheese. Other kinds live inside your body. Many are harmless, and some may be

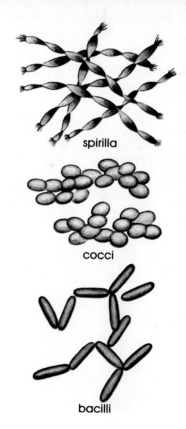

spirilla

cocci

bacilli

helpful. For instance, certain bacteria form vitamin K in your intestines. However, some bacteria cause disease and even death. For example, have you ever had strep throat? Strep throat is caused by one kind of cocci bacteria. Also, many kinds of food poisoning are caused by certain bacilli bacteria.

Science & Technology

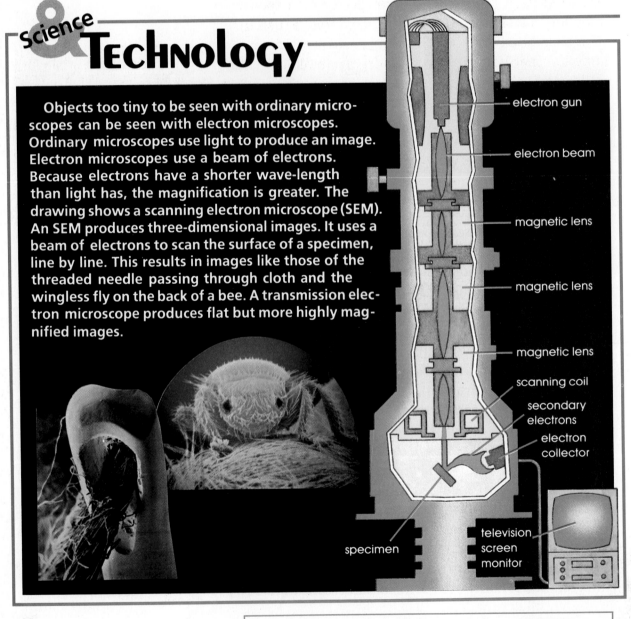

Objects too tiny to be seen with ordinary microscopes can be seen with electron microscopes. Ordinary microscopes use light to produce an image. Electron microscopes use a beam of electrons. Because electrons have a shorter wave-length than light has, the magnification is greater. The drawing shows a scanning electron microscope (SEM). An SEM produces three-dimensional images. It uses a beam of electrons to scan the surface of a specimen, line by line. This results in images like those of the threaded needle passing through cloth and the wingless fly on the back of a bee. A transmission electron microscope produces flat but more highly magnified images.

electron gun

electron beam

magnetic lens

magnetic lens

magnetic lens

scanning coil

secondary electrons

electron collector

specimen

television screen monitor

20

For Lesson Questions, turn to page 384.

Tissues, Organs, and Systems

How are cells organized in many-celled organisms?

Plants and animals are made of many cells. In most plants and animals, different cells perform different functions. Cells that perform the same function are like a team. A team of cells that performs a special function in a plant or animal is called a **tissue** (tish′ü). The cells in each tissue work together to perform a function that helps to keep the organism alive.

The cells that line the inside of your mouth form a tissue. The function of this tissue is to cover and protect the inside of your mouth.

The tissue that covers the outside of a leaf performs the same function as the tissue covering the inside of your mouth. The flat cells in that tissue protect the leaf. The cells also keep the leaf from losing water. This helps to keep the leaf moist.

Your body has many kinds of tissue. One kind is made of cells that can get longer and shorter. This is muscle tissue. Muscle tissue that is attached to your bones helps you to move. Muscle tissue in your stomach squeezes food and moves it into your intestine.

Another kind of tissue is nervous tissue. Nervous tissue is made of cells that carry messages between

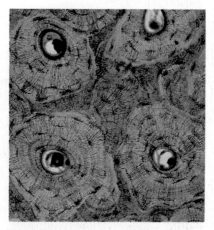

Bone tissue

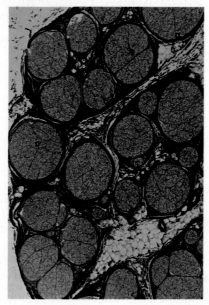

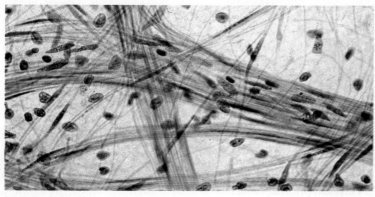

Muscle tissue

Nerve tissue

cell

tissue

organ

system

the brain and other parts of the body. Nervous tissue is found in the brain, the spinal cord, and the nerves.

Different kinds of tissue usually work together to carry out an important activity. A group of tissues working together to carry out a body activity is called an **organ** (ôr′gən). Your stomach is an example of an organ.

Look at the basketball players in the picture. Could one player do all the work for a team? No. The players work together to score points. Even the best player on a team needs the help of teammates.

In the same way, one organ alone cannot usually perform a major function in an organism. For example, the stomach cannot digest food all by itself. Other organs are also needed to help perform this function. In many plants and animals, organs work together to perform the functions that keep an organism alive. The organs are like the players on a team. Such a group of organs is called a **system.**

Your mouth, teeth, tongue, stomach, small intestine, and large intestine all work together. These organs, and others, work together to digest your food. Together they make up the digestive (də jes′tiv) system.

There are other systems in your body that perform major functions that help to keep you alive. The circulatory (sėr′kyə lə tôr ē) system carries food and oxygen to all parts of your body. The nervous system carries messages to all parts of your body. The respiratory (res′pər ə tôr ē) system takes in oxygen from the air and gives off waste gases. The muscular and skeletal systems support your body and help you to move. The excretory (eks′krə tôr ē) system removes waste materials from your body. Although each system performs a special function, all the systems work together. What systems are working to help the people in the picture as they exercise?

For Lesson Questions, turn to page 384.

Ideas to Remember

▶ All organisms need energy to carry out their life processes.

▶ All organisms are made up of one or more cells.

▶ Most cells have a nucleus, cytoplasm, and a cell membrane. Plant cells also have a cell wall and may contain chloroplasts.

▶ Single-celled organisms are called protists.

▶ A team of cells that performs a special function is called a tissue.

▶ A group of tissues working together to carry out an important body activity is called an organ.

▶ Organs working together to perform a major function in an organism make up a system.

Reviewing the Chapter

A. Use all the terms below to fill in the blanks.

mitosis   organism   chlorophyll   bacteria
chromosome   tissue   protist   protozoans

A living thing is called a/an __1__. A one-celled living thing is called a/an __2__. Two kinds of these one-celled living things are __3__ and __4__. All living things are made of cells. Cells that work together in a living thing form a/an __5__. Plant cells that make food contain __6__. Cells reproduce by a process called __7__. In this process, each __8__ makes a copy of itself.

B. Write the letter of the term that best matches the definition. Not all the terms will be used.

1. Cell part that contains the chromosomes
2. A group of tissues working together to carry out a body activity
3. Cell part that controls movement of materials into and out of the cell
4. Structures, found on chromosomes, that control a cell's activities
5. Cell part that gives strength and shape to a plant cell
6. Complex chemical link between living and nonliving things

a. genes
b. cell wall
c. system
d. virus
e. nucleus
f. cell
g. vacuole
h. cell membrane
i. organ
j. cytoplasm

UNDERSTANDING IDEAS

A. Label the numbered parts of the drawing. Use these terms: nucleus, cell membrane, cytoplasm, cell wall, vacuole.

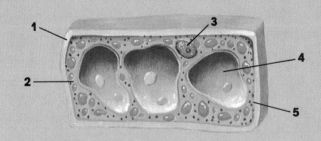

B. Arrange the names below in two groups: organisms that can make their food; organisms that cannot make their food.

diatoms   trees   grasshoppers
whales   amoebas   sunflowers
grass   zebras

C. These drawings of the stages of mitosis are out of order. Show the correct order, using the numbers under the drawings to identify the stages.

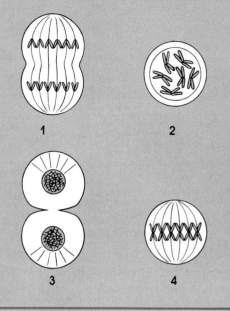

1   2

3   4

USING IDEAS

1. Your body contains many systems. Read about one of these systems. What organs make up the system? What important function does this system perform?

2. Certain human organs, such as kidneys and hearts, can be transplanted. But sometimes the new organ is rejected by the body. Read about organ transplants. Find out why rejection occurs.

THINKING LIKE A SCIENTIST

Answer the following questions. You may be able to answer some of the questions just by thinking about them. To answer other questions you may have to do some research.

1. Will robots ever be classified as living things? Robots can respond to the world around them. They use energy. In the future, robots may be used to design, construct, and service other robots. They grow by adding to their memory banks. Support your opinion with sound scientific reasoning.

2. Garden supply stores sell something called plant food. Each spring, gardeners feed their lawns with this substance. If plants make their own food in the chloroplasts of leaves, is "plant food" just a gimmick? Support your opinion with evidence.

CHAPTER 2
Plant Growth and Responses

Gardeners often compete with each other to grow the biggest vegetables or the tallest trees. But to the bonsai gardener, big things come in small packages. Bonsai (bon' sī) is the art of growing tiny trees in trays. The art of bonsai has been practiced in Japan for about 700 years. Today this special method of growing trees is becoming popular in this country.

On these pages are pictures of trees that have been grown by the bonsai method. Each of the trees is fully grown. Yet each is no more than 1 meter high. Some bonsai trees are very old. In fact, one bonsai tree brought to the United States in 1915 is now 300 years old!

How can these trees be fully grown and yet be so tiny? Gardeners prepare bonsai trees in a special way that holds back their growth. In the spring a gardener takes a young tree and plants it in a shallow pot. The tree is then given less water than usual so that it becomes limp. A heavy wire is then inserted into the soil near the base of the tree. The wire is wound around the young tree trunk in a series of coils. Then the limp tree trunk is bent into the shape desired by the bonsai artist. The upper branches are also wired into shape.

26a

The bonsai artist tries to make the tree look natural. In a natural setting, a mature tree might be twisted a little to one side or the other. It can have branches of various lengths and at different levels of the trunk. The shape of a tiny bonsai tree is very much like a full-size tree in the wild.

Besides wiring the trunk and branches, the bonsai grower also pinches off leaves. After doing this for many years, the grower produces a tree with tiny leaves. By cutting off certain branches, the grower can produce a tree of the desired shape and size. Having a bonsai tree is like having a beautiful landscape in a dish.

Bonsai trees can be grown in a variety of places. They can be placed in gardens, on balconies, and on rooftops. Bonsai are not indoor plants. They can stand the same kinds of weather conditions as full-size trees. Young bonsai plants should be watered once or twice a week when first planted. In wet weather they may not need any extra water. In dry weather they may need to be watered several times a day.

26b

What kinds of trees are grown in the bonsai style? In Japan the black pine is favored. In California the juniper is the favorite. Redwoods and pines are also popular. Maple and cherry trees are favored in the eastern United States.

Bonsai are often shown at flower shows. Some may be sold at your local florist. Clubs devoted to the growth of bonsai trees are now sprouting all over the United States. Perhaps you would like to try your hand at growing a bonsai tree. Remember, good things often come in small packages!

Now try this

Work with three or four other students. You will need four potted bean plants. They should all be about the same height. Record the height of each plant. For the next 3 weeks, you will be growing the plants. Your goal is to keep the plants alive but as small as possible. You can try any technique except cutting off the top leaves of the plant. Record everything you do to keep the plants alive but not growing tall. After 3 weeks, measure the plants. Only parts above the soil may be measured. The most successful student team is the one with the healthiest, but shortest, plants!

In this chapter you will learn how plants grow. You will also learn how plants respond to the world around them.

How Plants Grow

How do plants grow in size?

Growth takes place only in the **growth regions** of plants. There are two kinds of growth regions. One kind causes some parts of a plant to grow longer. This kind is located at the tips of stems, branches, and roots. The other kind of growth region causes a plant to get bigger around, or grow in circumference. Which kind of growth region is shown in the drawing?

In all growth regions, there is a special kind of tissue called growth tissue. Many of the cells in this tissue are dividing by mitosis. What stages of mitosis can be seen in the picture of growth tissue? After a cell divides, the two new cells grow larger. Finally they grow as large as the cell from which they formed. Then many of these cells also divide by mitosis.

As the size and the number of cells at the tips of stems, branches, and roots increase, those parts grow

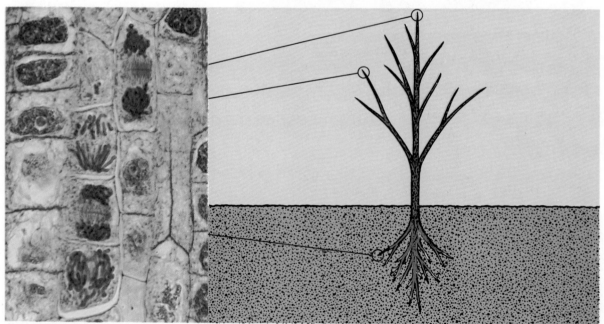

Growth tissue

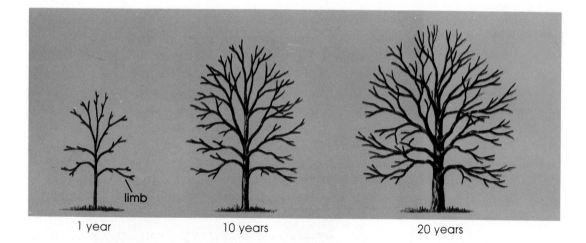

limb

1 year   10 years   20 years

longer. Compare the drawings of the tree. You can see that the trunk, or stem, grows taller. Also you can see that the limbs, or branches, grow longer. Notice, however, that as the tree grows, the location of a limb on the tree does not change.

Not only do stems, branches, and roots grow longer, but they also grow bigger around. Growth in circumference takes place in the other kind of growth region. The growth tissue in this region is arranged in a ring. Plants such as tulips and corn have nonwoody stems. Plants that have bark, such as trees and shrubs, have woody stems. Find the ring of growth tissue in the drawing of the nonwoody stem. Compare its location with the location of growth tissue in the drawing of a woody stem.

In a woody stem the ring of growth tissue is located just under the inner layer of bark. It is only one cell thick. This layer of growth tissue forms two kinds of new cells. As it does, the stem gets bigger around.

In places where the seasons change, the cells formed in the spring are large and have thin walls. Those formed in the summer are smaller and have thicker walls. The thin-walled cells are lighter in color and are called spring wood. The thick-walled cells are

Nonwoody stem (top)

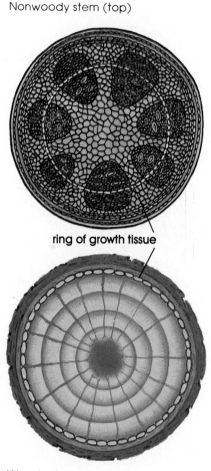

ring of growth tissue

Woody stem (bottom)

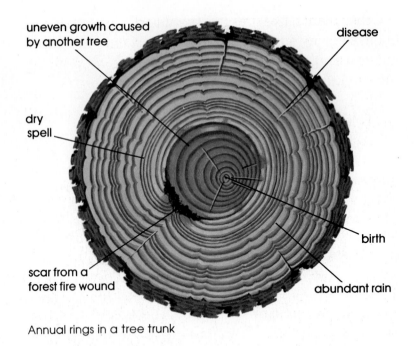

uneven growth caused
by another tree

disease

dry
spell

scar from a
forest fire wound

birth

abundant rain

Annual rings in a tree trunk

darker and are called summer wood. These two layers of cells appear as a ring in the stem. The ring represents a year's growth. For this reason the ring is called an **annual ring.** How could you tell the age of a tree from its stem? About how old is the tree?

Annual rings vary in width. Those formed during a rainy growing season are wide. During periods of drought, growth is much slower, so the annual rings are narrow. How do you think temperature might affect the size of annual rings? By studying growth patterns in annual rings, scientists can learn what the climate for a region was like hundreds of years ago.

The growth tissue of trees in cold northern regions becomes inactive in the fall. The trees, although alive, do not grow during the winter. They remain dormant (dôr′mənt), or inactive, until spring.

Some plants, such as corn and geraniums, grow from seeds in the spring and then die in the fall. Before they die, they form seeds that will grow into new plants the next spring. Such plants are called annuals.

Other plants, like grasses, seem to die in the fall but begin to grow again in the spring. It is only the parts above the ground that die—the roots stay alive. These plants are called perennials (pə ren′ē əlz).

Science & Technology

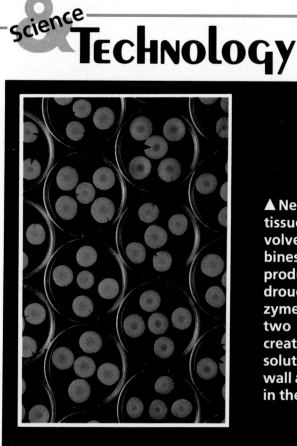

▲ New kinds of plants are being developed by tissue culture. One method of tissue culture involves genetic engineering. This process combines genetic materials from different plants to produce desirable traits. Such traits might be drought resistance or a certain color. First, enzymes are used to dissolve the cell walls. Then two cells from different plants are fused to create a new cell with the desired traits. Special solutions stimulate the cell to regenerate a cell wall and to grow into a new plant. The fused cell in the picture is undergoing its first cell division.

▲ Another method of tissue culture reproduces cells from tiny pieces of tissue. Each of these pieces of carrot tissue is capable of developing into a whole plant.

▶ Reproduction by tissue culture bypasses the use of seeds. It is the quickest way to mass-produce new varieties of plants.

For Lesson Questions, turn to page 386.

Growth and Survival

How can the way a plant grows help it to survive?

The survival of an organism depends on certain conditions. The conditions that are found where an organism lives are part of its environment (en vī′rən mənt). The **environment** includes all the living and nonliving things in a region. A plant's environment must have conditions suitable for growth. These conditions include sufficient light and water and a proper temperature range.

If a plant cannot grow in a certain environment, it will die. Often, however, conditions are not perfect, yet plants survive. The plants react to the environment in ways that help them survive. Some of the things that plants may react to are light, gravity, and water. The trees along the cliff in the picture live in a

rugged environment. But they are reacting to the available light and water and are growing.

The reaction of an organism to something in its environment is called a **response** (ri spons′). The response may be either positive or negative. Something in the environment that can cause a response is called a **stimulus** (stim′yə ləs). Pulling your hand away from a hot stove is a response. The stimulus is heat.

Plant responses to a stimulus often involve growth. Growth toward a stimulus is a positive response. Growth away from a stimulus is a negative response. Look at the picture of the plant that is leaning to one side. Perhaps you already know that plants grow toward light. On which side of this plant was the light probably the strongest?

Light was the stimulus for the plant. The growth of the plant toward the light was a positive response. Plant responses that involve growth are called **tropisms** (trō′piz əmz). The response of a plant to light is called **phototropism** (fō tō trō′piz əm).

How can growing toward light help a plant survive? Many plants grow from seeds that are scattered in the environment. Suppose a seed lands under a bush where there is little light. Does this mean the young plant will die? Not necessarily. As the stem of the plant grows, it may bend toward the light. The stem may bend enough so that the leaves get enough light for the plant to live.

What causes plants to bend toward light? There is a chemical in plants that speeds up cell growth. The chemical moves to the side of a plant stem that is away from the light. This causes the cells on the shaded side to grow faster and larger. The larger cells on the shaded side cause the stem to bend toward the light. Use the drawing to explain this stimulus-response reaction. What will happen if this plant is turned around?

Phototropism

light

Activity

How do plants respond to gravity?

Materials 2 small glass jars / paper towel / tape / 4 radish seeds / water / 2 pencils

Procedure

A. Tape a piece of paper towel to the inside of a glass jar, as shown.

B. Tuck 2 radish seeds between the towel and the jar. Put the seeds on opposite sides of the jar, near the top. Set up the second jar in the same way.

C. Half fill the jars with water, but do not let the water level reach the seeds. Only the paper towel should be wet to keep the seeds moist. Set the jars aside until the seeds sprout.

  1. In which direction do the stems and leaves grow?
  2. In which direction do the roots grow?

D. When the seedlings have grown so that the leaves are just above the jar tops, pour the water out of one jar. Then turn that jar upside down on top of two pencils. Be careful not to injure the seedlings as you do this. Keep the paper towel moist. Observe the seedlings in both jars daily for several days.

  3. What happens to the stems, leaves, and roots of the seedlings in the upright jar?
  4. What happens to the stems, leaves, and roots of the seedlings in the jar turned upside down?

Conclusion

1. The response of plant growth to gravity is called geotropism (jē ot′rə piz əm). Which plant part(s) show a negative geotropism?
2. Which plant part(s) show a positive geotropism?

Using science ideas

How do you think positive and negative geotropisms help plants to survive?

In addition to light and gravity, plants also respond to other things. Roots, for example, grow toward water. Roots respond to the stimulus of water more positively than they do to the stimulus of gravity.

Morning glories and peas grow long, thin parts called tendrils (ten′drəlz). When the tendrils touch a fence post, they twist around it. These plants respond to the stimulus of pressure, or touch. A mimosa plant, like the one in the pictures, also responds to touch. What evidence of that response can you see?

In addition to growth responses, a plant may have special structures that help it to survive. For example, the tough bark of a tree may prevent insects from eating into the tree and killing it. Any structure or response that helps an organism to survive is called an **adaptation** (ad ap tā′shən).

SKILLS: Experimenting, Using variables

Finding Out

Design an experiment to show whether a root will grow around objects blocking its path.

A true scientific experiment always has two setups. One setup, called the *control,* is kept under normal conditions. In the other setup, all but one of the conditions are the same as those in the control. This one condition is called the *variable.* Be sure to include both a control and a variable in the experiment you design.

First, state a scientific purpose for the experiment. Then make a list of all the materials you will use. Next write a step-by-step plan for carrying out the experiment.

After planning your experiment, try it out. Make observations and record data during the experiment. When you have finished, make a conclusion based on your data.

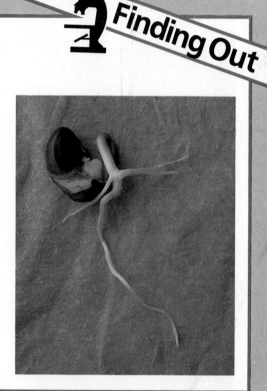

For Lesson Questions, turn to page 386.

Other Adaptations of Plants

How are plants adapted to their environments?

If a seed lands on the soil near its parent plant, it usually has very little chance to survive. As it grows, it must compete with the parent plant for water and light. So most seeds have adaptations that cause the seeds to be spread around.

Milkweed seeds are very light and can be carried by the wind. Maple seeds are "winged." The wings help to carry the seeds in the wind. Many seeds, such as apple seeds, are hidden in fruits. Animals eat the fruits and seeds, but the seeds are not digested. They pass out of the animals and into the soil. Some seeds, such as those of cocklebur, have stickers that cling to animal fur and to clothing. The seeds are carried on the fur or clothing for a time and then fall off.

Maple seeds

Milkweed seeds

Cocklebur

Black walnut tree

Locoweed

Some plants produce poisons that help them to survive. The wild cherry is such a plant. It produces an acid that will kill, in only a few minutes, animals that eat it. A plant called locoweed contains chemicals that are poisonous to animals that eat its leaves. Many plants produce chemicals that are not poisonous, but that give the plant a bad taste or odor. Among these are horsetails, rhododendron (rō də den′drən), and barberry. Certain plants give off chemicals that are poisonous to other plants. For example, black walnut trees give off a chemical that prevents seedlings from growing. Therefore new plants do not grow around them and compete for space.

The needles of evergreen trees are still another kind of plant adaptation. Pines, firs, and other evergreens have needles instead of broad leaves. The needles are compact and have a small surface area. Therefore these trees do not lose much water through their needles. Evergreen trees grow in places where there is little rainfall. The needlelike leaves are an adaptation for conserving water.

Horsetails

Activity

How does temperature affect the germination of seeds?

Materials 2 paper towels / 2 pans / 50 bean seeds / water / tweezers

Procedure
A. Fold the paper towels in half lengthwise twice. Put one towel in each pan.

B. Place 25 seeds between the first and second layers of each towel. Soak the towels with water.

C. Place one pan in a refrigerator at about 5°C. Store the other pan in a dark area at room temperature (20° – 25°C).

D. Keep the towels moist in both pans. Check the pans each day for 7 days for seed germination.
   1. In a table like the one shown, record the total number of seeds that have germinated in each container each day.

Results
1. Make a bar graph showing the total number of seeds that germinated in each container every day over the 7-day period.
2. At which temperature did the greater number of seeds germinate?

Conclusion
How did temperature affect the germination of seeds in this experiment?

Day	NUMBER OF SEEDS GERMINATED	
	At 20°-25°C	At about 5°C
1		
2		

Prickly pear cactus

Barrel and cardon cactuses

Beaver tail cactus

Some plants have adaptations that help them live in cold places. Others have adaptations that help them live in hot, dry places. Desert plants, such as cactuses, have many adaptations that help them survive. Cactus plants have thick stems in which water is stored for use during long dry spells. The stems often have a tough, waxy coating that prevents water from evaporating. They also are covered with needlelike spines. The spines prevent animals from biting into the stem to get water. Like the needles of evergreen trees, cactus spines have a small surface area. Therefore they do not lose much water. The spines and white hairs on the plants also help to reflect sunlight.

Cactus stem cross section

The seeds of many desert plants have chemicals in the seed coat. These chemicals keep the seeds from germinating until conditions are favorable. Water is necessary to dissolve the chemicals. If there is only a little rain, all the chemicals do not dissolve, and the seeds will not germinate. If the seeds did germinate, the young plants would probably die. Why? When

there is a lot of rain, all the chemicals in the seed coat dissolve. Then the seeds will germinate. There will probably be enough water in the soil for the plants to grow and survive.

Many desert plants have long roots that are close to the soil's surface. Such shallow roots are an adaptation for absorbing as much rainwater as possible. Being close to the surface, they can take in the water before it evaporates, runs off, or soaks deep into the soil. In this way, much water is absorbed quickly.

As the picture shows, a forest fire is very destructive. However, in some ways forest fires are helpful. For example, the seeds of a jack pine tree are held inside a cone. Normally the cones are tightly closed and hang on the tree. It takes a long time for the cones

to dry and open naturally. But when they are heated in a forest fire, the cones open and scatter thousands of seeds. Some of these fall on the bed of ashes from the fire and then germinate when there is enough moisture again. Since the fire has destroyed competing plants, the new jack pine seedlings grow rapidly. They do not have to compete with older and bigger trees for light and moisture. Also, the ashes from the trees that burned are a rich source of minerals. Before a fire in one part of Minnesota, there were only about six pines to an acre. After the forest fire, there were between 15,000 and 20,000 new seedlings to an acre.

The seeds of some kinds of shrubs are also adapted to forest fires. These seeds have such a hard seed coat that water cannot enter. The heat from a forest fire splits the seed coat. After a fire the seeds can absorb water and then germinate.

Jack pine cones and seedling

For Lesson Questions, turn to page 386.

41

Biological Clocks

How is the timing of blooming controlled in plants?

Look at the picture of the crocus in the snow. Crocuses bloom in the early spring. Other kinds of flowers, such as day lilies, bloom during the summer. Some flowers, such as mums, don't bloom until the fall. But nearly all the flowers of any one kind of plant bloom at the same time. As a result, pollen can be transferred among the flowers. Many seeds will then be produced.

Some kinds of flowers, such as morning glories, open in the morning. Other kinds, such as four o'clocks, open in the late afternoon. Still others, such as the moonvine, open just as it is getting dark. But nearly all the flowers of any one kind of plant are open at the same time. This allows pollen to be transferred and seeds to be produced.

What causes all the flowers of one kind to bloom at the same time of the year? What causes the flowers to

Crocus

Day lily

Morning glories, open and closed

open or close at certain times of the day? The answers to these questions are not fully known. Scientists do know that something causes plants to react in certain ways at certain times. That "something" is called a **biological clock.** A biological clock is not a specific part of a plant. Rather, it seems to be a kind of "chemical clock" in the plant cells. Something outside the plant sets the clock, much as an alarm clock is set. This clock setter for plants is usually light, but it can also be temperature. The chemical clock in the plant cells then cause certain activities to take place at certain times. The way that happens is not yet completely understood. What do you think sets the biological clock in a crocus? In a morning glory?

The biological clock in a plant may function almost as well as a real clock. In fact, flowers may actually be

Moonvine, open and closed

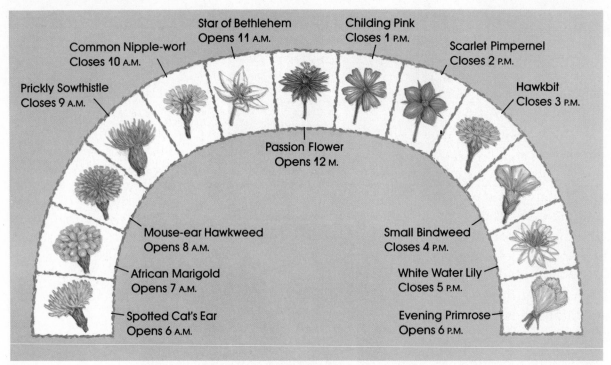

Common Nipple-wort
Closes 10 A.M.

Star of Bethlehem
Opens 11 A.M.

Childing Pink
Closes 1 P.M.

Scarlet Pimpernel
Closes 2 P.M.

Prickly Sowthistle
Closes 9 A.M.

Hawkbit
Closes 3 P.M.

Passion Flower
Opens 12 M.

Mouse-ear Hawkweed
Opens 8 A.M.

Small Bindweed
Closes 4 P.M.

African Marigold
Opens 7 A.M.

White Water Lily
Closes 5 P.M.

Spotted Cat's Ear
Opens 6 A.M.

Evening Primrose
Opens 6 P.M.

Flower clock

used to tell time. On a sunny day you can tell the time to within a half hour of the correct time with a flower clock. A flower clock consists of a series of flower beds arranged to form the face of a clock. Each bed is planted with a different kind of flower that is known to open or to close at a certain time. Time is read by noting which flowers are open or closed.

Growing an accurate flower clock is difficult. The variety of flowers that make up the clock must be selected carefully. Often, flowers that open or close at a certain time grow only in a particular region. When planted in a different region, the flowers may not bloom.

A plant's biological clock causes the plant to respond to changes in its environment. For example, a mum plant responds to changes in the length of day and night. In nature, mums usually produce flowers only in the fall. The short daylight period in the fall is a signal to the plants to bloom. Florists have learned how to fool the mum's biological clock by growing mums in artificial light. The length of time that the mums receive light each day is the same as the daylight period in the fall. Therefore, the plants can produce flowers all year.

A plant's biological clock may keep the plant from growing in certain places. Ragweed plants produce flowers when the daylight period is just about 14 1/2 hours long. In many places in the midwest, the days are the right length for ragweed to grow and produce seeds. But in northern Maine, daylight is longer than 14 1/2 hours for most of the summer. When daylight shortens to about 14 1/2 hours there, it is nearly fall. The weather has turned cool. So the ragweed plants die before they can produce seeds. As a result, there is little ragweed in northern Maine.

Ragweed

Ideas to Remember

▶ In plants, growth regions located at the tips of stems, branches, and roots cause these structures to grow longer.

▶ Rings of growth tissue near the outside of stems, branches, and roots cause these structures to increase in circumference.

▶ Plants respond to the environment in ways that increase their chances of survival.

▶ An adaptation is a structure or response that helps an organism to survive in its environment.

▶ Different plants have different adaptations. A plant's adaptations help it to survive.

▶ The biological clocks of plants control the timing of certain important activities.

For Lesson Questions, turn to page 386.

Reviewing the Chapter

SCIENCE WORDS

A. Use all the terms below to fill in the blanks.

annual rings   phototropism   environment   stimulus
adaptations   growth regions   tropism   gravity

In plants, growth takes place only in certain places called __1__.
Growth can be observed in many ways. For example, the yearly
growth patterns of trees can be observed in the __2__ produced in the
stem. Like all living things, plants respond to conditions in the __3__.
Something that causes a plant to respond is called a/an __4__. Any
plant response that involves growth is called a/an __5__. The growth
response of a plant toward light is called __6__. Both stems and roots
respond to __7__, but in opposite directions. Since these responses
help a plant to survive, they are called __8__.

UNDERSTANDING IDEAS

A. Study picture **A**. It shows a tree in early spring. Then study pictures **B, C,** and **D**.

1. Certain places on the tree in picture **A** are labeled. List the letters that identify the places where an increase in length can occur.

2. Which picture (**B, C,** or **D**) best shows how the tree in picture **A** might look the following spring?

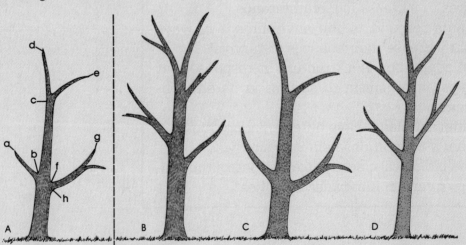

B. State whether each sentence is true or false. Rewrite false statements to make them true.

1. Cells on the lighted side of a stem grow faster than those on the shaded side.
2. Plant stems grow in the direction of the pull of gravity.
3. Growth regions are located at the tips of stems, branches, and roots.
4. The seeds of many kinds of desert plants will germinate only after a heavy rain.
5. A plant's biological clock is an organ in the stem.

USING IDEAS

1. The seeds of some plants, including many evergreens, must be frozen and then warmed before they will germinate. Find out how this adaptation helps the plants to survive.

2. Plan and carry out an experiment to find out if bean stems will grow downward if light only comes from below.

THINKING LIKE A SCIENTIST

Answer the following questions. You may be able to answer some of the questions just by thinking about them. To answer other questions you may have to do some research.

1. Why do many plants in tropical regions lack growth rings?
2. Using living trees, the Japanese have developed an art form called bonsai. Bonsai are miniature versions of common trees, such as maple, pine, oak, and many others. Although the bonsai trees may be over 100 years old, they rarely are taller than 1 m. Many are only 30 cm to 50 cm tall. Do these plants just mature slowly? Have the Japanese interfered with the plants' biological clocks? How are these miniature trees grown?

CHAPTER 3
Animal Adaptations

Merlin Tuttle is a real-life "batman." Tuttle's mission is to change people's image of bats. He has started a group for the support of bats. This group, called Bat Conservation International, is based in Austin, Texas. The main purpose of Tuttle's group is to spread the truth about bats.

Bats, like all animals, have structures that help them survive in their environment. These structures are known as adaptations. Unlike most other animals, bats have adaptations that make people think they are scary creatures. Some people think of bats as evil animals that come out at night and suck blood. They even believe bats can get tangled in your hair. What are the real facts about bats?

It is true that most bats fly at night. But there are a few kinds that fly in daylight. Many of the night-flying bats eat great numbers of insects. For example, a single gray bat can eat up to 3,000 insects in one night. Because they eat so many insects, bats can be helpful to farmers. The bats eat insects that could otherwise destroy farmers' crops.

Three species of bats do drink animal blood. One species also drinks human blood, but only rarely. The bite is very small and so painless that a person could sleep through the experience. Blood-drinking bats are found in Mexico and Central America.

Bats are unlikely to wind up in someone's hair. They have a built-in sonar system that keeps them from flying into objects. This sonar is an adaptation that enables bats to fly at night. Their sonar is so sensitive that bats can detect a mosquito!

Bats can pass on rabies to other animals. But most people are not likely to meet a bat with rabies. Only a sick bat would allow a person to come close to it. So if a bat lets you come close, beware! It is probably sick. Do not touch it! In the past 40 years, records have been kept on bat-caused rabies in North America. In that time, only 10 cases of rabies in humans have been reported. Remember, you need not fear bats if you do not handle them.

Bats are really useful, friendly, and intelligent mammals. Many bats pollinate the flowers of important food crops. These crops include bananas, avocados, mangoes, dates, figs, and cashews. Some people blame bats for destroying farmers' fruit crops. But bats seldom damage the crops. They eat only the ripe fruit. Most fruit is harvested before it is ripe. So any fruit eaten by bats was overlooked by harvesters or ripened early. Bats help farmers in one other way. In some parts of the world, bat droppings are used to fertilize crops.

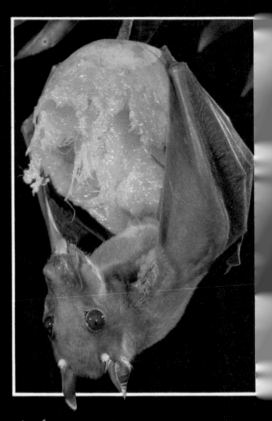

What about the myth that bats are ugly? Just look at the photographs on these pages. Have an open mind. Can't you see that bats have a certain charm? They could even be called good-looking!

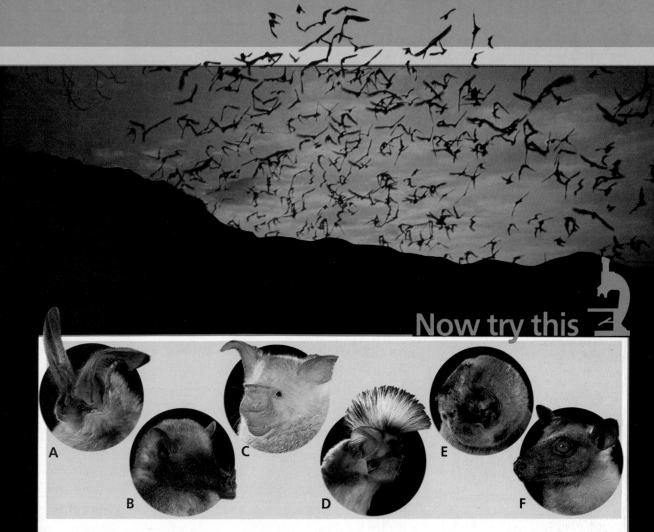

From the photographs you can see the bats vary in size, shape, and color. Bats adapt to their surroundings by means of these differences in their structure. Read the descriptions below. Match the descriptions to the bat pictures on this page. Indicate your answers by letter. Give reasons for your answers. You can compare your answers with those given on page 432.

1. This bat could be called the "peacock" of the bat world.
2. This bat has such keen hearing that it can hear the sounds of tiny insects.
3. The strange shape of this bat's nose helps to direct the sounds the bat makes.
4. This bat does not rely on sonar. It uses its eyes to find its way around.
5. The flaps of skin around this bat's mouth open up into a "megaphone."
6. The shape of this bat's face makes it easy for the bat to pollinate flowers.

In this chapter you will learn how many different animals adapt to their surroundings.

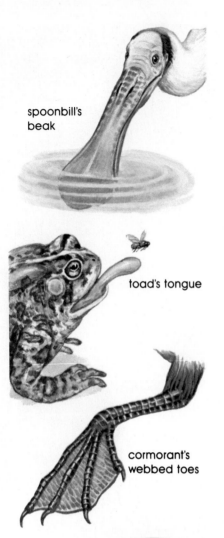

spoonbill's beak

toad's tongue

cormorant's webbed toes

Structural Adaptations

How can the structure of an animal's body help it to survive?

An adaptation can be something an organism does that helps it to survive. An adaptation can also be a certain part of an organism. The large ears of many bats allow these animals to use their sonar. An adaptation that involves some part of an organism's body is called a **structural adaptation.**

Different animals have different kinds of structural adaptations. Some adaptations help animals to feed. Other adaptations help animals to move. Such adaptations can help animals to catch food and to escape from enemies. Adaptations may also protect animals from other animals or from a harsh environment. Such adaptations often involve the body covering. Some adaptations are shown in the drawings. How might each adaptation help the animal to survive?

The first type of structural adaptation you will study is related to feeding. Different animals may have different kinds of teeth for chewing and eating different kinds of foods. Rodents, such as beavers, rats, and chipmunks, have two pairs of sharp front

Beaver and its incisor teeth

Cow and its molar teeth

teeth. These teeth, called **incisors** (in sī′zərz), work like a pair of shears. They enable rodents to chew and gnaw wood. As a rodent gnaws, its teeth wear down. But unlike the incisor teeth of other animals, the rodent's teeth keep growing. They continue to grow as long as the animal lives. The sharpness of the teeth and their ability to keep growing are adaptations. What do you think might happen if a rodent's incisor teeth did not wear down?

Grazing animals, such as sheep and cows, have large flat teeth along the sides of the mouth. These teeth are called **molars** (mō′lərz). Grazing animals use their molars to crush and grind tough plant materials. This makes the food easier to digest.

Look at the picture of the lion's teeth. How are the lion's teeth different from the teeth of the beaver and the cow? Meat-eating animals, such as lions and wolves, have sharp pointed teeth near the front of the mouth. These teeth are called **canines** (kā′nīnz). The teeth are useful in killing prey. The meat-eating animals then use their sharp incisor teeth to tear off chunks of flesh, which they then swallow with little chewing. Since meat is easier to digest than plant

Lion and its canine teeth

51

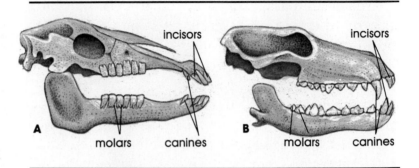

material, the molars of meat-eaters are small. Compare the two animal skulls in the drawing. Which one of these animals eats meat? Which animal grazes?

Insects also have specialized mouth parts for feeding. Some, like mosquitoes, have mouth parts adapted to feeding on the blood of animals. Other insects are adapted to feeding on plants.

Have you ever seen a butterfly move from flower to flower? The butterfly has a long tube-like mouth that it can coil and uncoil. This adaptation helps it to get the nectar that is deep inside the flowers.

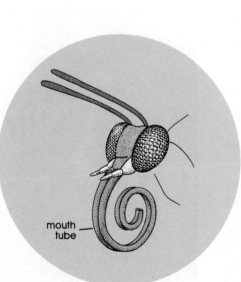

mouth tube

Pale clouded yellow butterfly

Birds lack teeth, but they have bills that are adapted to eating seeds, fruits, or animals. What is the woodpecker's structural adaptation for feeding? The woodpecker has a sharp beak that it uses to drill holes in trees. It then feeds on insects that live in the wood. Look at the picture closely. What other parts of its body is this woodpecker using to help it get food?

Another type of structural adaptation of animals is related to movement. Such adaptations include the ability to hop, run, climb, jump, swim, or fly. Body structures are related to adaptations for movement.

Kangaroos are plant eaters that hop about on powerful hind legs. If attacked, a kangaroo will bound away in great leaps. Powerful leg muscles enable a large kangaroo to take leaps of 10 m or more. Such jumps can help the kangaroo escape wild dogs and other enemies. Rabbits and frogs are other animals whose hind legs are similarly adapted to hopping. In addition to being powerful, the hind legs of hopping animals are longer than their front legs.

Woodpecker

Kangaroo

53

Gibbon

Gibbons are small apes that live in the forests of Asia. These animals spend most of their time in trees. Notice how long the arms of a gibbon are. Gibbons use their long, powerful arms to swing among the branches in search of the fruits they eat. Though clumsy on the ground, gibbons swing through the forest with amazing skill. Their arms are an adaptation mostly for locomotion but also for food getting.

The cheetah is a meat-eating animal that lives in Africa. It catches its prey, such as antelope, by running it down with a quick burst of speed. The cheetah's light build and long legs help it to build up speed quickly. In addition, the cheetah has a flexible backbone. As the cheetah runs, its backbone stretches and shortens like a spring. This action gives the cheetah a very long stride, which adds to its speed. Over a short distance the cheetah can run about 100 km/h.

Cheetah

Although awkward on land and unable to walk, frigate (frig′it) birds are masterful fliers. Airplane pilots have reported seeing them at an altitude of more than 1,200 m. Without landing, they often travel 1,600 km or more out to sea in search of food. They can hover like a hummingbird and swoop like a hawk. What structural adaptations make such feats possible?

Frigate birds have a wingspread of about 2.5 m. Their wing feathers are almost 30 cm long. Like other flying birds, frigates have strong breast and wing muscles and hollow, lightweight bones. Even with its great size, the total mass of the frigate is less than that of the average gull. Strong muscles and hollow, lightweight bones are adaptations for flight. Other adaptations include the shape and arrangement of feathers and the large wingspread.

Body coverings are structural adaptations that help various animals in different ways. Some kinds of animals, including worms and amphibians such as salamanders, breathe through their skin. In fact, some salamanders, like the dusky salamander, do not have lungs. Such salamanders can only breathe through their skin.

Frigate bird

Spotted dusky salamander

Short-horned lizard

Worms and salamanders have smooth, moist skin. The moist skin allows oxygen and carbon dioxide to pass through it. In this way the animals can take in oxygen as they breathe and can give off carbon dioxide. Perhaps you have seen worms on a driveway or sidewalk after a rainstorm. They were flooded out of their burrows. Once their skin dries, they have no way to get oxygen, so they die.

Some people think that salamanders are related to lizards. But lizards are reptiles, not amphibians. All reptiles have scales or horny plates covering their body. Oxygen cannot pass through this body covering, so reptiles cannot breathe through their skin. However, the scales or horny plates on their body keep these animals from losing water. For this reason, reptiles are well suited to life on land. Many live in the desert. Could a salamander live in the desert? Why?

Lizards have another interesting adaptation that keeps them from losing water. They do not store urine in a bladder as do some other animals. Neither do they excrete water in their urine. Their urine is pastelike, rather than liquid. The extra water is kept in the body, thus enabling lizards to live in dry places.

As you probably know, animals with hair are called mammals. Hair is an adaptation that helps mammals keep warm. Musk oxen and other mammals that live in cold regions have thick coats of hair. The long, thick

Musk ox

hair of the musk ox protects the animal from cold temperatures and arctic winds.

Mammals may shed hair as summer approaches and grow thicker coats of hair in the fall. The whitetail deer of the United States and Canada has a light coat of reddish-brown hair in the summer. In winter this deer has a thick coat of grayish hair.

Sometimes an animal's body covering is an adaptation that protects it against enemies. The porcupine is an animal whose body is covered with long, sharp quills. The armadillo (är mə dil'ō), which is found in the southern United States and Mexico, is covered with armor plates. The plates are a hard, horny material that is actually modified skin. They are connected by a flexible tissue. This makes it possible for the armadillo to bend and move. The hard plates help protect the armadillo from its enemies. The armadillo can also roll into a ball when attacked.

Armadillo

For Lesson Questions, turn to page 388.

SKILL: Inferring

Finding Out

What structural adaptations can help an imaginary animal to survive in this desert?

Think of an imaginary animal that lives in this desert. The animal feeds on insects in the early evening and morning. During the day it burrows into the ground to avoid the heat. It is food for a large ground-dwelling bird.

What structural adaptations would the imaginary animal have that would help it feed? What would its teeth be like? Describe any specialized mouth parts the animal would have.

What structural adaptations related to movement would the imaginary animal have? What would the imaginary animal's body covering be like? Explain your answers.

Activity

How does hair help to keep an animal warm?

Materials 2 tin cans of the same size / glue / cotton / hot water / 2 Celsius thermometers / clock or watch

Procedure

A. Remove the labels from two tin cans. Coat the outside of one can with glue.

B. Put a layer of cotton over the glued surface. Wait a few minutes for the glue to dry. Fluff the cotton outward.

C. Fill both cans with hot water from the same container. Make sure both cans have the same amount of water.

    1. What do you think will happen to the temperature of the water in each can?

D. Measure and record the temperature of the water in each can every 5 minutes for the next half hour.

Results

1. Make a bar graph of the temperature data to show how the water temperatures compare.
2. Which can lost heat more quickly?

Conclusion

1. In what way is the fluffed cotton like the hair of an animal's coat?
2. From your observations, explain how hair helps to keep an animal warm.

Using science ideas

Many marine mammals, such as whales, have little hair. How do such animals keep warm in cold water?

Looks That Protect

How can an animal's appearance help it to survive?

There are several kinds of structural adaptations that involve appearance, or how an animal looks. Often such adaptations help the animal to look like something else or to hide in its environment.

One structural adaptation involving appearance is **protective coloration** (prə tek′tiv kul ə rā′shən). An animal with protective coloration has a color similar to that of its environment. As a result, the animal is hard to see. This may give the animal some protection from its enemies. Or it may help to make the animal a successful hunter.

The chameleon (kə mē′lē ən) is a tree-dwelling lizard found in Asia and Africa. Chameleons can change color to match the color of their surroundings. For example, a chameleon will turn green when it is

Chameleons

Snowshoe hare in summer

Snowshoe hare in winter

among green leaves. But when on a brown branch, it will turn brown. This is due to special color cells. The cells contain black, yellow, and red pigments. When the pigments spread out in the cell, one color is seen. When the pigments shrink to one part of the cell, another color is seen. These changes seem to be controlled by nerves and chemicals. The ability to change color allows the chameleon to remain hidden as it hunts the insects that it feeds on.

Some animals change color with the seasons. An example is the snowshoe hare. What color is the hare in summer? What color is it in winter? These colors help the hare to blend in with its environment. Throughout the year the hare's enemies, such as the bobcat, have difficulty seeing it.

Can you see the insect on the branch in the picture below? It is called a walking stick. The walking stick has a color similar to that of the branches it lives on. It is also shaped like a small branch. These adaptations make it hard for lizards and birds that eat the walking stick to see it. An adaptation in which an animal looks similar to something in its environment is called **protective resemblance** (ri zem′bləns).

Walking stick

Certain harmless animals benefit by looking like poisonous or dangerous animals. Look at the pictures of the monarch butterfly and the viceroy butterfly. The body of the monarch contains a poison harmful to other animals. A bird that eats a monarch will become sick. Thereafter it will not eat monarch butterflies. The bird will also avoid viceroy butterflies. The viceroy benefits by looking like the poisonous monarch. Would you be able to tell the two butterflies apart if both were on a flower? An adaptation in which an animal looks like a dangerous or poisonous animal is called **mimicry** (mim´ik rē). Mimicry also includes imitating the sounds or habits of another animal.

For Lesson Questions, turn to page 388.

Monarch butterfly

Viceroy butterfly

Behavior and Instinct

How can instincts help animals to survive?

You have learned that body parts and coverings are adaptations. But an adaptation can also be something that an animal does. The activities and actions of an animal are called **behavior.** Behavioral adaptations include any activity that helps an animal to survive.

Some kinds of behavior are learned. For example, a wolf pup learns to hunt by imitating adult wolves. But animals are also born with certain patterns of behavior. Any behavior pattern that an animal is born with is called unlearned behavior, or **instinct** (in'stingkt). The behavior patterns involved in nest building and the raising of young are examples of instinct. Animals usually do not have to learn these behaviors.

Different birds build different kinds of nests. Look at the picture of the blue jay feeding its young. The blue jay builds its nest with small sticks. Then it lines the nest with roots. The nest may be from 2 m to 15 m above the ground. It is usually close to the trunk of a tree. This behavior pattern is the same for all blue jays.

Blue jay feeding its young

Grebe

Chimney swift

Kingfisher

Some birds, such as kingfishers, tunnel into the banks of rivers and streams to make nests. Others, like grebes (grēbz), build nests that float in the water. The chimney swift often builds its nest on the inside wall of a chimney. The nest is made of sticks. The chimney swift glues the nest to the wall with its own saliva. The saliva hardens and holds the nest in place.

Different nest materials may be used. But in all cases the nest increases the chance that the young birds will survive.

Nest building is a complex behavior. Some kinds of instinct, however, are simple. For example, a young fawn may remain still if something approaches it in the forest. Since it blends in with the forest, the fawn may not be seen. The simple act of keeping still is an instinct that may save the fawn's life. What are some other examples of simple instincts in animals?

Another interesting kind of behavior in animals is migration (mī grā'shən). **Migration** is the movement of an animal or a group of animals from one region to another. The animals later return to the original region. The timing of migration is often related to a change in the seasons. Migration is sometimes simply a journey to better feeding grounds. However, many animals migrate to certain regions to reproduce and to raise their young. These regions are called **breeding grounds.**

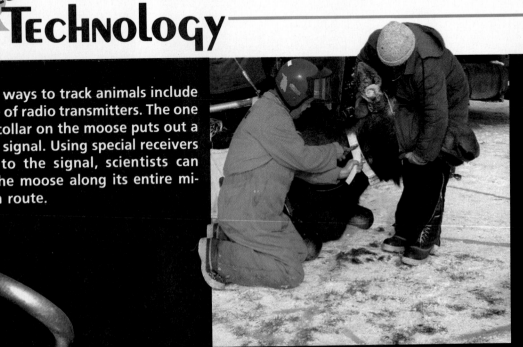

▶ New ways to track animals include the use of radio transmitters. The one in the collar on the moose puts out a certain signal. Using special receivers tuned to the signal, scientists can track the moose along its entire migration route.

◀ Some animals, such as this bushmaster, are "fed" a radio transmitter. With fish, the transmitter may be put under the skin or on the large upper fin. Transmitters have been put on birds that migrate over the oceans. These signals are picked up by satellites and relayed to receivers on the earth. Migrating birds and insects can also be tracked by radar. Radar can tell how high and how fast they travel. Radar can even identify the species and sex of migrating insects from their wingbeats. Of what value is tracking animals to learn about their movements? What do you think scientists expect to find out?

Gray whales migrating

One animal that migrates to breed is the gray whale. Gray whales spend the summer in the Bering Sea, north and west of Alaska. In the fall they migrate to Baja California, a part of Mexico. There the females bear their young. In the spring the adults mate again and then migrate back to the Bering Sea. The migration of the Alaska fur seal is similar. During the winter the males and females live far apart. The males live near the Gulf of Alaska, and the females, off the coast of California. Find these places on the map in the drawing. In June the males and females meet at the Pribilof Islands. There the young are born and the adults mate again. In the fall the females and their young migrate back to California.

Many kinds of birds are well known for their migratory behavior. The arctic tern makes the longest journey of any bird. During the summer in the Northern Hemisphere, this bird is found throughout the arctic region. It breeds in Alaska, Canada, Greenland, and northern Europe and Asia. In fall the birds travel all the way to the antarctic region. They arrive in time for the antarctic summer. The arctic terns fly north again as the antarctic fall begins and spring returns to the arctic.

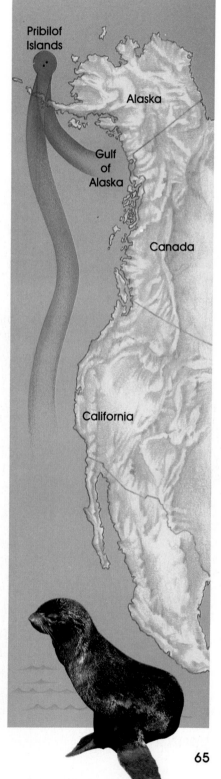

Wildebeests migrating

Wildebeests (wil'də bēsts) are grazing animals that migrate in search of water. Wildebeests live part of the year on the plains of East Africa. As the dry season begins in June, they move west looking for water. A journey of more than 300 km takes them to a region where water can be found. In December the rainy season begins in East Africa. Then the wildebeests return to the plains, where water is again available.

Some insects migrate, too. Monarch butterflies feed on milkweeds. From early spring they work their way north, following the milkweed season. They breed as they migrate, spreading over most of the United States. In the fall they gather in large flocks to make the long journey south. Monarchs travel from as far north as Canada to as far south as Mexico.

Migrating monarch butterfly flock resting

For Lesson Questions, turn to page 388.

Hibernation

Why do certain animals hibernate over the winter?

Many animals do not migrate in the winter. They have other ways to survive the cold and the scarcity of food. One adaptation for survival is the deep sleep called **hibernation** (hī bər nā′shən).

During hibernation, an animal's body temperature drops to about the temperature of the environment. However, it does not drop much lower than the freezing point of water. Body activities, such as breathing and heartbeat, become very slow. Because of its low temperature, a hibernating animal needs little food. It can live off the fat stored in its body.

Many of the animals that hibernate are cold-blooded. A **cold-blooded animal** is an animal whose body temperature changes as the temperature of the environment changes. A cold-blooded animals's body temperature is often close to the temperature of the environment. Snails, amphibians, and reptiles are examples of cold-blooded animals.

Bullfrog in pond in fall

Spotted salamander

Many kinds of animals that live in lakes and ponds hibernate in the mud. Turtles and frogs are among these animals. In the fall they bury themselves in the mud at the bottom of a lake or pond. They survive through the winter even though the lake or pond may freeze over. As spring returns, the frogs and turtles leave the mud and enter the water again.

Some amphibians and reptiles hibernate in the ground. Look at the picture of the spotted salamander. It has crawled into a space in a piece of wood well below the surface. Salamanders hibernate in places like this through the winter. When the weather warms in the spring, they become active again.

Many kinds of snakes hibernate in dens. Dens provide a certain amount of protection. The den may be a hole in the ground under a large rock. Or the den may be a small cave. Different kinds of snakes, such as copperheads and rattlesnakes, may hibernate together.

Some warm-blooded animals hibernate, too. A **warm-blooded animal** is an animal that has a fairly constant body temperature. Birds and mammals are examples of warm-blooded animals.

Copperhead snakes

Some kinds of rodents, such as the woodchuck and chipmunk, hibernate. The woodchuck gets fat during the summer and fall, then lives on its fat while it sleeps. The chipmunk stores food in its den during the summer and fall. It wakes up about once a week during the winter to eat.

Bears, raccoons, and skunks also go into a winter sleep. However, there is some question as to whether these animals are really hibernating. For example, the body temperature of a black bear remains near normal during its winter sleep. Some black bears even leave their dens and wander around for a time. They then return to their dens.

How is hibernation an adaptation? For some animals, hibernation is a way of surviving the extreme cold of winter. For others, hibernation may be a way of surviving during a season when food is scarce.

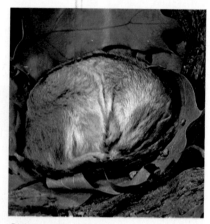

Chipmunk in den

For Lesson Questions, turn to page 388.

Grizzly bear in fall

Activity

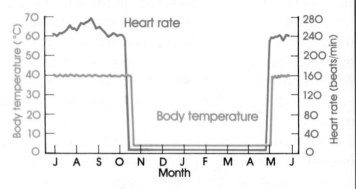

How are body temperature and heart rate related to hibernation?

Procedure

The graph shows the changes in body temperature and heart rate in the arctic ground squirrel. The data is for one year, beginning with the month of July. Use the graph to answer the questions.

1. During what month does the arctic ground squirrel go into hibernation?
2. During what month does the arctic ground squirrel awake from hibernation?
3. What is the arctic ground squirrel's body temperature when the animal is active?
4. What is the arctic ground squirrel's body temperature when the animal is hibernating?
5. What is the approximate heart rate of an active arctic ground squirrel?
6. What is the approximate heart rate of a hibernating arctic ground squirrel?

Conclusion

In an arctic ground squirrel, what is the relationship of body temperature and heart rate to periods of activity and hibernation?

Using science ideas

In some operations, doctors lower the body temperature of patients. They do this by packing the patient's body in ice. Why might this be done?

Learned Behavior

How does the ability to learn help an animal to survive?

Learning is a process that results in a change in behavior because of experience. For example, suppose your dog comes to eat when you shake the food sack each day. Now suppose you stop shaking the food sack at feeding time. Instead, you rattle a can of marbles each day just before you feed the dog. Will your dog learn to come and eat when it hears the marbles rattling? If it does, the dog's behavior will have changed because of a new experience. That is learning.

Since the environment is always changing, animals must be able to learn. For example, suppose raccoons begin feeding on garbage in cans in a park. For months they tip over the garbage cans and make a mess every night as they eat. Finally the park rangers decide to do something about the problem. They have the garbage cans emptied at the end of each day.

Will the racoons continue to look for food in the garbage cans and finally starve? No — the raccoons will learn that food is no longer available in the gar-

Raccoon searching for food

Elephants learning to stand on their hind legs

bage cans. Although their environment has changed, they will get food in other ways. They may eat more of their natural food, such as insects and wild berries. They may also learn to feed at a nearby garbage dump.

How does learning take place? For most kinds of learning, there are two important steps. The first step is to repeat the experience. This is called practice. For a circus elephant to learn to stand on its hind legs, it must repeat the experience. In other words, it must practice. For a person to learn to play the piano, he or she must practice.

The second step in learning is reinforcement (rē in-fôrs'mənt). This lets the learner know whether the practice is correct. One kind of reinforcement is punishment. A mother lion teaching her cubs to hunt may slap them if they don't follow her lead.

Another type of reinforcement is reward. If your dog performs a trick, you may reward it with food or a pat on the head. Wild-animal trainers often reward their animals with food. Words of praise from the teacher reward a piano student who has practiced a musical piece.

A guide dog must be taught to lead a blind person across streets and around objects. But in some animals a different and unusual type of learning takes place. It is called **imprinting.** Imprinting depends on only one experience. For example, newly-hatched geese will follow the first moving thing they see. Usually this is their mother. However, if they see a person or some object move first, it becomes the "mother." This imprinting results in the geese behaving as if the person or object is their real mother.

Some kinds of learning may take place only in humans. Learning that requires imagination and the making of mental pictures seems to occur only in humans. You use mental pictures to learn about the structure of matter. You make mental pictures of atoms, and the particles that make up atoms. In such learning you form one mental picture after another.

Training a guide dog

For Lesson Questions, turn to page 388.

Ideas to Remember

▶ Structural adaptations, such as protective coloration, help organisms to survive.
▶ Some adaptations involve activities or behavior patterns that help animals to survive.
▶ Animals are born with certain instincts that aid survival.
▶ Migration involves the movement of animals to better feeding or breeding grounds.
▶ Many cold-blooded animals and some warm-blooded animals survive through the winter by hibernating.
▶ Learning is the result of experience. Most types of learning are aided by practice and reinforcement.

Reviewing the Chapter

SCIENCE WORDS

A. Write the letter of the term that best matches the definition. Not all the terms will be used.

1. Behavior in which an animal goes into a deep sleep
2. Adaptation in which an animal looks like some dangerous or poisonous animal
3. A process that results in a change of behavior because of experience
4. An animal with a fairly constant body temperature
5. Behavior that involves the movement of animals over a long distance
6. Adaptation in which an animal looks similar to something in its environment
7. Any behavior pattern that an animal is born with
8. A region where animals go to reproduce and to raise their young

a. protective resemblance
b. warm-blooded animal
c. hibernation
d. protective coloration
e. breeding grounds
f. migration
g. cold-blooded animal
h. mimicry
i. instinct
j. learning

UNDERSTANDING IDEAS

A. Write the terms in two groups: behavioral adaptations; structural adaptations.

large canines	nest-building	webbed feet	hibernation
thick fur	pointed beak	migration	sharp quills

B. Study the graph. Then answer the questions that follow.

1. During which months are the caribou most likely to be migrating from one region to another?
2. During which month or months do the caribou travel the farthest?
3. Caribou live in northern Canada. In which general direction are they most likely to travel during the fall?

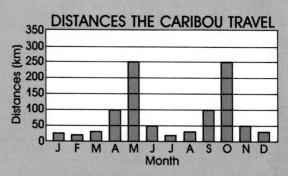

DISTANCES THE CARIBOU TRAVEL

C. Write the term that does not belong in each group. Explain why the term does not belong.

  1. bat's wings, frog's legs, lion's teeth, gibbon's arms

2. chameleon, kangaroo, snowshoe hare, snowy owl

3. eagle's beak, tiger's claws, cow's molars, musk ox's fur

USING IDEAS

1. Observe some of the animals in your community. Identify examples of protective coloration or protective resemblance.

2. You have five fingers on each hand. One finger is a thumb. How is your thumb a structural adaptation?

THINKING LIKE A SCIENTIST

Answer the following questions. You may be able to answer some of the questions just by thinking about them. To answer other questions, you may have to do some research.

1. An animal's feet are structural adaptations that help it move from place to place. How are the feet of animals that run fast different from those of slow runners? Study the drawings at the right. They show three basic types of feet. Form a hypothesis about how each type of foot is used.

2. Some animals, such as birds and fish, are darker colored on the top of their bodies than on the bottom. How do you think this coloring pattern is an adaptation for these animals?

3. You probably have heard someone say that you can't teach an old dog new tricks. What is the basis for such a saying? Can an old dog learn new tricks? Support your answer.

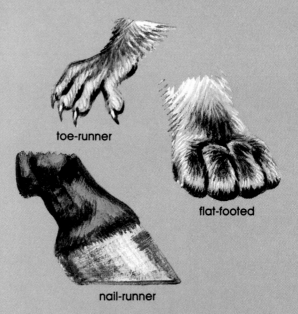

toe-runner

flat-footed

nail-runner

CHAPTER 4

Climate and Life

What became of the dinosaurs? As you may recall, some scientists believe that about 65 million years ago the earth was struck by a giant meteorite. When this object struck, it sent huge amounts of dust up into the air. Months, or perhaps years, passed before the dust settled. The dust blocked out the light of the sun, leading to the death of most plant life. With the death of plants, the death of most animals followed. Some scientists believe that the dinosaurs disappeared during the time of this great dust cloud.

About 10,000 years ago, giant animals that looked much like elephants roamed the earth. These animals, called woolly mammoths, were covered with long, coarse hair. They had huge curving tusks that they used for digging in the hard dirt. A tusk is a long curving tooth that sticks out of the side of the mouth.

Unlike the elephants, which live in hot climates, the mammoths lived in the Arctic. The mammoths had a thick layer of fat to protect them from the cold weather of their region.

Woolly mammoth   African elephant

Like the dinosaurs, the woolly mammoths are extinct. But the dinosaurs lived long before humans were on the earth. People could not leave drawings or written records of dinosaurs. The woolly mammoths and early cave people lived at the same time. The cave people drew pictures of the mammoths on the cave walls. These ancient people also told stories about the animals with the curving tusks.

In 1800 the chief of a tribe in Siberia came upon something scary. He found a huge tusk sticking out of a frozen mound of earth. The chief was scared because he thought the center of the earth was filled with dangerous animals. The chief did not do anything about his finding for many months. Finally he took a closer look. He began digging into the ground. Much to his surprise, the tusk was attached to a frozen dead animal! The animal was a woolly mammoth. At that time scientists guessed that the animal had been buried in the ice about 10,000 years.

Cave drawing of a mammoth

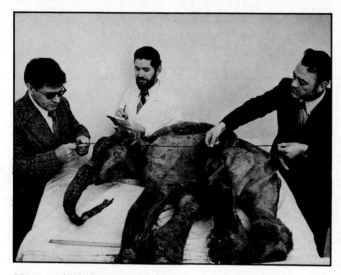
Mammoth skeleton

Word of the chief's discovery spread quickly. Soon other people were digging for mammoths. In fact, searchers dug for bones and dead animal bodies all over Siberia. Thirty-nine frozen mammoths were found. Only four were complete bodies. The rest were only body fragments.

The woolly mammoths' bodies were well preserved. Scientists thus believed the animals had died quickly. The mammoths were probably flash-frozen in place. What event could have frozen the mammoths where they stood? How had they remained preserved so well for so long?

Now try this

Work in a team of four or five students. You will need three fresh plant leaves, a hand lens, a microscope, a slide, a scalpel, and a plastic bag. Using the equipment you have, observe the leaves carefully. Record your observations. Then place the leaves in the plastic bag. Label the bag with your names and the date. Place the bag in a freezer at school.

By the next day the leaves will have been frozen. Look at the leaves. How have they changed? Which changes are the result of the freezing process? You may wish to freeze other materials that are available. For example, you could use a piece of lettuce leaf, a small tomato, and a slice of onion. Compare they way these items look after freezing with the way the leaves look.

After you have completed this activity, answer these questions: (1) Suppose the leaves had been placed in water and then frozen. Would they have been better preserved? (2) Which is a better process for preserving the leaves—slow freezing or fast freezing?

The woolly mammoths lived only in a very cold region of the earth. In this chapter you will find out about several regions of the earth. Each has a different climate. You will find out what types of plants and animals live in these regions.

Life Zones

What is a life zone, or biome?

Plants and animals are not distributed evenly over all the earth. Also, different kinds of plants and animals live in different places. What accounts for these differences?

All organisms need certain things to survive. They need food, air, water, space in which to live, and the right temperature range. These conditions for life are found in a relatively narrow region on, just above, and just below the surface of the earth. This narrow band or region is called the biosphere (bī′ə sfir). *Bios* means "life." Therefore the **biosphere** is the earth's life sphere. It extends only about 2 km above and 2 km below the earth's surface. In that narrow band there

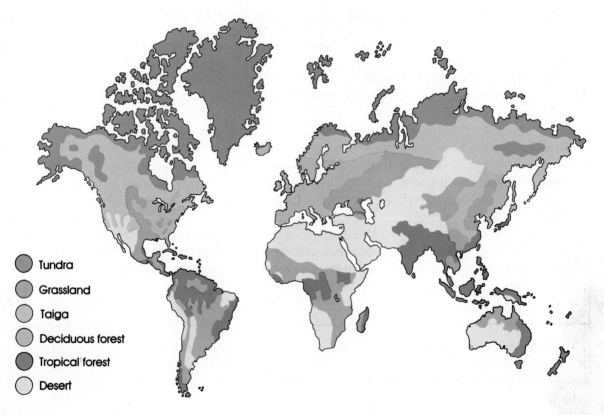

- Tundra
- Grassland
- Taiga
- Deciduous forest
- Tropical forest
- Desert

is enough air and water for life. There is also enough solar energy to warm the region and to enable green plants to make food.

The same amount of air and water is not available everywhere on the earth. Neither is the amount of solar energy nor the temperature range the same everywhere. As a result, different kinds and numbers of plants and animals exist in different places. These places, or life zones, are called biomes (bī′ōmz). A **biome** is a region of the earth where many of the same kinds of plants and animals live. All parts of a biome have about the same climate. **Climate** is the average weather for a large region over a long period of time.

The map on page 78 shows the locations of six major land biomes. Notice that the same biomes are found throughout the world. In addition the oceans are often referred to as a life zone, or biome. Some biomes are named after the most common types of plants that grow there. Others are named for the places where they are located.

The table below lists the average yearly precipitation for the land biomes. The average temperature range for the year is also given. Which one has the greatest range in temperature?

AVERAGE PRECIPITATION AND TEMPERATURE OF LAND BIOMES

Biome	Average precipitation (yearly)	Average temperature range (yearly)
Tundra	11 cm	−26°C to 4°C
Taiga	35 cm	−10°C to 14°C
Deciduous forest	115 cm	6°C to 28°C
Tropical forest	253 cm	25°C to 27°C
Grassland	90 cm	0°C to 25°C
Desert	16 cm	24°C to 32°C

For Lesson Questions, turn to page 390.

Activity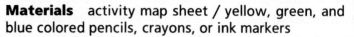

How is going up a mountain like traveling from the tropics to the North Pole?

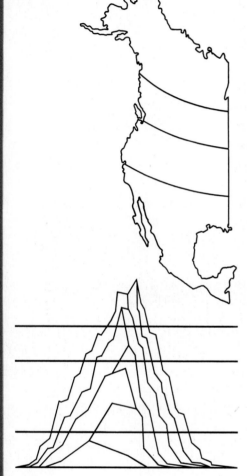

Materials activity map sheet / yellow, green, and blue colored pencils, crayons, or ink markers

Procedure

A. From your teacher, get a sheet of paper on which the maps that you will need for this activity are printed. The maps are like the ones shown here, only larger.

B. Several biomes are shown on the map of North America. Use the table on page 79 to find the temperature range for each of these biomes. On your map, write the temperature range for each biome.

C. Study both maps. Compare the kinds of plants that grow in the biomes with those that grow on the mountain.

1. Which part of the mountain best matches the desert biome of North America? Color both of these regions yellow.
2. Which part of the mountain is most like grassland and deciduous forest biomes? Color these regions light green.
3. Which part of the mountain is most like the taiga? Color these regions light blue.
4. Which part of the mountain is most like the tundra? Color these regions dark blue.
5. How do you think the top of a very high mountain is like the North Pole?

Conclusion

How is going up a mountain like traveling from the tropics to the North Pole? How is it different?

Using Science Ideas

How do you think the temperature will change as you go up a mountain?

The Tundra

How do living things survive in the tundra?

The **tundra** (tun′drə) biome is in the far north. It is the coldest of all biomes. Plants and animals of the tundra must adapt to sudden seasonal changes.

Winter in the tundra is very harsh. There are many months of cold and darkness, and food is scarce. Animals such as caribou, gulls, and foxes often must migrate in search of food. Some smaller animals, such as lemmings, burrow under the snow for protection from the cold and from predators. Others that can survive winter in the tundra include the snowy owl, ptarmigan (tär′mə gən), and musk ox. What adaptation may help musk oxen withstand the winter cold?

The tundra. Clockwise: musk ox, ptarmigan, collared lemming, arctic fox

The tundra summer lasts for only 6 to 8 weeks. There are long hours of daylight and no darkness. During the short summer a thin top layer of the earth thaws. Ponds and puddles form because water from the melting ice cannot seep into the frozen soil below.

The plants of the tundra grow quickly in summer, but they do not last long. Most of the plants are very small. They include grasses, lichens, and mosses. Some woody plants are only a few centimeters tall. There are no trees in the tundra. There is not enough water deep in the soil for trees to grow. Also, trees could not survive the strong winds.

The tundra. Clockwise: lichens, deer fly, sharp-shinned hawk, peregrine falcon

Millions of insects hatch in the ponds and puddles that form in the summer. The air is filled with swarms of black flies, deer flies, and mosquitoes. The insects irritate some animals, but are food for many birds that nest in the tundra during the summer. Other birds, such as eagles, falcons, and hawks, feed on lemmings and other small mammals. Why do these birds migrate to other areas in winter?

Black fly swarm

Science & Technology

▼ The Trans-Alaska Pipeline is built on permafrost — permanently frozen ground beneath the earth's surface. Stretching for 1,280 km, some of the pipeline is aboveground and some is underground. The oil it carries is hot — about 58°C. The pipeline is designed to keep the permafrost from melting.

▲ Over 640 km of the pipeline rest on specially made metal supports. In the supports are thin tubes containing liquid ammonia (a). The ammonia absorbs heat from the soil, and vaporizes. It rises to radiators (b), where the heat is released harmlessly into the air. As the ammonia cools and condenses, it runs down the tubes and the cycle begins again. Sliding "shoes" (c) on the crossbars of the supports allow the pipeline to move sideways to prevent damage during earthquakes or thermal expansion and contraction. The pipeline itself is well insulated, Where the pipeline runs underground, it is surrounded by small pipes through which refrigerated brine is pumped. This keeps the ground frozen. Why is it environmentally important to keep the permafrost frozen? What do you think would happen if it thawed?

For Lesson Questions, turn to page 390.

The Taiga

What are the features of the taiga?

The **taiga** (tī′gə) is the largest biome. It is south of the tundra. This biome spreads across North America, northern Europe, and northern Asia. *Taiga* is a Russian word that means "swamp forest." This name is used because the melting snow often causes swampy conditions in early summer.

The taiga forests are an important resource. Many trees are cut for lumber and for pulp from which paper is made. The main trees of this biome are conifers (kō′nə fərz), such as spruce, fir, and pine. **Conifers** are trees that produce seeds in cones. Most conifers are evergreens and have needlelike leaves. Conifers are an important link in the food chain in the taiga. During the long winter, deer, elk, and other animals browse on the branches of these trees. Squirrels and some birds eat the seeds from the cones.

Taiga and pinecones

Much of the ground under the trees is shaded. The limited amount of sunlight prevents many kinds of plants from growing. Only a few grasses and other small plants can survive. These grow mostly in small meadows and clearings. During the summer they are food for large grazing animals, such as moose, elk, and deer. Also during the summer there are many small insects. These are food for a variety of birds. Beavers live in small ponds and streams all year long.

For Lesson Questions, turn to page 390.

In winter many of the taiga animals are less active. Insects hibernate, and squirrels and bears sleep much of the time. Certain birds and other animals migrate out of the taiga. Predators, such as lynxes, wolves, and wolverines, remain active. They hunt snowshoe hares and other small animals for food.

Clockwise: beaver, elk, lynx

The Deciduous Forest

What are the characteristics of the deciduous forest?

A very different biome is found south of the taiga. There are fewer conifer trees in this biome. Instead of trees with needles, most of the trees have broad leaves. This is the **deciduous** (di sij′ü əs) **forest** biome. It is named after the broad-leaved trees that are most common there.

Deciduous trees lose their leaves at some time during the year. Most deciduous trees lose their leaves in the autumn months. The climate in the deciduous forest biome is moist, with rain in summer and snow in winter. The winter is cold and the summer is hot. There are four seasons in the deciduous forest biome. In order to survive in this biome, the plants and animals must adapt to the seasonal changes.

The deciduous forest. Clockwise: hydrangeas, ferns, rhododendrons

Great horned owl

Raccoon

Tennessee warbler

Black bear

The deciduous forest has several layers. In a way the forest may be compared to a large city. The largest and most dominant form of life is the tall trees of the forest. They are like the skyscrapers in a city. There may be more than 100 different kinds of large trees in the forest.

Next are the smaller trees. They are like the large hotels in a city. Beneath them are flowering bushes, such as rhododendrons and hydrangeas. Beneath these flowering shrubs are as many as 100 kinds of smaller plants, including ferns. Finally, on the forest floor there is a thick undergrowth of small plants. To what parts of a city might ferns, and the plants on the forest floor be compared?

Animals also live at different levels in the forest. Birds live at different levels, depending on their nesting and feeding habits. What reasons can you think of for the animals shown to live where they do?

In spring, when sunlight reaches the forest floor, many wild flowers bloom. In summer the broad leaves of the trees shade the ground. Some light filters through the leaves—enough for shrubs to grow. Mosses and ferns grow in the deep shade.

Gray squirrels

There are many kinds of trees in the deciduous forest. Some of these are maple, oak, walnut, elm, and beech. Many of these trees produce fruits and nuts that are eaten by animals.

In autumn the leaves change from green to red, gold, or brown. The leaves fall and cover the ground. As the leaves decay, the minerals they contain are released and help to enrich the soil.

The animals of the deciduous forest include deer, squirrels, chipmunks, raccoons, and skunks. There are many small birds. Larger birds, such as grouse and wild turkeys, are also common. Near ponds and streams you might find snakes, turtles, and frogs.

In winter many animals are less active. Some birds migrate from the taiga to pass the winter in the deciduous forest. Other birds migrate from the deciduous forest to warmer areas. Many reptiles hibernate.

Turkey

Deciduous forest

Oak leaf

For Lesson Questions, turn to page 390.

The Tropical Forest

What are the characteristics of the tropical forest?

The biome that is the richest in plants and animals is the **tropical forest.** Scientists believe that many plants and animals in this biome are still undiscovered and unclassified. Like the deciduous forest, the tropical forest also is organized in layers. Plants and animals are present in huge numbers. More than 1,000 different kinds of plants may grow in an area about the size of three football fields.

Most trees in the tropical forest have broad green leaves. The leaves stay green all year. The reason for this is that the climate does not vary. It is almost always hot and rainy. There is little change in temperature throughout the year.

Cashew apple and nut   Tropical forest   Candle bush

89

Blue-crowned motmot

The tropical forest biome is a valuable resource. It is important in many ways. At one time, tropical forests covered large areas of land. Today, almost half of them have been destroyed. There is some evidence that this is having a world-wide effect on temperature and on rainfall. In addition, tropical forests are the source of many useful products that cannot be found anywhere else in the world.

What is it like in the tropical forest? Outdoors, you would feel as if you had a roof over your head. The leaves of the tall trees actually form a kind of roof. This roof keeps out sunlight, so few plants grow on the forest floor.

Many strange and beautiful plants, such as orchids, grow on the tall trees. These plants are vines that climb toward the sunlight. What adaptations do such plants have? Most of the plants have beautiful and colorful flowers that attract insects and birds. Many of the birds are brightly colored.

Most animals of the tropical forest live in the trees. These animals include many kinds of insects, lizards, snakes, frogs, birds, and mammals such as monkeys. All the animals have a good supply of food. Many feed on seeds and fruits from the trees. Some snakes, such

Toucan

Orchid

Python

Tiger beetle feeding

Squirrel monkey

as the huge pythons and anacondas, prey on the large animals of the forest.

The soil of the tropical forest is very poor. Almost all the nutrients are in the plants themselves. There are few leaves to decay and enrich the soil. When a plant or animal dies, it decays quickly. The roots of the forest plants grow close to the soil's surface. The nutrients are immediately taken up by the growing plants.

SKILL: Making a model

Finding Out

How can you make a model biome?

Choose one of the biomes discussed in this chapter. It may be a biome that you have not studied yet. Use reference books to find out as much as you can about the biome—its plants and animals, its soil, its climate, and so on.

Get an empty 3- to 4-L glass jar with a tight-fitting lid. Be sure that the jar is clean. Collect the materials needed to make a "mini" biome. Include both plants and animals. Be sure that the living things have enough space, food, air, and water to survive. In what ways is your model like the real biome? In what ways is it different?

For Lesson Questions, turn to page 390.

The Grassland

What is the grassland like?

The largest **grassland** biome is in North America. It covers most of the central United States and a large part of Canada. This region is also called the prairie. The term *prairie* means "farm field" or "meadow."

The climate in the grassland biome is similar to the climate in the deciduous forest. However, there is less rain and snow than in places where deciduous forests are found. Also, the summers are hot and the winters are cold.

Many years ago most of the grassland biome was covered with native grasses. Some of the grasses grew as much as 2 m tall. Growing among the grasses were hundreds of kinds of wild flowers and some woody shrubs. Many of the same kinds of animals that lived there then still live there today.

Quail (top) and prairie grasses and flowers

Grassland   Wheat

Cattails

Prairie dog

Over the last few hundred years the grassland biome changed greatly. The changes were caused by humans. Today very little of this biome exists in its natural state. Now the grasslands are used in two major ways. In those areas with the highest rainfall, the native grasses have been plowed under. Cereal grains — such as wheat, corn, oats, barley, and rye — are planted in their place. Here the upper layers of soil are deep, dark, and fertile. The roots and other plant parts that remain after harvesting decay and enrich the soil. Drier grasslands not suitable for growing grain are used as grazing land for cattle and sheep. In some places, overgrazing has ruined the land by causing wind erosion. Much of the fertile soil has blown away, making the land unsuitable even for grazing.

Cattails and sedges grow where there is enough moisture to form marshes, and near lakes and ponds. There are few trees, mainly cottonwoods, oaks, and willows. They are mainly in the river valleys where there is enough moisture to support their growth.

Meadowlark

Bison

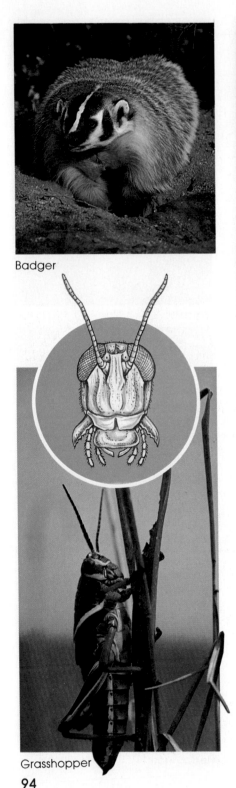
Badger

Grasshopper

Animals of the grassland eat the leaves, seeds, and roots of the many plants, or they prey on other animals. Some representative animals are bison, coyotes, wolves, and jack rabbits. Prairie dogs, mice, and badgers live in underground burrows. Birds such as meadow larks, quail, and sparrows nest among the plants. Larger birds, such as owls and hawks, prey on the smaller birds and mammals.

Insects, such as the grasshopper, are also common. Grasshoppers are well adapted to eating plants. They have two lips and two powerful jaws with sharp teeth. The jaws, or chewing mouth parts, move from side to side, cutting and grinding the food. How else are grasshoppers adapted to eating plants? Grasshoppers can do much damage to grain crops and other plants. Often they will invade orchards and fully strip the leaves from fruit trees, sometimes killing the trees. Swarms of grasshoppers may migrate hundreds of miles in search of food. But all grasshoppers are not pests. Some eat only plants that are weeds.

94

For Lesson Questions, turn to page 390.

The Desert

What are the features of the desert?

The **desert** is a region that receives little or no rain. The rain that does fall evaporates quickly. The largest desert biome in the world is the Sahara, in Africa. It receives almost no rain and has almost no plant life.

Some of the deserts in the United States are very different from the Sahara. Compare the deserts shown in the pictures. How are the two deserts different? The deserts of northern Nevada and northern Utah may get up to 25 cm of precipitation per year. This is enough to support the growth of shrubs, such as sagebrush. These deserts are called cold deserts because the winter temperatures are very low.

Scorpion

Sahara

Arizona desert

Kangaroo rat

Collared lizard

All deserts have one thing in common besides their dryness. There is always a wide range in temperature between day and night. Often the days are hot and the nights are cold.

Plants and animals of the desert have many adaptations that allow them to live there. Some plants, such as cactuses, store water that can be used during dry periods. Other desert plants have thick leathery leaves. Little water is lost from such leaves. The roots of desert plants are shallow. But they extend very far in all directions.

All animals that live in the desert have adaptations that prevent water loss from their bodies. Reptiles, such as snakes and lizards, have tight waterproof skin. Some animals, such as the kangaroo rat, can live without drinking any water. They get their moisture from the plants they eat. And they prevent water loss by staying underground during the day.

Insects and birds are common in the desert. The birds eat the insects. Lizards and scorpions also eat insects. Coyotes, hawks, and rattlesnakes prey on small animals, such as rabbits and mice.

Some deserts in Arizona and southern California have been changed into lush farms and resorts by bringing water to them. This is called irrigation. Many other deserts could be used for growing food if people could find ways to irrigate them.

Irrigation of the desert

96

For Lesson Questions, turn to page 390.

Activity

How are these animals adapted to conditions where they live?

Materials reference books

Procedure

A. Six animals are pictured in this activity. Some are found in only one biome. Others live in more than one biome. Each is able to survive because it obtains the necessities of life from the region or regions where it lives.

B. Design a table in which to record the following information for each animal.
  1. The biome or biomes in which it lives
  2. The environmental conditions where it lives
  3. What it eats
  4. Any predators it has

Conclusion

1. For each animal, identify any adaptations it has to **(a)** survive environmental conditions, **(b)** obtain food, and **(c)** defend itself.
2. Which animal is adapted to the widest range of conditions?

Using Science Ideas

Suppose each animal were transferred to a biome in which it is not normally found. What survival problems would be faced by the animal?

wolverine

striped skunk

desert iguana

giraffe

muskox

anaconda

Aquatic Habitats

What are the features of aquatic habitats?

The term *biome* is usually used only for land regions. Yet water covers most of the earth. And many plants and animals live in water. A body of water where organisms live is called an **aquatic** (ə kwat′ik) **habitat.** A habitat is like a biome.

One type of aquatic habitat is the **freshwater habitat.** Ponds, lakes, and streams are freshwater habitats. Many kinds of plants are found in or near the water. Cattails may grow at the water's edge. The roots of water lilies anchor at the bottom. But their leaves and flowers float on top of the water. Other plants may live under the water.

Some animals that live in or near fresh water are birds and insects, such as dragonflies and mosquitoes, frogs, toads, turtles, and snakes.

Dragonfly

Mosquito larvae Pond

Shrimp (top), blue crab, and oysters

Another aquatic habitat is the **marine habitat.** The marine habitat includes all the water in the oceans and seas. This water is salt water. The marine habitat is a huge one, for the marine waters cover about 70 percent of the earth. Many kinds of fish live in marine waters. Crabs, shrimp, and lobsters also live in marine waters. The oceans and seas supply much of the world's food.

Lobster

Most life in marine waters is found in shallow water or near the surface. There is a good reason for this. The source of all food in the oceans is the plants that carry out photosynthesis. To do this they need sunlight. But plants cannot get sunlight if they are deep in the water. Microscopic plants float on the surface. These plants belong to a group of organisms called **plankton** (plangk′tən). Other plants, such as kelp and other types of seaweed, are very large. These plants live on or near the surface of the water.

Some animals in the marine habitat feed on producers, which are living things that make their own

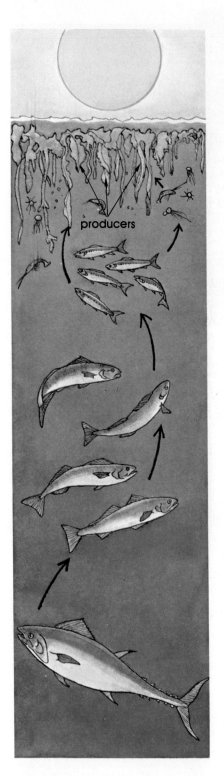

producers

food. Others feed on animals that eat producers. Therefore every animal in a marine habitat depends on producers. The food chain formed by this relationship can be seen in the drawing.

In addition to sunlight, producers need nutrients. In shallow water, nutrients from decaying organisms are available. In deep water, nutrients on the bottom are a long way from the producers. But there are some areas where nutrients from the bottom are brought to the surface. In these areas, water from the bottom rises to the surface in a process called **upwelling.** In regions where there is upwelling, there are large numbers of living things.

There are areas within the marine habitat that have certain characteristics that support living things. These characteristics are determined in part by the temperature of the water and the shape of the coast. Coral reefs are found in tropical waters, such as those near Florida. The Florida Keys are islands that have been built up by coral. Many beautiful tropical fish are found near coral reefs.

Along rocky coasts, such as in California and New England, small pools form during low tide. Starfish, mussels, and barnacles are often found in these pools.

Coral reef

Estuary

A third type of aquatic habitat is the estuary (es'chü er ē). An **estuary** is a place where a freshwater river flows into an ocean or a sea. The estuary is a good habitat for many forms of life. So the estuaries of the world are also important sources of food for people. That is why we must not pollute the streams that empty into estuaries.

Ideas to Remember

► A biome is made up of all the living things that are found in a certain region with a particular climate.

► Certain plants and animals are adapted to the conditions found in each biome.

► The six major land biomes are the tundra, the taiga, the deciduous forest, the tropical forest, the grassland, and the desert.

► Many of the plants and animals in one biome could not survive in another biome.

► Aquatic habitats are bodies of water in which certain kinds of plants and animals live. They are like land biomes.

► Like the grasslands, aquatic habitats are important sources of food for people.

Tide pool

For Lesson Questions, turn to page 390.

Reviewing the Chapter

A. Use all the terms below to complete the sentences.

deciduous forest   biome   grasslands
tropical forest   desert   taiga
aquatic habitat   tundra

A region of the earth where the same kinds of plants and animals live is called a/an __1__. In the __2__ the soil is frozen and no large plants are found. In the __3__, however, conifers are an important resource. The __4__ is named after the broad-leaved trees that grow there. The __5__ is rich in plant and animal life, yet the soil there is poor. The __6__ receives little precipitation and can support only specialized plants, such as the cactus. Prairies, or __7__, are now often used to grow grain or to graze animals. A body of water in which organisms live is called a/an __8__.

B. Unscramble each group of letters to find a science term from the chapter. Write a sentence using each term.

1. gaita   **2.** klontnap   **3.** etamlic
4. staryue   **5.** glinwuelp   **6.** nierfsco

UNDERSTANDING IDEAS

A. The graph on the left shows the average monthly temperature in a certain biome. The graph on the right shows the average monthly precipitation in a certain biome.

1. Which biome does the temperature graph apply to?
2. Which biome does the precipitation graph apply to?

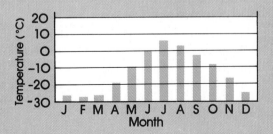

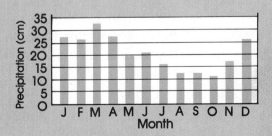

B. List the six land biomes, starting with the biome that has the most severe winter weather and ending with the one that has no winter season. How does the vegetation change as the weather conditions change from one biome to another?

C. Explain why most marine life is found in shallow water or near the surface of the ocean.

D. Identify the biome in which each of the following groups of animals lives.

1. eagles, falcons, snowy owls, caribou
2. deer, raccoons, turkeys, frogs
3. wolves, lynxes, squirrels, moose
4. kangaroo rats, scorpions, rattlesnakes, lizards
5. monkeys, pythons, insects, toucans

USING IDEAS

1. In the Science & Technology feature on page 83, you learned about one problem that engineers faced in building the Trans-Alaska Pipeline. Find out what other problems they had to overcome in building the pipeline.
2. Explain why an aquatic habitat is like a biome.
3. Desert plants usually grow apart rather than close together. Find out why this is so.
4. Find out about the problems that engineers face in building an irrigation system for desert regions.

THINKING LIKE A SCIENTIST

Answer the following questions. You may be able to answer some of the questions just by thinking about them. To answer other questions, you may have to do some research.

1. You have learned that the biome covering the northernmost region of the world is the arctic tundra. The major biome in the Antarctic, the southernmost region of the world, is not tundra. It is classified as an arctic-alpine desert. How would the climate of this biome differ from that of the tundra? What differences would you expect to find in the plants and animals of the two biomes?
2. The tide-pool area along the immediate shoreline of an ocean is a unique aquatic habitat. Why is it so difficult for sea plants and animals to survive in this habitat? Describe a tidepool animal and its adaptive structures.

Science in Careers

The general name for the science that studies living organisms is *biology*. However, there are many fields in biology.

Some biologists study cells. These people investigate the inner workings of cells and the chemistry of life at the level of the cell. The study of cells is called *cytology* (sī tol'ə jē). Some biologists study tissue. They are interested in identifying different kinds of tissue.

A **botanist** is a person who studies plants. Some botanists study plant growth. Botanists also attempt to develop new types, or strains, of plants. Botanists may develop strains of food plants that give higher yields. Or the new strains may be resistant to diseases.

A person who studies animals is called a **zoologist.** Some zoologists specialize in the study of animal behavior. They try to identify the factors that control animal behavior. In some cases, they try to learn the meaning of an animal's movements or actions. They have learned that many animals communicate through their actions. There are many interesting fields in the life sciences.

Botanist

Zoologists

People in Science

EUGENIE CLARK
(1922–)

Dr. Clark is a professor of zoology at the University of Maryland. Her major interest is marine life. Much of her recent research has involved studies on the behavior of sharks. Her studies have indicated that sharks, like many other animals, can learn. For instance, some sharks can be trained to push a target to obtain food as a reward. Dr. Clark, along with other scientists, is also investigating the mating behavior and migration patterns of various kinds of sharks.

A scientist observing the feeding behavior of a shark

Developing Skills

WORD SKILLS

At the back of this book is a section called the Glossary and another section called the Index. A glossary lists the important terms in a book and their definitions. An index lists the main topics covered in a book and the pages on which information about the topics can be found. Subtopics and their page numbers are listed under some main topics.

Use the Glossary and Index of this book to answer the questions.

1. In what order are the terms and topics listed in the Glossary and Index?
2. What other helpful information is contained in the Glossary?
3. Find the term *tissue* in the Glossary and write the definition. Now find this term in a dictionary and write the definitions. How does a glossary differ from a dictionary?
4. Suppose you wanted to obtain information on the topic of how cells reproduce. Which topics and subtopics would help you locate this information?
5. Find the term *hormone* in the Glossary. How is this term pronounced? What is the meaning of this term?
6. Find the term *cell*, in the Glossary. What are two definitions for this term? On what pages can this term be found?

READING A LINE GRAPH

A line graph can be used to show how things change. For example, the line graph on the next page shows how the amount of the earth covered by forests has changed. The forests shown on this graph are deciduous forests and tropical forests. Use the graph to answer the following questions.

1. What is the first year shown in this graph? What is the last year shown?
2. How much of the earth was covered by tropical forests in 1950?
3. How much of the earth was covered by deciduous forests in 1975?
4. How will the amount of the earth covered by tropical forests change by 2000 if the pattern continues?
5. What will happen to the amount of the earth covered by deciduous forests by 2000?
6. Suppose you measured a tree every year for six years. The first year it was 90 cm tall. The second year the tree was 160 cm tall. It was 280 cm tall the third year, 420 cm tall the fourth year, and 550 cm tall the fifth year. The sixth year the tree was 650 cm tall. Use this data to make a line graph. Put the measurements along the side line. Put the year along the bottom line.

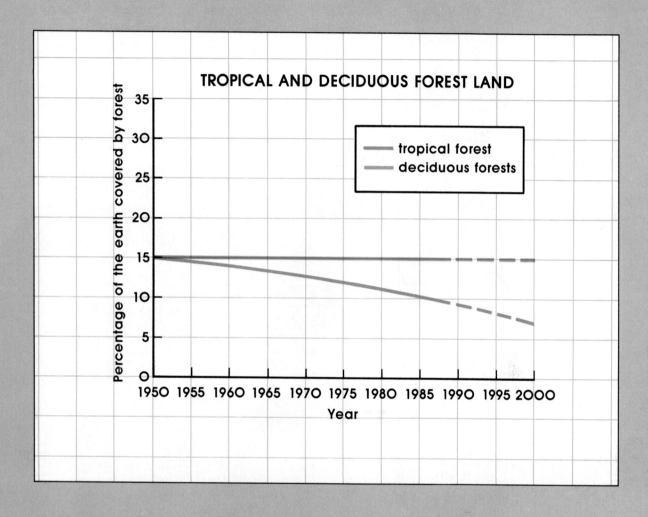

TROPICAL AND DECIDUOUS FOREST LAND

Percentage of the earth covered by forest

— tropical forest
— deciduous forests

Year

USING THINKING SKILLS

Forests are an important source of many resources. But forests also use up land that might be used for housing or farming. Think about this as you do the following.

1. Use reference books to find out what resources are obtained from forests.
2. Why, do you think, has the amount of land covered by deciduous forests not changed since 1950? Use reference books to help you find out.
3. Should the same methods used to save deciduous forests be used to save tropical forests? Explain your answer.
4. Should forests be allowed to remain or should more forests be destroyed to make room for farmland? Explain your answer.

UNIT TWO

Investigating Our Physical World

Chapter 6—Chemical Changes in Matter A fireworks display is an example of a chemical change. What forms of energy are released by this chemical reaction? An insight into different kinds of chemical reactions and other changes in matter is presented in Chapter 6.

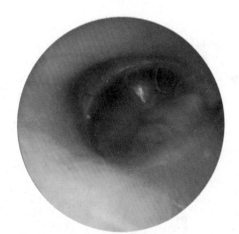

Chapter 8—Sound Energy Have you ever had an inflamed eardrum? If so, it may have looked like the one in this picture, as seen through fiber optics. In Chapter 8 you will learn about the only form of energy that you can hear.

Chapter 9 — Using Electricity This chapter will help you realize how important electricity is. From simple electric circuits found in a home to microchips like the one in the picture, electricity affects the way you live, work, and play.

Chapter 5 — Matter and Atoms
A scanning tunneling microscope produced this highly magnified image of the surface of graphite. The bumps or "hills" in the image are believed to represent carbon atoms. In Chapter 5 you will find out more about the atomic structure of matter.

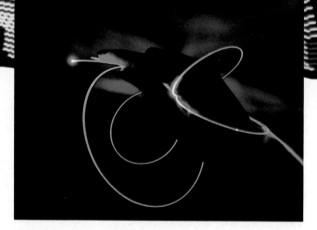

Chapter 7 — Light Energy Twisted into any shape, fiber optics transmits images without distortion. The light is conducted by thin glass or plastic fibers enclosed in a flexible tube. In this chapter you will learn about the characteristics and behavior of light.

CHAPTER 5
Matter and Atoms

In the next four pages, you will take a journey with your eyes. Some of the things you will see are ordinary. You may see some of these things every day. Yet they will not look ordinary. You will be seeing them with "new eyes." Come, let's begin the trip.

▲ What is in this photograph? Suppose you could put yourself in the picture. How big would you be? This photograph was taken from a distance of 800 km from the earth. Huge canyons and rivers on earth look like wiggly lines here. Suppose you were standing on a cliff above a river. You would be too small to be seen in the picture.

Now imagine that you are on a cliff ▶ by the sea. You might see this nest with a mother bird, a just-hatched bird, and an egg.

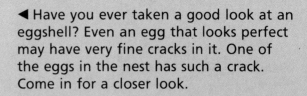

◀ Have you ever taken a good look at an eggshell? Even an egg that looks perfect may have very fine cracks in it. One of the eggs in the nest has such a crack. Come in for a closer look.

With a powerful microscope you can make the crack in the eggshell look much larger. In the picture the crack has been magnified ◀ 20 times.

The picture below was made with the same powerful microscope. The crack has been magnified 70 times its normal size. Does the photograph still look like a picture of a crack in an eggshell? Does it remind you of anything you have seen before? ▼

◄ On this page the appearance of the eggshell has really changed! The two views here show the crack greatly enlarged. Notice how different the crack looks. It looks almost like a deep canyon on the surface of the earth. Perhaps tiny living things could perch on the edge of the eggshell "cliff"!

▲ Crack magnified 923 times

Crack magnified 3,543 times ▶

110b

Matter is found in three forms—gas, liquid, and solid. How far apart are the units that make up these forms of matter? You can make models that show how the distance between units differs in gases, liquids, and solids.

You will need 3 empty cups, 3 cups of peas, and several toothpicks. The peas should have been soaked overnight in water. You probably know that the units in gases are spread far apart. In liquids the units are closer together. In solids they are even closer together. Use the peas and toothpicks to show how the arrangements of units compare in gases, liquids, and solids. Explain why you built your models as you did. Let your models stand overnight. You may be surprised to see how the models look the next day..

The picture shown on this page does not look like anything you have already seen. You are now looking at crystals. The eggshell is made up of a substance called calcium carbonate. This substance exists in the form of crystals. As you can see, the crystals have angular shapes.

Can the crack be magnified still more? And are there units in the eggshell that are smaller than the crystals? Yes. Crystals are made up of even smaller units.

In this chapter you will learn about some of the tiny units that make up matter. You will find out about the behavior of these units and how they join to form larger units.

Matter and Mass

How do scientists define matter?

Everything in the world is made of matter. Rocks, soil, buildings, and cars are all made of matter. So are animals and plants. You, and even the invisible air around you, are made of matter.

To define matter, one must know some characteristics of matter. Matter takes up space. It is easy to see that a rock or a building or a living thing takes up space. Does air take up space? If you have ever blown up a balloon, you know that it does. Which balloon in the picture takes up more space?

Matter also has mass. **Mass** is a measure of the amount of matter in an object. An object's mass can be measured by using a balance like the one in the picture. Which object has the greater mass? How do you know? Mass is usually measured in grams or in kilograms. The mass of a large paper clip is about 1 g. The mass of this book is about 1 kg. **Matter,** then, can be defined as anything that takes up space and has mass.

The mass of an object is always the same, regardless of where the object is. An object would have the same mass on the moon as it has on the earth.

People are often confused by the terms *mass* and *weight*. They use the terms as if mass and weight were the same thing. But they are not. **Weight** is usually defined as a measure of the earth's pull of gravity on an object. But it can also refer to the pull of gravity between other bodies.

Weight depends on where an object is in relation to the center of gravity of the other body. For example, suppose that you weighed yourself in a mine deep in the earth. You would weigh more than at sea level. You would weigh more because you would be closer to the earth's center of gravity. If you weighed yourself on a very high mountain, would you weigh more or less than at sea level? Why? Weight is also slightly greater at the North Pole and the South Pole than at the equator. This is because the poles are about 20 km nearer the center of the earth than is the equator. Where do you think you could jump higher — on a high mountain or in a deep valley? Why?

You can see that weight varies depending on where an object is on the earth. It can also vary depending on where an object might be in other parts of the solar system. If you could travel to Jupiter, you would weigh 2.5 times more on Jupiter than on the earth. What would your weight be on Jupiter?

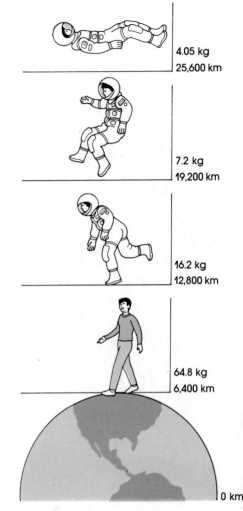

4.05 kg
25,600 km

7.2 kg
19,200 km

16.2 kg
12,800 km

64.8 kg
6,400 km

0 km

Astronaut John Young leaping on the moon's surface

For Lesson Questions, turn to page 392.

113

Activity

How is a balance used to determine mass?

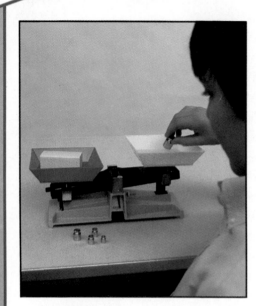

Materials balance / set of metric masses / variety of objects

Procedure

A. Look at the drawing of the balance. Identify the main parts of a real balance by finding them in the drawing.

B. The balance is zeroed when the pointer lines up with the center mark on the scale. Zero the balance.
  1. Why must the balance be zeroed before it is used?

C. Place an object whose mass you are to find on the left pan. Add masses to the right pan until the balance is zeroed again. The mass of the object is equal to the combined mass of the masses.
  2. Record the mass of the object in a table like the one shown.

D. Repeat step **C** for the other objects assigned to you.

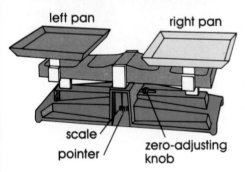

left pan   right pan

scale
pointer   zero-adjusting
knob

Conclusion

1. Which object had the greatest mass?
2. Which object had the least mass?
3. Compare the size of the object having the greatest mass with the size of the object having the least mass. Is size the same as mass? Explain.

Using science ideas

1. How would the results be affected if this activity were done on the moon? On Jupiter?
2. Suppose you have a box of 500 straight pins. You want to know the mass of 1 pin. However, the smallest mass in your set of masses is too great to measure 1 pin. What could you do to measure the approximate mass of 1 pin?

Object	Description of object	Mass (g)
1		
2		
3		

Atoms

What are atoms, and what are they made of?

You know that matter is anything that takes up space and has mass. You also know that all matter is not the same. What causes one kind of matter to be different from other matter? Scientists have learned that the small particles, or building blocks, that form matter cause these differences. The small particles are called atoms. There are many kinds of atoms.

Atoms are too small to be seen, even with the most powerful microscope. You may wonder, then, how scientists know about atoms. Scientists use very large machines called particle accelerators (ak sel′ə rā tərs) to study atoms. The one shown here is over 1 km wide. In an accelerator, particles are made to travel in circles at very high speeds. At their highest speed the particles are released to hit target atoms. The high-speed particles smash the target atoms into the still smaller particles that form the atoms.

Particle accelerator

115

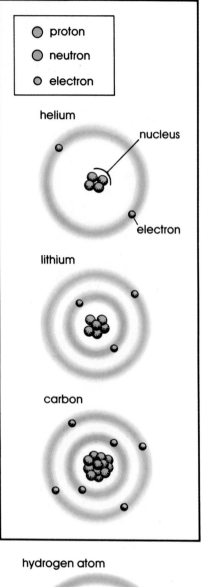

proton
neutron
electron

helium

nucleus

electron

lithium

carbon

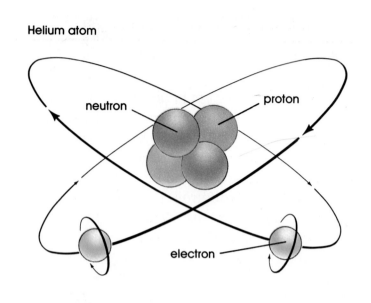

Helium atom

neutron

proton

electron

hydrogen atom

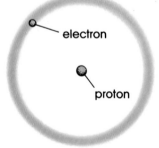

electron

proton

Scientists use the information they get from machines such as accelerators to form ideas about what atoms look like. These ideas are called models. Models help scientists understand how atoms behave. One model is the Bohr model. It is named after the scientist who suggested the model. Bohr models of atoms are shown at the left. Compare them with the three-dimensional model above.

The central part of an atom is called the **nucleus** (nü′klē əs). Two kinds of particles are found in the nucleus. They are called **protons** (prō′tonz) and **neutrons** (nü′tronz). Particles called **electrons** (i lek′-tronz) move around the nucleus. Electrons move in paths called **orbits.** Study the models. How many electrons does an atom have for each proton in its nucleus?

The models show that there is space between the nucleus and the electrons. But how much space? What is the actual size of an atom? The simplest atom is the hydrogen (hī′drə jən) atom. Suppose that the nucleus of this atom were the size of a table-tennis ball. Then the electron would be the size of a pinhead. It would be orbiting about 125 m from the ball.

For Lesson Questions, turn to page 392.

Grouping the Elements

What are the basic kinds of matter?

Think of the thousands of kinds of matter around you. For example, there are foods, clothing, plastics, medicines, and living things. You know that different kinds of matter are made of different kinds of atoms. Does this mean that there are thousands of kinds of atoms? No. There are fewer than 100 kinds of atoms that occur naturally. Matter that is made of only one kind of atom is called an **element** (el'ə mənt). An **atom,** then, can be defined as the smallest bit of an element. Different elements are made of different kinds of atoms. The models of atoms on page 116 are of the atoms of different elements.

There are 92 natural elements. In addition, scientists have been able to make some artificial elements. So now there is a total of about 109 known elements. This means that there are about 109 different kinds of atoms known today. A few elements and some of the things that are made from them are shown here. Which of these items can you find around your home? Gold and aluminum are other elements. What are some items made from these elements?

LEAD   (Pb)
82 protons
125 neutrons
82 electrons

SILVER   (Ag)
47 protons
61 neutrons
47 electrons

COPPER (Cu)
29 protons
35 neutrons
29 electrons

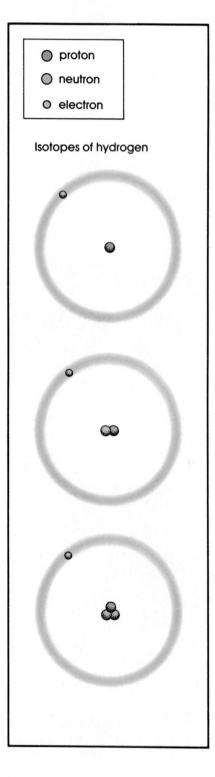

proton
neutron
electron

Isotopes of hydrogen

How do atoms of the various elements differ? Perhaps you have already noticed that each kind of atom has a different number of protons in its nucleus. Look again at the models of atoms on page 116. How many protons does helium have? How many does lithium have? How many does carbon have? These atoms are different from one another because each has a different number of protons. A scientist would say that they are different because they have different atomic numbers. The **atomic number** of an atom is the number of protons in the nucleus of the atom. Atoms of different elements have different atomic numbers. But all atoms of the same element have the same atomic number.

Protons have a positive charge (+). Electrons have a negative charge (−). The positively charged protons attract and hold an equal number of negatively charged electrons. Therefore the atomic number — the number of protons — also tells you the number of electrons in an atom.

But how do you know the number of neutrons in an atom? Scientists use a second number to describe atoms. It is called the mass number. The **mass number** is the total number of particles in the nucleus of an atom. For example, the mass number of helium is 4. This means that there are 4 particles in the nucleus. Some of the particles are protons, and some are neutrons. The atomic number of helium is 2, so helium has 2 protons. How does knowing the mass number and the atomic number of an atom tell you how many neutrons are in the nucleus of the atom?

Earlier you learned that matter takes up space and has mass. Since matter is made of atoms, atoms have mass. Protons and neutrons have about the same mass. A proton has a mass 1,836 times greater than that of an electron. A neutron has a mass 1,837 times greater than that of an electron.

All atoms of the same kind have the same number of protons, but the number of neutrons may vary. An atom of the same element that has a different number of neutrons is called an **isotope** (ī′sə tōp). Isotopes occur naturally in most elements. Three isotopes of hydrogen are shown in the drawings. Which isotope has the greatest mass?

Science & Technology

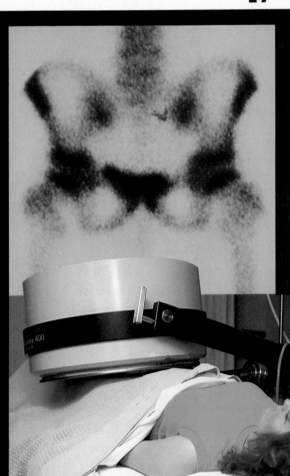

Some isotopes of elements are radioactive. These isotopes, called radioisotopes, may be used in different ways. The pictures show one way that radioisotopes are used. In this case the woman is undergoing a pelvic scan. The image produced will aid her doctor in making a diagnosis. The greatest single use of radioisotopes is in medical science. When a radioactive compound is given to a patient, it is absorbed in various amounts in different organs. The extent to which the radioactive atoms move through the body can be followed and measured with special instruments. Some radioisotopes are used to treat cancer. They kill cancer cells but do not affect surrounding healthy cells in the same way. Other uses of radioisotopes include tracing the path of ocean currents, detecting whether or not a painting is a forgery, preserving food, and making some kinds of plastics.

Many facts about the elements and their atoms are found in a chart called the **periodic table.** A simple periodic table is shown below. The elements are listed in rows, in the order of their atomic numbers. Find carbon in the table. What is carbon's atomic number? Each element also has a symbol. The symbol is usually one or two letters that stand for the name of the element. Look at the symbols for the elements in the table.

The periodic table can tell us other things about elements. For example, many elements fall into groups, or families. All elements in the same family

The periodic table

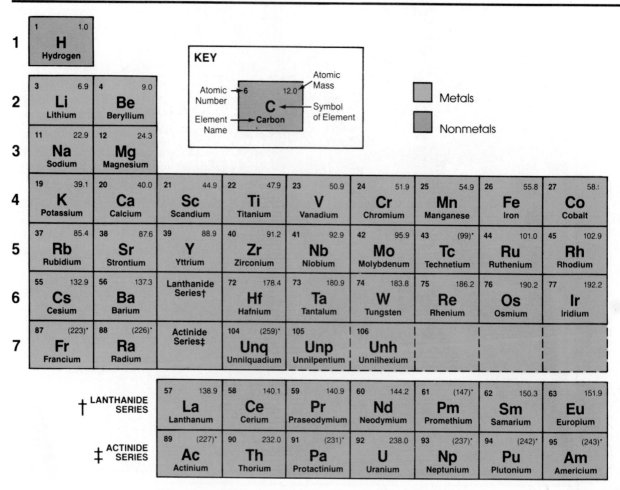

*Atomic masses appearing in parentheses are those of the most stable known isotopes.

are alike in some ways. Most elements in a family behave, or react, in the same way. They also have similar characteristics. But like the members of a human family, the elements in a family are not exactly alike. The families of elements are shown in the columns in the table.

Find the element fluorine (flü'ə rēn) in the periodic table. What is fluorine's atomic number? Fluorine and all the elements listed below it belong to the same family. These elements all behave in a similar way. All the elements in the fluorine family are poisonous gases. What elements belong to the helium family?

For Lesson Questions, turn to page 392.

							2　　4.0 He Helium
		5　　10.8 B Boron	6　　12.0 C Carbon	7　　14.0 N Nitrogen	8　　15.9 O Oxygen	9　　18.9 F Fluorine	10　　20.1 Ne Neon
		13　　26.9 Al Aluminum	14　　28.0 Si Silicon	15　　30.9 P Phosphorus	16　　32.0 S Sulfur	17　　35.4 Cl Chlorine	18　　39.9 Ar Argon
28　　58.7 Ni Nickel	29　　63.5 Cu Copper	30　　65.3 Zn Zinc	31　　69.7 Ga Gallium	32　　72.5 Ge Germanium	33　　74.9 As Arsenic	34　　78.9 Se Selenium	35　　79.9 Br Bromine	36　　83.8 Kr Krypton
46　　106.4 Pd Palladium	47　　107.8 Ag Silver	48　　112.4 Cd Cadmium	49　　114.8 In Indium	50　　118.6 Sn Tin	51　　121.7 Sb Antimony	52　　127.6 Te Tellurium	53　　126.9 I Iodine	54　　131.3 Xe Xenon
78　　195.0 Pt Platinum	79　　196.9 Au Gold	80　　200.5 Hg Mercury	81　　204.3 Tl Thallium	82　　207.1 Pb Lead	83　　208.9 Bi Bismuth	84　　(210)* Po Polonium	85　　(210)* At Astatine	86　　(222)* Rn Radon

64　　157.2 Gd Gadolinium	65　　158.9 Tb Terbium	66　　162.5 Dy Dysprosium	67　　164.9 Ho Holmium	68　　167.2 Er Erbium	69　　168.9 Tm Thulium	70　　173.0 Yb Ytterbium	71　　174.9 Lu Lutetium
96　　(247)* Cm Curium	97　　(247)* Bk Berkelium	98　　(251)* Cf Californium	99　　(254)* Es Einsteinium	100　　(257)* Fm Fermium	101　　(258)* Md Mendelevium	102　　(255)* No Nobelium	103　　(256)* Lr Lawrencium

**No names have been given and no mass data is available.

Atomic masses based on C-12 = 12.0000

Compounds and Molecules

What is formed when atoms are chemically joined?

How can there can be thousands of kinds of matter when there are only 92 natural elements? The reason is that most elements combine with other elements. Each different combination of elements is a different kind of matter. For example, the ore that iron comes from is a combination of iron and oxygen. Sand is a combination of silicon and oxygen.

When the atoms of two or more elements combine chemically, they form a **compound** (kom′pound). The smallest unit of most compounds is a molecule (mol′ə kyül). A **molecule** is two or more atoms that are joined in a certain way. Several compounds and some items made from these compounds are shown

POTASSIUM DICHROMATE
(used in glues and dyes)

made of: potassium
chromium
oxygen

COPPER NITRATE
(used in varnishes
and enamel paints)

made of: copper
nitrogen
oxygen

IRON OXIDE
(used in paint
pigments and in inks)

made of: iron
oxygen

NICKEL SULFATE
(used in ceramics)

made of: nickel
sulfur
oxygen

in the pictures. Have you heard of any of these compounds before? Find the elements in each compound in the periodic table on pages 120–121.

As you have learned, the smallest particle of an element is an atom. In some elements the atoms are chemically joined with atoms of the same kind. For example, the element oxygen is made of pairs of oxygen atoms. The two oxygen atoms making up a pair are chemically joined. The paired atoms act as a chemical unit. Such a pair of oxygen atoms makes up an oxygen molecule. The element hydrogen is also made of paired atoms. The paired hydrogen atoms act as a chemical unit. Two hydrogen atoms that are chemically joined make up a hydrogen molecule.

Not all atoms form molecules. The atoms of some elements act as single particles. That is, the atoms are not chemically joined with other atoms to form larger units. For example, helium is a gas made up of single helium atoms. The other elements in the helium family are also gases made up of single atoms. These gases usually do not combine with any other atoms.

A compound always contains at least two different kinds of atoms. Scientists use a formula to show the kinds and numbers of atoms in a compound. The formula gives the symbol for each element and the number of atoms of each element.

You have probably heard of the compound carbon dioxide. The formula for carbon dioxide is CO_2. This means that each molecule of carbon dioxide contains 1 atom of carbon and 2 atoms of oxygen. The formula for glucose (glü′kōs), a kind of sugar, is $C_6H_{12}O_6$. What are the elements in glucose? How many atoms of each element are there in a molecule of glucose? Water is a compound made of hydrogen and oxygen atoms. There are 2 atoms of hydrogen and 1 atom of oxygen in a molecule of water. How would you write the formula for a molecule of water?

hydrogen molecule
formula: H_2

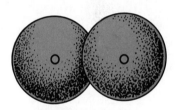

oxygen molecule
formula: O_2

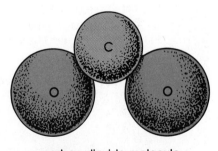

carbon dioxide molecule
formula: CO_2

For Lesson Questions, turn to page 392.

123

Kinds of Compounds

How are compounds classified?

All compounds are formed by elements that are chemically joined. But all compounds are not alike. Compounds are classified into groups according to certain characteristics. One group of compounds is called **acids.** All acids contain the element hydrogen (H). Acids have a sour taste. Vinegar and lemon juice are acids. The pictures show some other substances that contain acids. There are acids in many foods. But they are weak acids. Some acids are dangerous or even poisonous. Strong acids can burn skin and destroy other materials. **Never taste a substance to find out if it is an acid.**

Have you heard of hydrochloric (hī drə klôr′ik) acid? It has many uses in chemistry. But hydrochloric acid can be very dangerous. The formula for hydrochloric acid is HCl. What elements make up hydrochloric acid? Acids are used either directly or indirectly in making many products. Some acids and their uses are listed in the table.

SOME COMMON ACIDS AND THEIR USES

Acid	Formula	Some Uses
Sulfuric	H_2SO_4	Making medicines, fertilizers, pigments, paper pulp, alcohol, dyes, other acids and chemicals Refining petroleum Car batteries
Nitric	HNO_3	Making fertilizers, explosives, drugs, dyes Cleaning metals
Carbonic	H_2CO_3	Soft drinks
Acetic	$HC_2H_3O_2$	Making plastics, medicines, photographic film, rubber, other chemicals As a solvent

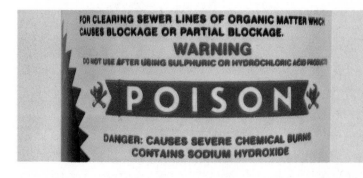

Bases make up another group of compounds. All bases contain the elements oxygen and hydrogen (OH). Bases have a bitter taste, and many strong bases feel slippery. The pictures show some items that contain bases. Like acids, strong bases can be very dangerous or poisonous. **Do not taste or touch a substance to find out if it is a base.**

Many cleaning products, such as ammonia and lye, are strong bases. Lye is usually used in drain cleaners. Lye contains the base sodium hydroxide. The formula for sodium hydroxide is NaOH. What elements are in sodium hydroxide? Like acids, bases are used in making many products. Some common bases and their uses are listed in the table.

SOME COMMON BASES AND THEIR USES

Base	Formula	Some Uses
Sodium hydroxide	NaOH	Making soap, textiles, paper, rubber Tanning Refining petroleum and vegetable oils
Ammonium hydroxide	NH_4OH	Making deodorants, cleaning and bleaching compounds, fertilizers, other chemicals
Potassium hydroxide	KOH	Making soaps, drugs, dyes, alkaline batteries, adhesives, fertilizers Purifying industrial gases
Calcium hydroxide	$Ca(OH)_2$	Making plasters, cements

Scientists use an indicator (in'də kā tər) to tell if a substance is an acid or a base. An **indicator** is a substance that changes color when it is mixed with an acid or a base. One indicator is litmus (lit'məs) paper. Litmus paper can be red or blue. Blue litmus paper turns red in an acid. Red litmus paper turns blue in a base. A substance that is neither an acid nor a base is said to be **neutral** (nü'trəl). Neutral substances do not change the color of indicators. The picture shows an acid and a base being tested with litmus paper.

You have learned that acids and bases are two groups of compounds. Salts make up still another group. A **salt** is formed when an acid and a base combine chemically. When that happens, water is also formed. The process is called neutralization (nü trə lə zā'shən). Can you tell why? One salt that you are probably familiar with is table salt. It is used to flavor food. Its formula is NaCl. What elements make up table salt?

There are many salts in addition to table salt. Salts are not always white and salty. Some salts are green, pink, or blue. Also, some salts are poisonous. **Never taste a substance to find out if it is a salt.**

Activity

How can acids and bases be identified?

Materials tape / 6 small jars / safety goggles / vinegar / lemon juice / ammonia / baking soda solution / boric acid solution / plastic spoon / red-cabbage juice / tap water

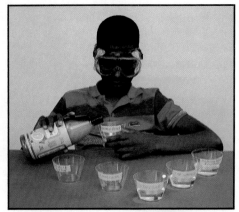

Procedure

A. Put a strip of tape on each jar. Label the jars *Vinegar, Lemon juice, Ammonia, Baking soda solution, Boric acid solution,* and *Tap water.*

B. Put on safety goggles. Pour the liquids into the labeled jars. The liquid in each jar should be about 2 cm deep.

C. Observe the color of each liquid. Also smell each liquid. **Caution** *Smell the liquids carefully. Your teacher will show you how.*

    1. In a table like the one shown, record the color and odor of each liquid.

D. Test the liquids with red-cabbage juice. Put about 2 spoonfuls of juice in each jar. Red-cabbage juice turns blue-green in a base. It turns dark red or purple in an acid.

    2. Record in the table any color changes that you observe.

    3. What is the red-cabbage juice?

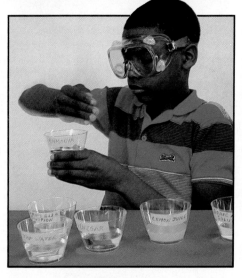

Conclusion

1. Which of the liquids were acids?

2. Which of the liquids were bases?

3. Were any of the liquids neutral? If so, which ones? How could you tell?

Using science ideas

Predict how each of the liquids that you tested would react with litmus paper. Then test the liquids with litmus paper.

Sample tested	Color and odor	Color with red cabbage juice

127

Using calcium chloride

Salts are used in many ways. The pictures show some common materials that contain salts. Which of these might be used for cooking? What are some other uses for salts? If you live in a cold climate, you may have seen a salt used to melt ice. Usually this salt is calcium chloride (kal′sē əm klôr′īd), $CaCl_2$. What two elements form this salt?

Another group of compounds are called oxides (ok′sīdz). As you might guess, **oxides** are compounds formed when oxygen combines with another element. Oxygen is an active element and combines easily. Rust is an oxide formed when the element iron combines with oxygen. The formula for water is H_2O. Could water be classified as an oxide? Why?

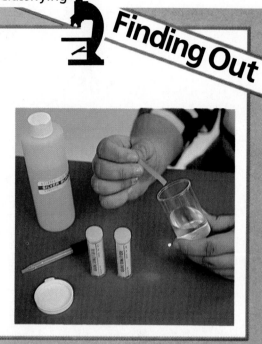

Finding Out

How can you make a neutral solution?

You know that indicators can be used to test for acids and bases. Predict if they can also be used to test when a solution is neutral.

Get some fresh limewater solution, and test it with both red and blue litmus paper. Is limewater solution an acid or a base? Test some white vinegar in the same way. Is the vinegar an acid or a base?

Pour a small amount of limewater into a clear-plastic pill bottle. Put a piece of red litmus paper and a piece of blue litmus paper in the bottle. What happens to the color of the litmus papers? Use a medicine dropper to add white vinegar, drop by drop, to the limewater. Watch what happens to the litmus paper. How will you know when your solution is neutral?

Ideas to Remember

▶ Matter is anything that has mass and takes up space.

▶ Matter is made up of small particles called atoms.

▶ Atoms are composed of particles called protons, neutrons, and electrons.

▶ Matter that contains only one kind of atom is an element.

▶ There are 92 natural elements on the earth.

▶ Most elements are combined with other elements, forming compounds.

▶ There are many kinds of compounds, including acids, bases, salts, and oxides.

For Lesson Questions, turn to page 392.

Reviewing the Chapter

SCIENCE WORDS

A. Use all the terms below to complete the sentences.

periodic table	nucleus	molecule	weight	mass
atomic number	neutrons	electrons	orbits	element

Anything that has __**1**__ and takes up space is matter. A measure of the force of gravity on matter is called __**2**__. All matter is made of atoms. The central part of an atom is called the __**3**__. It contains protons and __**4**__. Particles called __**5**__ travel in paths around this central part. These paths are called __**6**__. The number of protons in an atom is known as the __**7**__. A substance made of only one kind of atom is called a/an __**8**__. A chemical unit made up of two or more atoms is a/an __**9**__. Information about these substances can be found in a chart called the __**10**__.

B. Write the letter of the term that best matches the definition. Not all the terms will be used.

1. Two or more elements that are chemically joined
2. A substance that changes color in an acid or a base
3. A substance that tastes sour
4. A substance that turns red litmus paper blue
5. A substance made from an acid and a base
6. The smallest particle of an element
7. The total number of particles in the nucleus of an atom

   a. mass number
   b. indicator
   c. salt
   d. acid
   e. base
   f. atom
   g. compound
   h. neutral

UNDERSTANDING IDEAS

A. Use the periodic table on pages 120–121 to find the number of protons and electrons in each of these elements.
   1. calcium   2. aluminum
   3. silicon   4. sodium

B. Use the tables of acids and bases to find the elements in each of these compounds.
   1. acetic acid   2. sulfuric acid
   3. ammonium hydroxide

C. Why does this parent keep household cleaners locked in the cabinet?

D. In your own words, compare the meaning of the terms *mass* and *weight*. Explain why the mass of an object is always the same but the weight of the object may vary.

USING IDEAS

1. Read the ingredients listed on several foods and household products in your home. Write the name of each product and the name of any acid, base, or salt that it contains. Be sure to tell whether each substance is an acid, a base, a salt, or an oxide.
2. Make a model of an oxygen atom, using construction paper or clay.

THINKING LIKE A SCIENTIST

Answer the following questions. You may be able to answer some of the questions just by thinking about them. To answer other questions, you may have to do some research.

1. The National Aeronautics and Space Administration is predicting that astronauts will explore other planets in our solar system before the year 2030. Do you think that the structure of atoms on Mars will be identical to the structure of atoms on Earth? Do you think the space explorers will discover new, naturally occuring elements?
2. You probably have seen advertisements on TV for products that relieve acid indigestion or "heartburn." Some ads show a person who claims to have an upset stomach placing a tablet in a glass of water. The tablet fizzes and creates bubbles in the water. After drinking the bubbling water, the person reports that he or she no longer suffers from acid indigestion. Explain how the tablet brings relief from acid indigestion.

CHAPTER 6
Chemical Changes in Matter

Have you ever seen a group of buildings devoted to the study of science? How did these buildings look? Were they big and very serious? Some people feel that buildings that house important ideas should also look serious. Robert Rathbun Wilson does not agree. Dr. Wilson is a physicist, a scientist who studies the behavior of matter. But he is also a sculptor. A few years ago, Wilson had the chance to combine the two great loves of his life—physics and sculpture. Wilson was the designer, and for many years, the director, of Fermilab.

Fermilab is the short name for the Fermi National Accelerator Laboratory. It is a research center in Batavia, Illinois. Scientists there study the nature of matter. They can find out a lot about matter by accelerating, or speeding up, the particles that make up matter. Particles from within atoms are sent racing through a long circular track. These particles move at a speed of 99.99 percent the speed of light. By moving at such a great speed, the particles destroy themselves by crashing into each other. In the process, great amounts of energy are released. For a fraction of a second, new particles are formed. They are of great interest to scientists. The brief lives of the particles give scientists a look into the nature of matter. The formation of these particles may also tell something about the history of matter. It may show which particles first combined to form atoms.

Very serious work takes place at Fermilab. But the environment there tells a lot about the humor of its designer, Dr. Wilson. The photographs on these pages show the unique architecture of the buildings and other structures at Fermilab.

The entrance to Fermilab is unique. Visitors are welcomed by a giant piece of sculpture. Wilson calls it *Broken Symmetry*. (Symmetry is a balanced arrangement of parts on either side of a line.) He explains the meaning of the sculpture: Scientists often look for symmetry in the things they study. But once scientists find symmetry, they look for tiny ways in which these things are not quite symmetrical.

▼Accelerator track

▼*Broken Symmetry*

▼ Tunnel inside accelerator

Electric power lines around the buildings are held up by
structures that look like the Greek letter pi (π). One building
contains two orange spiral staircases. The staircases are Dr.
Wilson's tribute to DNA, the molecule that contains the code
of life.

The main structure at Fermilab is the accelerator. When Dr.
Wilson had to decide on the size of the accelerator track, he
did not use complex numbers. He decided that the track
would have a radius of 1 kilometer. In Dr. Wilson's words, "It
was a nice round number, neither too big nor too small. It
was a number everyone could remember, so lots of dumb
mistakes wouldn't creep in."

Are you surprised by Dr. Wilson's words? His reasons for
deciding on the track size might not sound scientific. But scientists are people, too. Sometimes they make decisions to
help keep things simple.

Fermilab is a unique place. Some of the greatest scientists
in the world are at work at Fermilab. Yet, in spite of the serious side of the science, the environment is one of beauty
and playfulness. Fermilab is a place where science and art
come together.

Inside an accelerator, particles are moving very quickly. These particles often crash into each other and split into smaller units. The data from these collisions help scientists understand more about the structure of matter.

In your classroom you cannot build a particle accelerator. But you can study the way in which some objects collide.

You will need five marbles, each of a different color; three large sheets of newsprint; a felt-tip marker; and a cardboard tube from paper towels or gift-wrapping. Cover a desk top with newsprint. Arrange four of the marbles in a cluster on the newsprint. With a marker, mark the position of each marble. Point one end of the cardboard tube toward the marbles and rest the other end on a book. Roll a shooter marble down the tube. Watch the way the marbles move as they collide. Record the position of the shooter marble and the four other marbles after they have come to rest.

Repeat the activity three times. Each time, cover the desk with a new sheet of newsprint. Use the marker to record the final position of all the marbles. Look at the marks on each sheet of newsprint. Is there any pattern? Can the movement of the marbles be predicted?

You can vary this activity in several ways: (1) Change the way you first set up the marbles on the desk top. Does the arrangement affect the way they move? (2) Use larger or smaller marbles. (3) Use a longer or shorter tube. What else can you change?

▼ **Dr. Robert Rathbun Wilson**

In this chapter you will learn about the different ways in which matter changes. You will also learn about the parts of atoms that are involved in changes in matter.

Properties and Changes

In what ways does matter change?

Matter may change in many ways, but all the changes can be classified as either physical or chemical. A **physical change** is a change in the size, shape, or state of matter. During a physical change the particles of which matter is made do not change. For example, a molecule of water remains H_2O when water changes state. It is H_2O regardless of whether the water exists as ice, as liquid water, or as water vapor.

In a physical change, only the physical properties of matter change—not the chemical composition of the matter. Therefore a **physical property** is one that can be identified without causing a chemical change in the matter. In addition to the size, shape, and state of matter, other physical properties include color, odor, hardness, and shape.

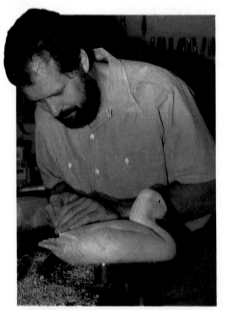

Wood carver

Gold pellets

Liquid gold

Gold bars

What physical changes are shown in the pictures on page 134? What other examples of physical changes can you give?

Now look at the pictures of the egg frying and the wood burning. They show both physical and chemical changes. A **chemical change** is a change in the chemical composition of a substance. In a chemical change, matter is changed into one or more different kinds of matter. In other words, the chemical properties of matter are changed. A **chemical property** is one that determines how an element or compound reacts with other elements or compounds. Burning wood is a chemical change. When matter burns, it combines with oxygen in the air. The ashes, gas, and smoke that are formed are different from the original wood and oxygen. How do you know that some of the changes shown in the pictures are chemical changes?

Density is also a property of matter. It can be used to identify materials or to compare two different objects or substances. **Density** is defined as the mass of a certain volume of a substance. The density of a substance may be stated in any unit of mass or volume.

DENSITIES

	Matter	Density (g/cm³)
Gases	hydrogen	0.00009
Gases	oxygen	0.0014
Liquids	bromine	2.93
Liquids	chlorine	3.21
Solids	aluminum	2.7
Solids	silver	10.5
Solids	gold	18.9
Solids	platinum	21.5
Solids	sodium	0.97
Solids	ebony wood	1.2
Solids	balsa wood	0.12

Usually, mass is stated in grams, and volume, in cubic centimeters. The density of water is 1 gram per cubic centimeter (1 g/cm³). Mercury has a density of 13.6 g/cm³. The bottles in the drawing each contain 1 L of a liquid. The liquids have different masses. Which liquid has the lowest density?

The densities of several substances are listed in the table. Which state of matter — solid, liquid, or gas — seems to be the most dense? Which is the most dense material listed? Which is the least dense?

Sometimes a comparison is made between the density of a substance and the density of water. Such a comparison is called **specific gravity.** When figuring specific gravity, you divide the mass of a certain volume of the substance by the mass of an equal volume of water. For example, the specific gravity of alcohol is as follows.

$$\frac{\text{mass of 1 L alcohol}}{\text{mass of 1 L water}} = \frac{0.81 \text{ kg}}{1 \text{ kg}} = 0.81$$

What is the specific gravity of the other liquids in the bottles in the drawing below?

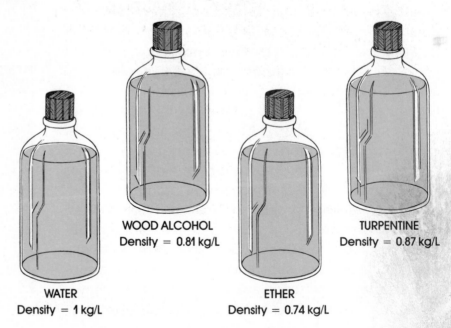

WATER
Density = 1 kg/L

WOOD ALCOHOL
Density = 0.81 kg/L

ETHER
Density = 0.74 kg/L

TURPENTINE
Density = 0.87 kg/L

For Lesson Questions, turn to page 394.

Activity

How is specific gravity related to sinking and floating?

Materials 6 objects to be tested / dishpan / water / metric ruler / measuring cup / salt / spoon

Procedure

A. Objects that have a specific gravity of less than 1 (1−) will float in water. Those that have a specific gravity of more than 1 (1+) will sink. Objects that have a specific gravity of about 1 (1) will float just below the surface of the water.

List in a data table the objects to be tested. For each, predict whether its specific gravity is 1, 1−, or 1+.

  1. Record your predictions in the table.

B. Fill a dishpan with tap water to a depth of 5 cm. Carefully place each object in the water. Observe whether the object sinks, floats high in the water, or floats just below the surface of the water.

  2. Record your observations in the table.

  3. For how many objects was your prediction correct?

C. Remove the objects from the water. Make a saturated solution of salt water by adding about 2 cups of salt to the water. Stir until you have dissolved as much of the salt as possible.

D. Repeat step **B**, using the solution of salt water.

  4. Record your observations in the table.

Results

How does the density of salt water compare with the density of tap water? Why?

Conclusion

How is the specific gravity of an object related to whether it sinks or floats in water?

Chemical Reactions

What happens during a chemical change?

You know that new substances are formed during a chemical change. Another name for a chemical change is a **chemical reaction.** Chemical reactions may be rapid or slow. Also, many chemical reactions give off energy. In a rapid reaction much energy is released quickly. Where is a rapid reaction shown here? Some rusted objects are shown in the picture on pages 132–133. Do you think that the rust formed during a rapid reaction or a slow reaction? Why?

Look at the picture of the silver cup. The cup has turned black because the silver reacted with an impurity in the air. This chemical reaction, called tarnishing, is a slow reaction. The silver polish in the bowl removes the tarnish. This is a rapid reaction.

One or more different kinds of matter are always formed during a chemical reaction. There are several kinds of chemical reactions. In one kind of reaction,

Tarnish on a silver cup

Fireworks

two elements combine to form a new substance. Carbon plus oxygen forms carbon dioxide. The chemical equation for the reaction is written like this.

$$C \quad + \quad O_2 \quad \longrightarrow \quad CO_2$$

| 1 atom of carbon | 2 atoms of oxygen | 1 molecule of carbon dioxide |

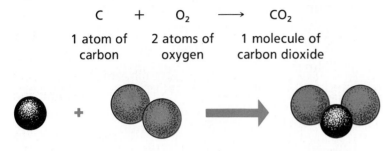

Some of the symbols for elements have a little number after the symbol. The number tells how many atoms of the element are in a molecule. If there is no number after a symbol, there is only 1 atom of that element in a molecule. The number 1 is not written.

No matter is ever lost or gained during a chemical reaction. This means that there must be the same number of atoms of an element on each side of the arrow. Look at the equation. The carbon molecule has 1 atom. The oxygen molecule has 2 atoms. The carbon dioxide molecule has 1 carbon atom and 2 oxygen atoms. Is the number of atoms of each element the same on both sides of the arrow?

In a second kind of chemical reaction, the molecules of a substance split. When that happens, two or more new substances are formed. For example, an electric current can split water molecules into hydrogen gas and oxygen gas. The equation looks like this.

$$2H_2O \quad \longrightarrow \quad 2H_2 \quad + \quad O_2$$

| 2 molecules of water | 2 molecules of hydrogen | 1 molecule of oxygen |

In order to have a balanced number of atoms, a chemical reaction often involves more than one molecule of each substance. The number of molecules is shown by the number that appears in front of an element or compound. Number 1 is not written.

There is a third way that new substances are formed during a chemical reaction. Have you ever watched square-dancers? A caller gives the dancers instructions. One instruction is "All change partners!" In a way, the third kind of chemical reaction is like this. Substances change partners. Sometimes one element takes the place of another element in a compound, as in the example shown here.

$$CuSo_4 + Fe \longrightarrow FeSO_4 + Cu$$

copper   iron   iron   copper
sulfate   (steel wool)   sulfate

The element iron changes places with the copper in the compound copper sulfate. What new partnership is formed? What happens to the copper?

In other cases, two sets of partners change places. For example, this happens when an acid and a base are combined.

$$HCl + NaOH \longrightarrow NaCl + H_2O$$

hydrochloric   sodium   sodium   water
acid   hydroxide   chloride
                     (table salt)

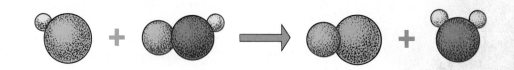

With what element did sodium change places? With what element did the OH change places? What two new materials were formed? What is another name for this type of reaction?

Study the equations on these pages. Although the equations are for different kinds of chemical reactions, they each show two things. They show that in a chemical reaction, matter is always changed to one or more different kinds of matter. They also show that the amount of matter present, both before and after the reaction, does not change.

By comparing the matter that reacts and the products formed in a chemical reaction you can see that matter can change. But matter cannot be created or destroyed by any chemical reaction. This fact is called the **law of conservation of matter.**

There is one other important law that relates to chemical reactions. This is the **law of conservation of energy** which states that energy is neither created nor destroyed during a chemical reaction. Like matter, however, energy can change form.

SKILLS: Measuring, Interpreting data

Finding Out

How can you demonstrate the law of conservation of matter?

Use a funnel to carefully pour a spoonful of baking soda into a bottle. Use a second funnel to pour some vinegar into a balloon. Attach the balloon to the bottle without letting any of the vinegar pour into the bottle. Use a balance to find the mass of this setup. Record the mass. Now lift the end of the balloon so that the vinegar pours into the bottle. When the chemical reaction is completed, find the mass of the setup again. Has matter been conserved?

For Lesson Questions, turn to page 394.

Activity

How can you identify a chemical reaction?

Materials safety goggles / wide-mouthed bottle / 1-hole rubber stopper / rubber tubing / 2 small pieces of glass or metal tubing / jar / limewater / baking soda / spoon / small paper cup / vinegar

Procedure
A. Put on safety goggles. Set up the materials as shown. The open jar should contain limewater. Limewater turns milky white when carbon dioxide is added to it. Be sure that the end of the glass or metal tube is in the limewater.

B. Put 2 spoonfuls of baking soda in the bottle.

C. Half-fill a small paper cup with vinegar. Pour the vinegar into the bottle containing the baking soda. Quickly close the bottle with the rubber stopper. Observe what happens.

Results
1. What evidence did you see of something happening?
2. Describe what happens to the limewater.
3. What is one product produced when baking soda reacts with vinegar? How do you know?

Conclusion
Why is this reaction a chemical reaction?

Using science ideas
How could limewater be used to indicate that a chemical reaction is taking place inside your body?

142

Chemical Bonds

What holds the atoms in a compound together?

You know that in some chemical reactions, compounds may be formed. You also know that compounds are formed when atoms of different elements combine. What holds the atoms together? The atoms are held together by forces called **chemical bonds.**

Chemical bonds are formed when atoms are attracted to other atoms. Some atoms attract many different atoms. Carbon and oxygen atoms easily react with other atoms. So carbon and oxygen can form many kinds of compounds. Some atoms, such as those of helium, do not attract any other atoms. So helium does not form chemical bonds.

What are chemical bonds? Scientists have learned that the forces that attract atoms involve electrons. Remember that electrons are found in orbits outside the nucleus of an atom. Only the electrons in the outermost orbit of an atom can form a chemical bond.

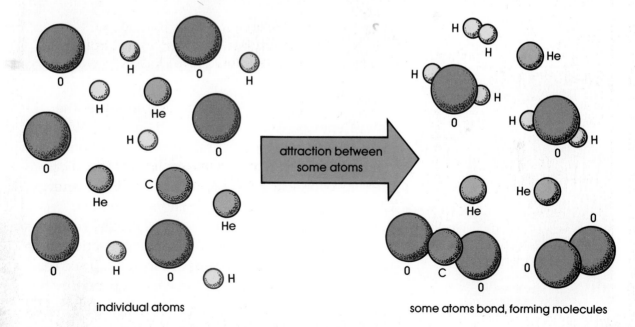

individual atoms

attraction between some atoms

some atoms bond, forming molecules

The number of electrons in that orbit determines whether the atom can form a chemical bond with another atom.

Making a compound is something like building a model with plastic blocks. The blocks are like the atoms. The plastic blocks hook on to one another. The way the blocks are held together may be compared to the way atoms are bonded together. By hooking the blocks together, you can build many different objects. If you want to change an object, you must take the blocks apart. Then you can combine them in a different way. You still have the same blocks, just arranged differently. In a similar way, atoms can be rearranged to form different compounds.

Breaking the bonds that hold atoms together involves energy. Making new bonds also involves energy. When bonds are broken and new bonds are made, energy is either released or used up. The energy in chemical bonds is called **chemical energy.** Chemical energy is stored in chemical bonds.

Now you can understand why chemical reactions may release energy. During a chemical reaction some bonds are broken. New bonds are formed. If the reaction releases more energy than it uses up, energy will be given off. Heat and light are usually produced.

144

For Lesson Questions, turn to page 394.

Other Changes in Matter

What kinds of changes involve the nuclei of atoms?

As you know, chemical reactions involve the breaking and forming of bonds between atoms. Bonds involve the outer electrons. The nuclei (nü′klē ī) of atoms are not involved in ordinary chemical reactions. (The term *nuclei* is the plural of *nucleus*.) A reaction involving the nuclei of atoms is called a **nuclear** (nü′klē ər) **reaction.** In a nuclear reaction, elements are changed into different elements.

Earlier you learned that most of the mass of an atom is in the dense nucleus. That is also where most of the atom's energy is. The nucleus is a tightly packed bundle of energy. Recall that the nucleus is made of protons, which have a positive charge, and neutrons, which have no charge. You know that unlike charges attract and like charges repel. Why do the protons not repel each other? They cannot because of the binding energy that holds the nucleus together.

When the nuclei of atoms are split apart in a nuclear reaction, the binding energy is released. Another name for the binding energy is **nuclear energy.** Scientists learned how to split the nuclei of atoms to release nuclear energy in the early 1940s.

Nuclear submarine

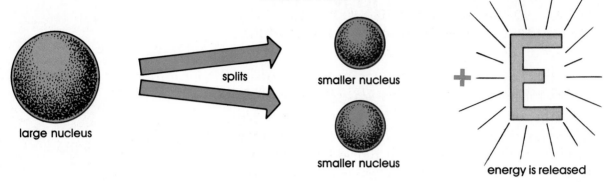

large nucleus

splits

smaller nucleus

smaller nucleus

+ E

energy is released

In one kind of nuclear reaction, large nuclei are split apart. When this happens, smaller nuclei are formed and energy is released. This kind of reaction is called **nuclear fission** (fish′ən). The fission of many atoms in a short period of time releases a large amount of energy. The energy from fission has many uses. Nuclear submarines run on energy from nuclear fission. A nuclear power plant produces electric power from

Nuclear power plant

the energy of nuclear fission. In these cases the reactions are controlled. So the energy is released slowly.

Recall that matter and energy cannot be created or destroyed. So where does nuclear energy come from? It comes from the mass in the nuclei of atoms. Suppose that you were to add the amounts of the masses of the small nuclei formed during fission. You would find that the total is a little less than the mass of the large nucleus from which the small ones were formed. The "lost" mass was released as energy. This is another law of science called the law of conservation of mass and energy. The **law of conservation of mass and energy** states that neither mass nor energy can be created or destroyed, but they can be changed from one to the other.

Another kind of nuclear reaction is called **nuclear fusion** (fyü′zhən). In a way, fusion is the opposite of fission. Instead of beginning with large nuclei, fusion starts with very small nuclei. It starts with the smallest of all nuclei — those of hydrogen atoms.

Fuse means "to put together." During one type of fusion, 4 hydrogen nuclei are fused at very high pressures and temperatures. They form 1 helium atom. Look at the drawing. How does the mass of 1 helium nucleus compare with the total mass of 4 hydrogen nuclei? How does this explain where energy comes from during fusion?

NUCLEAR FUSION

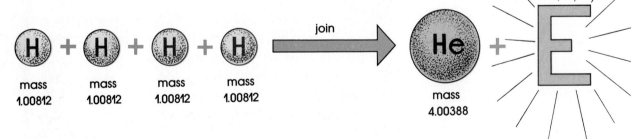

energy is released

As you know, it is possible to get energy from gasoline. But did you realize that you could also get energy from water? Obviously, water cannot be used to power your family car. But water is a source of a fuel called deuterium (dü tir′ē-əm), which can be used in nuclear fusion.

If nuclear fusion is ever a major source of energy on the earth, large amounts of fuel will be needed. Water, which covers three fourths of the earth, can provide one of these fuels. Do you think deuterium can be used to solve the energy shortage? Explain your answer.

Scientists have not yet learned how to control nuclear fusion. When they do, however, it is believed that nuclear fusion will be the solution to many of today's energy problems.

For centuries, people have wondered how the sun produces energy. Today, scientists know that the answer is by nuclear fusion. Fusion has been taking place in space for billions of years. The sun and all luminous stars are made mostly of hydrogen. Day after day, on every star, billions of tons of hydrogen are fusing. As the hydrogen forms helium, it releases the energy that we see as light. When all the hydrogen is used up, the star can no longer be seen. Scientists estimate that there is enough hydrogen left for the sun to continue to fuse for at least 4 billion years.

Many kinds of nuclear reactions take place naturally. The nuclei of certain elements break down into simpler nuclei. During such reactions, elements change into other elements. Elements that break down into other elements are called **radioactive** (rā dē ō ak'tiv) **elements.**

Uranium is a radioactive element. The element uranium breaks down and changes into the element lead. Most natural radioactive elements break down slowly. So the energy is released over a long period of time.

For Lesson Questions, turn to page 394.

Uranium ore

Ideas to Remember

▶ When matter changes, the properties of matter change.

▶ Specific gravity is a comparison between the density of a substance and the density of water.

▶ A chemical change is also called a chemical reaction.

▶ Matter and energy are neither created nor destroyed in a chemical reaction.

▶ A chemical reaction can be expressed with an equation. There are three main kinds of chemical reactions.

▶ Atoms in a compound are held together by chemical bonds.

▶ A change in the nuclei of atoms is called a nuclear reaction.

▶ The nuclear reactions called fission and fusion supply large amounts of energy.

▶ In a nuclear reaction, mass is changed to energy.

Reviewing the Chapter

SCIENCE WORDS

A. Write the letter of the term that best matches the definition. Not all the terms will be used.

1. A property that determines how an element or compound reacts with other elements or compounds
2. Forces that hold atoms together in compounds
3. The combining of atomic nuclei
4. A change in the size, state, or shape of matter
5. The splitting of a nucleus into smaller nuclei
6. A property such as color, odor, or hardness
7. A change in which different kinds of matter are formed
8. The mass of a given volume of a substance

a. nuclear fusion
b. physical property
c. chemical bonds
d. nuclear energy
e. chemical change
f. nuclear fission
g. density
h. chemical property
i. physical change

B. Copy the sentences below. Use science terms from the chapter to complete the sentences.

1. Any reaction involving the nuclei of atoms is a/an _____.
2. Elements that break down into other elements are called _____.
3. A property that can be identified without causing a chemical change in matter is a/an _____.
4. A chemical change is sometimes called a/an _____.
5. _____ is a comparison between the density of a substance and the density of water.

UNDERSTANDING IDEAS

A. Energy may be released as a result of chemical reactions and nuclear reactions.

1. Compare chemical and nuclear reactions as to where the energy is stored before it is released.
2. How do the laws of conservation of mass and energy apply to chemical reactions? How do they apply to nuclear reactions?

B. Write these three headings: (1) *Nuclear reaction,* (2) *Chemical reaction,* (3) *Physical change.* Write each of the following terms under the correct heading.

decaying leaves
mixing oil and vinegar
combining of small nuclei
breakdown of an
   element into another
   element

producing energy in the
   sun
dissolving salt in water
rusting of iron
digesting food
sifting gold from sand

changing hydrogen to
   helium
splitting water into
   hydrogen and
   oxygen

C. Study the following diagram.

 + join + ?

small nucleus   small nucleus   larger nucleus

1. What kind of reaction is shown in the diagram?
2. What else is produced as a result of this reaction?

USING IDEAS

1. Use your library to find out how you can use physical properties to identify such minerals as quartz, mica, and garnet.

2. Describe two physical changes and two chemical changes that can occur in your body.

THINKING LIKE A SCIENTIST

Answer the following questions. You may be able to answer some of the questions just by thinking about them. To answer other questions, you may have to do some research.

1. Spontaneous combustion is a dangerous chemical change. Spontaneous combustion occurs when something burns without having been ignited by a heat source. Describe the chemical properties that change in spontaneous combustion. How can spontaneous combustion be prevented?

2. Argon is a useful gas. It is used to surround the filament in some light bulbs. It also is used as an atmosphere for welding certain metals. What properties must argon have to make it useful in these ways?

CHAPTER 7
Light Energy

Are you tired of seeing the same old face in the mirror? If you are, there is a device that can help you change your face. This device is painless and fun to use.

You can find the face-changer at a museum in San Francisco, California. The museum is called the Exploratorium. There, you and a friend can sit on opposite sides of a special glass. This glass is both a mirror and a window. The image that you see in

the glass is a mixture of your face and that of your friend. How does this glass work? Equal amounts of light bounce off and pass through the glass. Both faces appear on the glass and blend into one face.

Look at the images shown on this page. A man and a woman sat on opposite sides of the glass. Through the "magic" of this special glass, their faces merged. You can

see how their images blended into one. Imagine how your face and the face of your best friend would look when combined in this glass.

No doubt you are sometimes very busy. At such times you could use an exact copy of yourself. The children in the photograph seem to have many copies of themselves. They are standing inside a giant kaleidoscope (kə lī′ də skōp). Perhaps you have

seen a toy kaleidoscope. The toy has three mirrors placed at angles to each other. The mirrors are inside a tube that has an eyepiece, which is held up to the light. There are small bits of paper at the bottom of the tube. As the tube is turned, the bits fall into different patterns. The bits are reflected off the three mirrors, forming designs.

Now try this

You can have fun with the photographs shown below. Use a small, square mirror. Place the mirror lengthwise along each photograph so that it passes through the nose. Look at the image formed in the mirror. Does the image differ from the photograph? Move the mirror to the right and to the left. How does the image change?

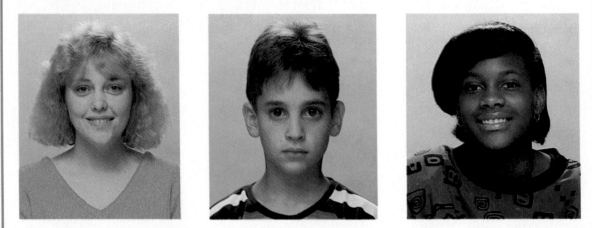

Below are several figures that have strange shapes. Take the same mirror and move it along each figure. Start at the far left of the figure and move the mirror to the far right. Notice the shape of the figure formed in the mirror. How does the figure change as you move the mirror?

At the museum is another special mirror that creates strange images. Two examples of these images are shown on this page. In the picture on the left, the man seems to be floating in air. In the picture shown below, he seems to have two pairs of arms and legs! How are these images formed? The man is sitting on a stool behind the mirror. He sticks his arms and legs out. Only parts of his arms and legs are reflected in the mirror, forming the strange image you see. How is this museum exhibit like the activity you just did?

Reprinted from GAMES Magazine. Copyright © 1986.

In this chapter you will learn how light behaves. You will find out how it acts when it strikes mirrors and different kinds of surfaces. You will understand more about the "magic" of the exhibits at the Exploratorium.

153

Radiant Energy

What forms of energy make up the electromagnetic spectrum?

Light is energy that you can see. Light energy is part of the electromagnetic spectrum (i lek trō mag-net'ik spek'trəm). The **electromagnetic spectrum** is made up of all forms of radiant (rā'dē ənt) energy. All radiant energy travels in waves. Radiant energy is always moving. When radiant energy stops moving, it changes to another form of energy. Often that energy is heat. Look at the drawing of the electromagnetic spectrum. What other forms of radiant energy make up the electromagnetic spectrum?

All forms of radiant energy travel at the same speed in a vacuum (vak'yüm). A **vacuum** is any space that contains little or no matter. Radiant energy travels about 300,000 kilometers per second (km/s). Think of how long it takes you to say "One hundred one." In that time, any form of radiant energy can travel a distance equal to seven orbits around the earth.

Electromagnetic spectrum

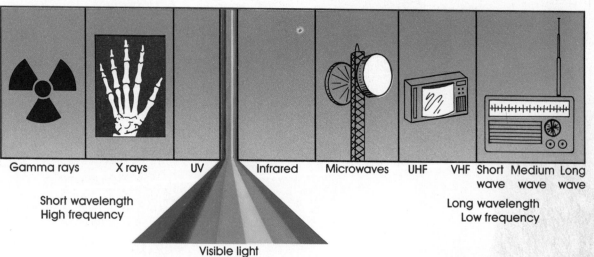

| Gamma rays | X rays | UV | | Infrared | Microwaves | UHF | VHF | Short wave | Medium wave | Long wave |

Short wavelength
High frequency

Long wavelength
Low frequency

Visible light

154

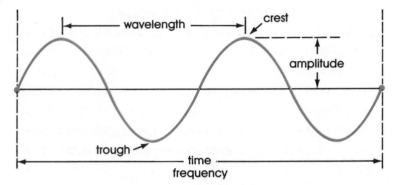

There are three characteristics that describe the wave motion of radiant energy. They are wavelength, amplitude (am′plə tüd), and frequency (frē′kwən sē). **Wavelength** is the distance between a point on one wave and the same point on the next wave. In the drawing this is the distance from one crest to the next. **Amplitude** is the amount of energy in the wave — the wave's strength. It is shown as the height of the wave. **Frequency** is the number of waves produced each second. Frequency is usually expressed as cycles per second (c/s).

How the characteristics of the wave motion are related can be seen in the following example. Imagine that the different forms of radiant energy are passing by you. Do they all have the same frequency? No, the shorter waves have the higher frequencies, since more of these waves pass by you in one second. This difference may be compared to a bullfrog and a tree-toad traveling at the same speed. The bullfrog takes long hops (long wavelength), so it only needs to make a few hops (low frequency). The tree toad

makes a great number (high frequency) of very short hops (short wavelength) to travel the same distance. In the same way, the forms of radiant energy with long wavelengths have low frequencies. The forms with short wavelengths have high frequencies. What represents amplitude in this example?

The relationship between wavelength and frequency is shown by the following equations.

$$\text{speed} = \text{wavelength} \times \text{frequency}$$

Wavelength equals speed divided by frequency.

$$\text{wavelength} = \frac{\text{speed}}{\text{frequency}}$$

Frequency equals speed divided by wavelength.

$$\text{frequency} = \frac{\text{speed}}{\text{wavelength}}$$

The frequencies of the different forms of radiant energy vary greatly. The lowest frequency is about 10 c/s. The highest frequency is about 100,000 billion billion cycles per second (100,000,000,000,000,000,000,000 c/s). What can you tell about the wavelengths of each of these forms of radiant energy?

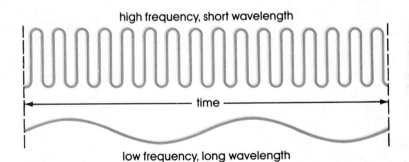

high frequency, short wavelength

time

low frequency, long wavelength

Radio and television waves are at the long-wavelength end of the electromagnetic spectrum. What does this tell you about their frequencies? Radio waves have frequencies as low as 10,000 c/s. Some television waves are as high as 300,000,000 c/s. Cycles per second are called hertz (Hz).

Science & Technology

Food may be cooked quickly with microwaves, a form of electromagnetic radiation. Microwaves penetrate the food, causing the molecules in the food to vibrate rapidly — as many as 5,000,000,000 vibrations per second. Friction among the rapidly moving molecules produces heat that cooks the food quickly and evenly. Microwaves are produced in a microwave oven by a device called a magnetron (a). From the magnetron, the microwaves pass through a metal tube (b) to a stirrer (c). The blades of the stirrer work like an electric fan, scattering the microwaves into the oven. Although microwaves pass easily through glass and paper, they do not pass through metal. They are reflected by the metal walls of the oven. As the waves bounce back and forth, they penetrate the food from all directions. Although the cooked food is hot, the oven itself remains cool. How does the way food is cooked in a microwave oven differ from the way food is cooked in gas or electric ovens? Why does it take more time to cook food in a gas or an electric oven?

Two forms of radiant energy, infrared (in frə red′) waves and ultraviolet (ul trə vī′ə let) waves, have frequencies close to the frequencies of visible light. These waves are named for their positions in the electromagnetic spectrum. *Infra* means "lower than." **Infrared waves** are radiant energy with frequencies lower than that of visible red light. When infrared waves strike matter, their energy causes the particles to vibrate faster. As the particles vibrate faster, the matter becomes hotter. For this reason, infrared lamps are often called heat lamps. They are used in restaurants to keep food warm until it is served. In factories where cars are made, infrared lamps are used to quickly dry the freshly painted cars.

All warm objects also give off some infrared waves. This energy can be photographed, using special infrared-sensitive film. Warmer objects give off more waves than do cooler objects. The warmer an

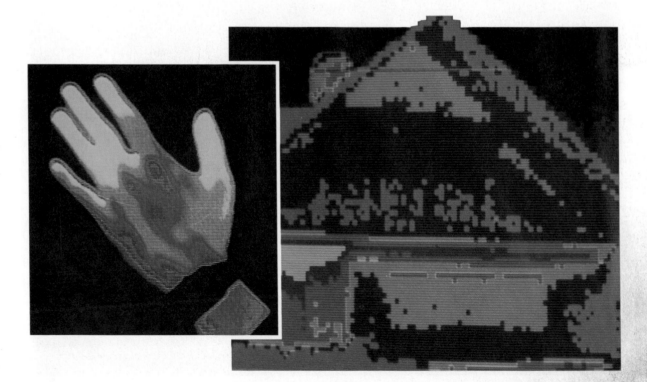

object is, the more red it appears in a picture taken with the special film. Which are the warmest areas in the pictures of the house and the hand on page 158? What may be some important uses for such film?

Ultraviolet waves are also named for their position in the electromagnetic spectrum. *Ultra* means "beyond." **Ultraviolet waves** are radiant energy with frequencies beyond that of the waves of visible violet light. They have higher frequencies and shorter wavelengths than visible violet light.

The sun gives off large amounts of ultraviolet radiation. Fortunately, only a small amount of this radiation passes through the atmosphere. Long exposure to small amounts of ultraviolet radiation can damage living things. Some molecules in your body have probably been changed by these waves. Sunburn is an example of such damage. Skin cancer can also result from too much exposure to ultraviolet radiation.

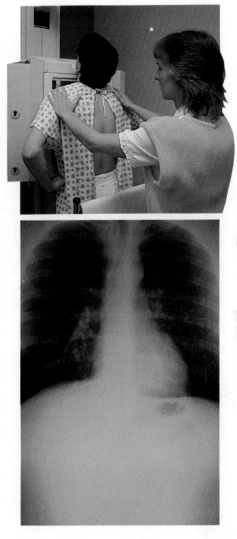

Beyond ultraviolet in the electromagnetic spectrum are X rays and gamma rays. These two forms of radiant energy can also be dangerous. Both X rays and gamma rays have very high frequencies and very short wavelengths. High-energy X rays may damage living cells. But the great penetrating power of X rays is important in medicine. How are X rays being used in the picture? Why do you think doctors and dentists are careful not to expose people to these rays any longer than is necessary?

Gamma rays have the highest frequencies of any form of radiant energy. They also have the shortest wavelengths. These rays have very high energy and great penetrating power. Gamma rays can be very destructive. They easily shatter the atoms and molecules they strike. During a nuclear reaction, atomic nuclei break down and give off gamma rays. In a controlled reaction the gamma rays can be held back through proper shielding.

159

For Lesson Questions, turn to page 396.

The Behavior of Light

What happens to light when it strikes matter?

Visible light, the radiant energy you can see, is about in the middle of the electromagnetic spectrum. Scientists have learned much about light by studying how it behaves. They have found that light waves travel in straight lines. You cannot see an object that is around the corner from you because light waves do not bend around corners.

Light waves can change direction. When light waves strike an object, some of the waves bounce off. But the paths of the waves to the object are straight lines. And the paths of the waves away from the object are also straight lines.

Scientists have also found that light travels in all directions from a source. Suppose you place a lighted lamp in the center of a room. Light will travel out from the lamp in all directions. No matter where in the room you are, some light waves will reach you.

Light could travel forever if it did not strike some form of matter. When light strikes matter, one or more things may happen, as shown in the drawings. Light energy may be **reflected.** When light energy is reflected, it does not go into the matter it strikes. Instead the light waves bounce off the surface of the matter. Light energy that is not reflected goes into the matter it strikes. If the light waves pass through the matter, the light is **transmitted.** If the waves do not pass through the matter, the light is **absorbed.**

Look at the picture of the airplane being serviced before take-off. Where is light being reflected? Where is it being transmitted? Where is it being absorbed?

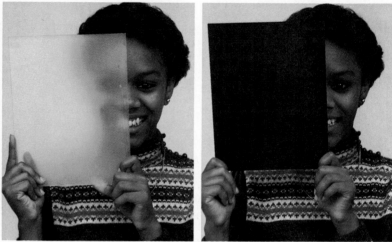

The windows of the jet airplane are clear glass. You can see through clear glass because it transmits light waves without scattering them. Matter through which light can pass without being scattered is said to be **transparent.** Other kinds of matter scatter light waves that pass through them. Matter that scatters light that passes through it is said to be **translucent** (trans lü′sənt). One translucent material is frosted glass. Many light bulbs are made of frosted glass. The light from such a bulb is less harsh than if the bulb were made of clear glass. Frosted glass is also used in windows and doors, for privacy. Objects look blurry when viewed through a translucent material, such as frosted glass. Matter through which light cannot pass is said to be **opaque** (ō pāk′). A brick is opaque. In the pictures, which of the materials held by the girl is transparent? Which is translucent? Which is opaque?

Transparent matter may also reflect some light. So you may be able to see yourself in a window. Translucent and opaque matter also reflect some light. In addition, all kinds of matter absorb some of the light that falls on them. So both a window and a brick will absorb some light. Which do you think absorbs more?

For Lesson Questions, turn to page 396.

Activity

How do light waves travel and change direction?

Materials metric ruler / large file cards / hole punch / scissors / tape / string, about 20 cm long / flashlight / 3 small mirrors

Procedure

A. Using a ruler, draw a line from top to bottom through the center of each of four file cards. With a hole punch, make a hole in three of the file cards. Center the hole on the line and 3 cm from the top of the card.

B. Cut three triangles from the fourth file card, as shown. Fold over about 4 cm of the top of each triangle. Tape each triangle to a file card. Be sure that the right angle of the triangle aligns with the center line and the bottom edge of the file card.

C. Stand the file cards about 10 cm apart on a table. Line up the holes. A piece of string threaded through the holes will help align the cards.

D. Darken the classroom. Have a classmate shine a flashlight through the hole in one end card. Close one eye. Then look toward the flashlight through the hole in the card at the other end.

  1. How does the light get from the flashlight to your eye?

E. Move the middle file card a few centimeters to the right or the left. Close one eye and look toward the flashlight through the hole in the end card.

  2. What do you observe? Why?

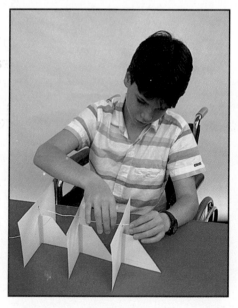

F. Do this step in a darkened classroom. With the aid of two classmates, each holding a mirror, try to make the beam of light travel in a zig-zag path.

Conclusion

1. How do light waves travel?
2. How can the direction in which light waves travel be changed?

Seeing Colors

Why are there different colors of light?

Visible light is one part of a large group of energy. *Visible* refers to light that can be observed with the eyes. Visible light itself is a group, or spectrum, of energy. The spectrum of visible light is made of all the colors of the rainbow. Together these colors form white light. How does one color of light differ from another? The different colors of light have different frequencies. Red light has the lowest frequency. Violet light has the highest frequency. White light is a mixture of waves of different frequencies.

White light can be separated into the colors from which it is formed, by passing the light through a prism (priz′əm). A **prism** is a specially shaped transparent object used to separate light. As white light passes through a prism, it is separated into bands of color. Together the bands are called the **visible light spectrum.** A spectrum formed by one prism is shown here. What are the colors of the spectrum?

red orange yellow green blue violet

Your eyes are special organs for receiving light. Special cells near the back of your eyes are sensitive to different frequencies of light. Color is really a sensation formed in your brain. No one really knows how color sensations are produced.

An object has color because it is either producing light, reflecting light, or transmitting light. An object that is producing light will be the color of the light that it is giving off. For example, neon gas produces red light when electricity is passed through the gas. You have probably seen red neon lights.

If copper is heated in a flame, green light is given off. If sodium is heated, yellow light is given off. If a material gives off all colors of light, what color will you see?

Some objects do not give off their own light. You can still identify their color because they reflect some of the light that strikes them.

Do You Know?

Sometimes you can see the light spectrum in the sky. It is called a rainbow. A rainbow can form when tiny raindrops are in the air. Waves of sunlight are bent as they enter the drops, much as light is bent as it enters a prism. The sunlight is separated into the colors of the spectrum. Some of the light is then reflected from the raindrops to your eyes. As a result, you see a rainbow.

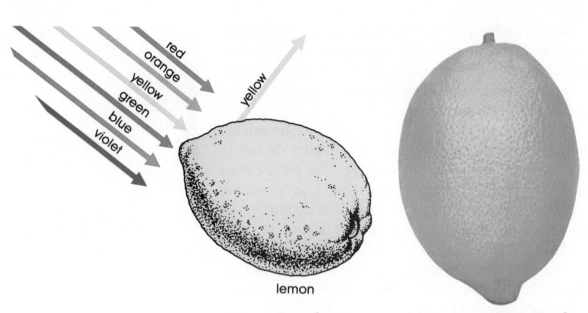

lemon

The color of an opaque object depends on the frequencies of light it reflects. If the object reflects all the frequencies of light, it will look white. A lemon looks yellow because it reflects the yellow frequencies of light. All the other frequencies are absorbed by the lemon. Similarly, an object looks green because it absorbs all the frequencies except green, which it reflects. The color of most opaque objects can be explained in this way. Why, then, do some objects look black? An object looks black because it absorbs most frequencies of light.

The absence of light is darkness. In a room where there is absolutely no light, you will not be able to see at all. Even in a dark room, however, there is usually some light. Why is it difficult to tell the color of an object in a dark room?

When white light passes through matter, many of its frequencies may be absorbed. But some frequencies may be transmitted. The light that is transmitted by such matter is colored. You probably have seen a car with a broken cover on the tail light. What color was the broken cover? What color light did the bulb inside give off?

Suppose the cover on the tail light is not broken. What happens? The bulb gives off white light. The white light passes through the red plastic cover of the tail light. The plastic absorbs all the frequencies except red. The red frequencies are transmitted, so the light that reaches your eyes looks red. Similarly, the green filter in the picture transmits only the green frequencies of light.

Sometimes your eyes and brain play tricks on you. Look at the flag shown here. Look at the white spot in the middle of the flag while you slowly count to 30. Now look quickly at a piece of white paper. What do you see? This is called an optical illusion.

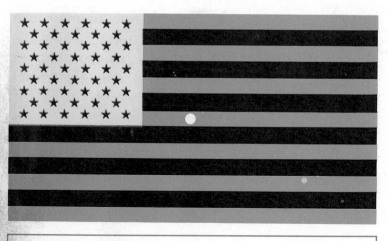

For Lesson Questions, turn to page 396.

Reflection and Mirrors

What happens to light that strikes a smooth surface?

There is a big difference in the way light is reflected from sand and from a mirror. As you can see in the drawing, light waves are reflected from a mirror at the same angle in which they strike the mirror. Light that strikes the sand is scattered and reflected in many different directions.

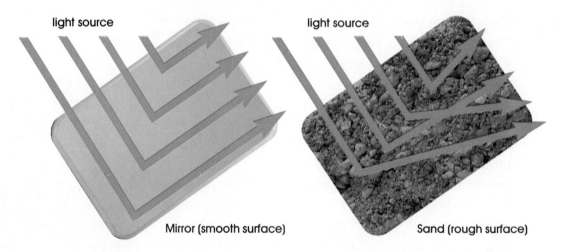

Mirror (smooth surface)

Sand (rough surface)

Since light reflected from a mirror has the same pattern as the light that strikes the mirror, reflections called images can be seen in a mirror. An image in a mirror *appears* to be the same distance behind the mirror as the object is in front of the mirror. Look at the drawing. Notice that the image is reversed from right to left. Because the image appears to be behind the mirror, it is called a **virtual image.**

Another kind of image is called a **real image.** A real image can be focused on a movie screen or on camera film. Lenses are usually used to form real images.

The mirrors in the drawings on this page are flat. Most mirrors in homes and schools are flat. A mirror with a flat surface is called a plane mirror. But some mirrors have curved surfaces. A mirror in which the reflecting surface curves outward is called a **convex** (kon veks') **mirror.** A convex mirror is shaped like the back of a spoon's bowl. A convex mirror makes things look smaller. However, the mirror reflects light from a large area. The side-view mirrors on trucks are usually convex mirrors. Such a mirror provides a wide field of vision behind the truck.

A mirror in which the reflecting surface curves inward is called a **concave** (kon kāv') **mirror.** A concave mirror is shaped like the inside of a spoon's bowl. The images formed by concave mirrors look bigger than the real objects. What is the advantage of such a mirror? Is the image real or virtual?

For Lesson Questions, turn to page 396.

Convex mirror

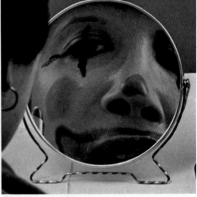

Concave mirror

Bending Light Waves

How can you change the path of light waves?

Light travels at a speed of about 300,000 km/s. But when light travels through different kinds of transparent materials, its speed may change. As its speed changes, the direction of the light may also change.

Imagine that as a car travels along a straight, smooth road, it moves at the same speed. Now suppose that the right wheels of the moving car slip off the road onto a soft, sandy shoulder. The car will slow down and be pulled sharply to the right. The driver would need to turn the steering wheel sharply to the left to again have the car move straight ahead. The drawings illustrate this.

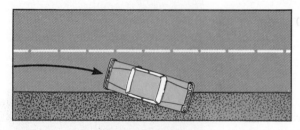
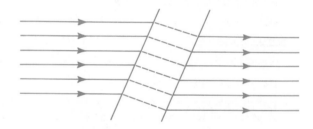

The example of the car is similar to what happens to light when it moves from one kind of transparent matter to another. As light moves from air to water, its speed and the direction in which it travels will change. Look at the pencil in the water. The light waves moving from the water to air change direction. This causes the pencil to look bent. The bending of light waves is called **refraction** (ri frak′shən).

When people want to bend, or refract, light, they use a lens. A lens is a piece of glass or plastic shaped so that it will bend light. Light travels faster through air than through a lens. When light strikes a lens, it slows down and bends. It acts much like the car whose wheels slipped onto the soft shoulder of the road.

The drawings show two kinds of lenses. How are they alike? How are they different? The lens that is thicker in the center than at the edges is called a **convex lens.** What happens to light waves when they travel through a convex lens? A **concave lens** is thicker at the edges than in the center. What happens to light waves that pass through a concave lens?

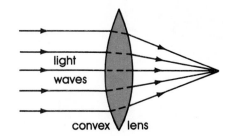

light waves

convex lens

Notice in the drawings that a convex lens focuses light, or brings it to a point. A convex lens is used in a movie projector to focus light on a screen. Convex lenses form real images. Telescopes and magnifying glasses also contain convex lenses.

Concave lenses spread out light. Images seen through a concave lens seem smaller and farther away than they do without the lens. Concave lenses are used in eyeglasses to correct a condition called near-sightedness. People who are near-sighted have in their eyes lenses that focus the light in front of the retina. The retina at the back of the eye is like the eye's movie screen. Concave lenses in glasses help move the image back to the retina.

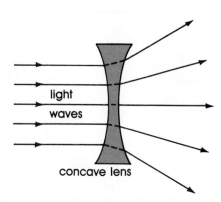

light waves

concave lens

SKILLS: Observing, Experimenting

Finding Out

How can you change the direction of light waves?

You can demonstrate the refraction of light. Put a coin in the bottom of an empty cup. Stand away from the cup so that you can just see the edge of the coin. Have a classmate slowly pour water into the cup until the cup is full. Keep your eye on the edge of the coin. What do you observe happening? Explain your observation.

What will happen if you use a liquid other than water? Repeat the procedure, using another clear liquid such as cooking oil. Does cooking oil refract light more or less than water?

171

For Lesson Questions, turn to page 396.

Activity

What are some properties of a convex lens?

Materials   magnifying glass (convex lens) / book / sheet of white paper / lamp

Procedure

A. Place a magnifying glass over a page of type in a book. While looking through the magnifying glass, slowly lift it to about 4 cm above the page.

　1. Describe what happens.
　2. What do you think will happen if you move the magnifying glass away from the paper? Try it.

B. Darken the room. Stand about 1.5 m from a lamp, with your back to it. Hold a sheet of white paper in one hand and the magnifying glass in the other.

C. Hold the magnifying glass about 5 cm in front of the paper. Look at the paper. (Do not look through the magnifying glass.) Move the magnifying glass slowly back and forth until an image forms on the paper.

　3. Describe the image that you see.

D. Experiment with the paper and magnifying glass to produce a larger image. Then try to produce a smaller image.

　4. How did you produce larger and smaller images?

Conclusion

Identify two properties of a convex lens.

Using science ideas

The lenses in your eyes are convex lenses. Why don't you see things upside down?

1.5 m

Modern Uses of Light

How is light being put to work in new ways?

Much of our work and play occurs under the natural light of the sun. Artificial light from bulbs and lamps allows many activities to continue after sunset. Headlights and tail lights on cars and trucks make night driving safer. The electric lights in your home make it possible for you to read and study at night. Many baseball games are played at night, ''under the lights.'' People have learned to produce light so that they can see when sunlight is not available.

Today, light is also being used for other purposes. Look at the beam of colored light in the picture. It is the artificial light of a laser (lā′zər). A **laser** is a device that strengthens light. A laser can produce a very powerful, very thin beam of light. A laser beam spreads out very little as it moves. The light of a laser is also very pure. This means that it is made up of light waves of a single color. In ordinary light of a certain color, such as blue, other colors are also present. The color of laser light depends on the kind of laser used.

A laser beam is sometimes referred to as concentrated light. A laser beam can be powerful enough to burn through metal. So laser beams can be used to

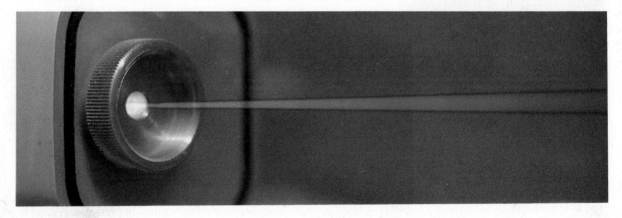

Laser used in welding

An optical fiber in a coil

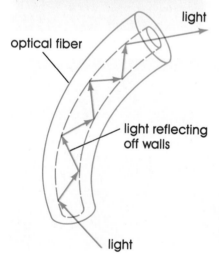

optical fiber

light

light reflecting off walls

light

drill holes in machine parts or to cut metal into shapes. Laser beams can also be used to weld metal parts together.

Laser beams are now being used in medicine. Very thin laser beams can be used to destroy diseased tissue. Laser beams are being used to treat an eye disorder in which the retina becomes detached. An eye surgeon can use a laser beam to "weld" the retina back into place.

Laser light is also used to carry voice signals. The light travels through a very thin glass tube called an optical fiber. The light reflects, or bounces, along the inner walls of the fiber, as shown in the drawing. In the future, most telephone calls may be carried in this way. In fiber optics communications, a beam of laser light can carry thousands of telephone calls at the same time.

People are also finding new uses for sunlight. Solar cells convert the energy of sunlight to electrical energy. Such solar cells are used on spacecraft.

Sunlight is also used to heat buildings. Solar panels receive the sunlight and change it into heat energy. The heat energy may be stored or be used to warm

Solar panels on a house

air or water that is then pumped throughout the building. Solar energy may supply a large part of the world's energy needs in the future.

For Lesson Questions, turn to page 396.

Ideas to Remember

▶ Light is a visible form of radiant energy.
▶ Together all the forms of radiant energy make up the electromagnetic spectrum.
▶ Some invisible forms of radiant energy include radio, television, infrared, ultraviolet, X rays, and gamma rays.
▶ All forms of radiant energy travel at the same speed, but they differ in wavelengths and frequencies.
▶ Light may be reflected, transmitted, or absorbed by matter.
▶ Different colors of light have different frequencies.
▶ Mirrors and lenses can be used to change the paths of light waves.
▶ A laser can produce concentrated light.

Reviewing the Chapter

SCIENCE WORDS

A. Copy the sentences below. Use science terms from the chapter to complete the sentences.

1. Light is a visible form of _____ .
2. A change in the direction of light as it passes from one material to another is called _____ .
3. Light that is trapped by matter is said to be _____ .
4. Light that passes through matter is said to be _____ .
5. Light that bounces off matter is said to be _____ .
6. Matter that allows light to pass through without being scattered is said to be _____ .
7. Matter that scatters light that passes through it is said to be _____ .
8. Matter through which light cannot pass is said to be _____ .

B. Write the letter of the term that best matches the definition. Not all the terms will be used.

1. A device that can produce concentrated light
2. The distance between a point on one wave and the same point on the next wave
3. The bands of color that make up white light
4. A lens that bends together waves of light
5. The number of waves that pass a point in a period of time

a. concave lens
b. frequency
c. laser
d. wavelength
e. spectrum
f. convex lens

UNDERSTANDING IDEAS

A. What is a lens? Identify the concave lens and the convex lens in the drawing. How does each type of lens change the path of light waves passing through it? Name three objects that contain lenses.

B. Explain why a banana appears yellow. Why does a yellow traffic light appear yellow?

C. Write the term that does not belong in each group. Explain your answers.

1. transmit, reflect, absorb, decay
2. space, infrared waves, X rays, ultraviolet waves
3. prism, lens, mirror, window
4. amplitude, wavelength, frequency, laser

D. Identify each material as *opaque, translucent,* or *transparent.*

1. gold
2. wood
3. ice
4. air
5. waxed paper
6. magnifying glass

USING IDEAS

1. Attach a rope to a doorknob. Produce waves in the rope by flicking it. How can you produce high-frequency waves? How can you produce low-frequency waves? How does wavelength change as you change the frequency?

2. Use your library to find out about animals that give off light. Choose one such animal, and explain how it uses its light to survive.

THINKING LIKE A SCIENTIST

Answer the following questions. You may be able to answer some of the questions just by thinking about them. To answer other questions, you may have to do some research.

1. Thirty-six years after inventing the first electric light bulb, Thomas Edison remarked, "No invention is perfect, and the incandescent lamp is no exception. Light without heat is the ideal, and that is far off. There is a good deal of truth in the saying that the firefly is the ideal." Why was Edison dissatisfied with his invention? Why is a firefly the ideal?

2. Why does the sky appear black to astronauts in space and blue to people on Earth?

3. Whole olives always appear larger in a jar than they do when taken out of the jar. How can you explain this? Support your reasoning.

CHAPTER 8

Sound Energy

The craftsman tightened the strings and polished the shiny wood one more time. Then he tucked the instrument under his chin and began to play. The rich tones of the violin filled the room. Another Stradivarius (strad ə vär′ ē əs) had been made.

Antonio Stradivari ▶

A Stradivarius is a violin made by members of the Stradivari family in Italy about 300 years ago. Cremona, Italy, was a center for the making of fine violins. In that small town, several now-famous families made violins. All the violins were of superb quality. Most young violinists today dream of owning a violin made long ago in Cremona. But there are very few of these instruments left. These few are very costly.

Some people feel that the instruments made today can never compare with those made hundreds of years ago. When the last of the violin makers of that era died, the secret of great violin making died also. None of the craftsmen passed on the art of producing those fine instruments.

Over the years, many scientists have worked to solve this mystery: How did those old violins produce such beautiful tones? Was it the wood? The glue? The varnish? (Varnish is the clear coating on the wood.) At least one person feels he has solved the mystery. He is Joseph Nagyvary, a chemist at Texas A & M University.

To solve the mystery, Nagyvary had to understand how a violin produces sounds. The sounds begin with the vibration of four tightly stretched strings. But these sounds are not very loud. The strings must be attached to a box that increases the loudness of their sounds.

◀ Joseph Nagyvary (left)

Many things happen when the strings are plucked or bowed. The strings vibrate. The air inside the violin vibrates. The wood of the violin also vibrates. All these vibrations add to the kinds of sounds that are made. New violins look very much like those made centuries ago. But they do not sound like the old violins. The mystery remains: What causes the difference?

Nagyvary thinks the difference lies in the way the wood is treated. He has studied the structure of the wood of old instruments and new instruments. The pictures on page 179 show the cells inside the wood of an old cello (chel´ ō). (A cello looks like a large violin and produces lower sounds.) You can see that the wood is made of tubelike cells. In old instruments, these cells were open at the ends.

▲ Construction of a violin
178b

Construct a stringed instrument that produces musical sounds. You may want to use a box with a lid, several rubber bands of different thicknesses, and a pair of scissors. You can also use a small block of wood and several nails. Add to this list of materials if needed. The design of the instrument is up to you. Keep in mind that it must produce sounds that are musical. But it does not have to sound like any instruments you now know. After you build your instrument, create music with it!

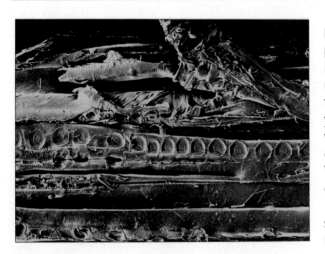

▲ Plugged-up wood cells (top);

▼ Unplugged wood cells (bottom)

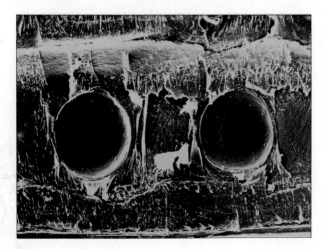

In the new instruments, the cells are plugged up. Nagyvary thinks that the old instruments were soaked in a special liquid for a long time. The soaking caused the ends of the cells to drop out. In recent years violin makers have not been soaking wood in this way. The ends of the wood cells in these violins are still plugged up. Violins made of wood with plugged-up cells produce sounds of a lower quality.

Nagyvary soaks his wood in much the same way as did the violin makers of Cremona. So the wood cells in his violins are open. He also coats the wood with a varnish made of chitin (kīt´ ən). Chitin is a substance found in the hard covering of certain animals that have an outer skeleton. The varnish is made from shrimp broth. This coating gives the violin a clear, pure sound.

Several musicians have tested Nagyvary's violins. They have found that his instruments sound as good as any Stradivarius. Perhaps the mystery of the violins has been solved.

In this chapter you will study some properties of sound. You will learn how sound is produced, how it travels, and how it sometimes is used in unusual ways.

Energy You Can Hear

What are sound waves like?

Sound is produced only when matter vibrates. Like light, sound is a form of energy. It is the only form of energy that you can hear.

Both sound and light travel in the form of waves. The waves travel outward in straight lines from their source. You may be wondering why waves can be described as energy. Do you remember how energy is defined? Energy is the capacity to do work, or to move an object. For example, the boy in the picture is making waves by disturbing the water. As the waves spread out, they will hit the boat and cause it to move. Thus, energy is used to move the boat.

All energy is transferred in one of two ways. It may be transferred by the movement of an object. Or it may be transferred by a wave that moves out from the source of the energy. Light waves, sound waves, water waves, and earthquake shock waves are examples of energy moving as waves.

The way that energy is transferred by different kinds of waves varies. For example, the picture shows the waves that were formed by something falling into the water. Note that the waves spread out in circles from the point where the water was disturbed. Water waves move only over the surface of the water.

Consider what happens when a firecracker explodes in air. The firecracker disturbs the air in much the same way that the water was disturbed. Energy from the explosion is carried through the air as sound waves. Unlike water waves, sound waves travel in all directions from the point of the disturbance. The waves move outward like an expanding ball.

Water waves and sound waves also differ in the way that their particles move. In water waves the particles move up and down. But with sound waves the particles move back and forth. Because of this back and forth motion, sound waves are called longitudinal (lon jə tü′də nəl) waves. A **longitudinal wave** is a wave in which particles of matter vibrate along the same path in which the wave travels.

Suppose that you struck a tuning fork to make it vibrate. The prongs of the fork would move back and forth. As a prong moves away from the center, the air particles ahead of it are crowded together. This re-

Water waves

region of crowded air particles

region of fewer air particles than usual

LONGITUDINAL WAVE MOTION

gion of crowded particles is called a **compression** (kəm presh'ən). When the prong moves back toward the center, it leaves a region that has fewer particles than usual. This region is called a **rarefaction** (rär ə fak'shən). In the drawing on page 181 note how the compressions and rarefactions form. The air particles disturbed by the fork prong bounce back and forth, or vibrate. They go nowhere. Only the energy they were given is passed along. How many compressions are shown? How many rarefactions?

Usually a sound wave is drawn as a wavy line, like this one. Imagine that the straight line of particles shown here with it came from the drawing on page 181. What do the humps in the wavy line represent? What do the hollows represent?

SKILLS: Making a model, Observing

Finding Out

How does a sound wave travel?

You can use a Slinky toy to demonstrate how a sound wave travels. Have a partner hold the Slinky by one end while you hold the other end. Stretch the Slinky along the floor. Pinch several coils together at one end of the Slinky and then release them. What happens along the length of the Slinky? Do the coils from one end actually move to the other end? How does this demonstrate the way a sound wave travels?

For Lesson Questions, turn to page 398.

The Behavior of Sound

What happens when sound waves strike matter?

You know that sound travels through air, which is matter. But what happens when sound waves strike other matter? Does the energy of the sound waves pass through the matter? Depending on the kind of matter the waves strike, three things may happen. Some of the sound energy may be **transmitted,** or passed through the matter. Some may be trapped, or **absorbed,** and some may be bounced back, or **reflected.** In these ways the behavior of sound waves is the same as the behavior of light waves.

What happens when sound waves strike a solid, such as a wall? Some of the sound energy may pass through the solid. That is why when you are inside a house, you can hear a dog barking outside. The barking that you hear is transmitted sound.

Not all the energy of a sound wave is transmitted. Some of it is absorbed. When sound energy is absorbed, it goes into matter but does not pass through. This is why a band playing in the next room is softer than it would be if you were in the same room.

The amount of sound energy absorbed by matter depends on how hard or soft the matter is. Soft matter usually absorbs more sound energy than does hard matter. Look at the picture of this room. Why would much sound energy be absorbed here?

To understand what happens to absorbed sound, think about what happens when sound waves strike matter. All matter is made of tiny particles. When a sound wave strikes one of those particles, it moves that particle. In hard materials the particles of matter are close together — they cannot move very far. They spring back into their original position.

Particles of matter in soft materials move about more easily. They absorb much of the sound energy that strikes them, because they move more. Therefore, soft materials absorb sound better than do hard materials. Sound energy makes the particles in matter vibrate. When sound energy is absorbed, this vibration is changed into heat. Do you recall the law of conservation of energy? It states that energy cannot be created or destroyed — it can only be changed from one form to another. In this case the sound energy is changed to heat.

Sound energy that is neither transmitted nor absorbed is reflected. The loudness or softness of reflected sounds also depends on the matter that the sound waves strike. When sound waves strike a hard smooth surface, most are reflected in one direction. These reflected sounds seem loud. This is because most of the waves reach a person's ears. When sound waves strike a hard rough surface, they are reflected in many directions. Because the waves are scattered, the sound does not seem so loud. Look at the pictures. In which of these places would sounds be the loudest? Why? What is another name for a sound that is reflected directly back to its source?

For Lesson Questions, turn to page 398.

Sound reflection from a hard smooth surface

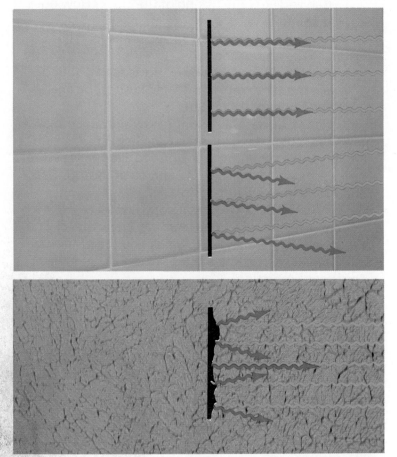

Sound reflection from a hard rough surface

Activity

How is sound reflected?

Materials activity angle sheet / tape / 2 cardboard tubes / small alarm clock

Procedure

A. Push your desk against a wall. The wall and the top of the desk should form a right angle.

B. Get an activity angle sheet from your teacher. Lay the angle sheet on your desk. The point where the angle lines meet should just touch the wall. Tape the sheet to your desk to hold it in place.

C. Lay one cardboard tube along line 1a. Put a clock near the outer end of the tube. Lay another tube along line 3b. Hold your ear near the outer end of this tube.

   1. Can you hear the ticking of the clock? How does it sound?

D. Move the tube from line 3b and lay it along line 2b. Listen at the end of the tube.

   2. Can you hear the ticking? How does it sound?

E. Move the tube from line 2b and lay it along line 1b. Listen at the end of the tube.

   3. Can you hear the ticking? How does it sound?

   4. Was the ticking loudest along line 3b, 2b, or 1b?

F. Move the tube and the clock to line 2a. Lay the other tube along lines 3b, 2b, and 1b as in steps **C, D,** and **E.** Each time, listen to the ticking.

   5. Was the ticking loudest along line 3b, 2b, or 1b?

G. Suppose that the tube and the clock are placed along line 3a. Predict along which line the other tube must be placed for the ticking to sound the loudest. Test your prediction.

Conclusion

1. How did sound travel from one tube to the other?

2. At what angles were the tubes when the ticking was the loudest?

3. How is sound reflected?

Describing Sound Waves

What are some characteristics of sound waves?

There are many differences among sounds. Some sounds are loud and some are soft. Some sounds are high; some are low. Some are pleasant; some can even be painful. The differences among sounds result from the different characteristics of sound waves.

Sound waves have some of the same characteristics as light waves. One of those characteristics is wavelength. **Wavelength** is the distance from the crest of one wave to the crest of the next wave. For sound waves this is the same as the distance from one compression to the next compression.

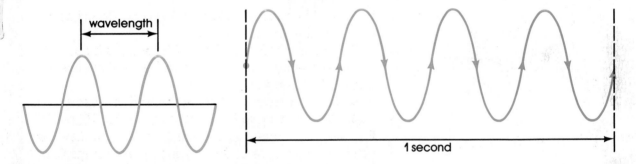

Another characteristic of both sound and light waves is frequency. **Frequency** is the number of waves that pass a point in a certain period of time. The frequency of sound is measured in vibrations per second. Vibrations per second may also be called cycles per second. Many things affect the frequency of sound. These include the kind of matter producing the sound, its shape, and its temperature.

All sounds of the same frequency have the same wavelength. Long waves have low frequencies, and short waves have high frequencies. Most people can hear sounds that have wavelengths between about 2 cm and 17 m.

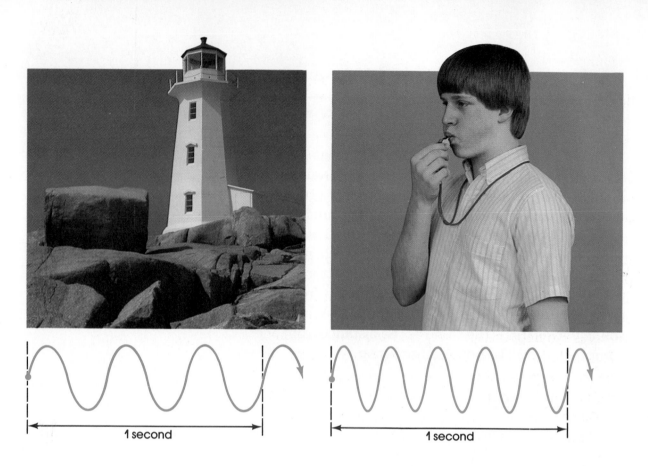

1 second   1 second

Perhaps you have heard the term *pitch* used to describe sound. **Pitch** is how high or how low a sound seems. Which of the objects shown here produces a high-pitched sound? Which produces a low-pitched sound? Pitch is a characteristic that depends on frequency. The faster a material vibrates in one second, the more sound waves it produces. The more sound waves there are, the higher the pitch. In other words, high-frequency sound waves produce sounds with a high pitch. Low-frequency sound waves produce sounds with a low pitch.

Have you ever been on a street corner as a car has sped by with its horn blowing? If so, perhaps you have noticed how the pitch of the horn seems to change. What is the reason for this? Does the speed of the sound waves change? The drawing on page 189 will help you to understand what does happen.

Think of how sound waves spread out in all directions from the source of a sound. You can see in the drawing that sound waves from the car horn spread out like an expanding ball. When the car is moving toward you, the waves are crowded together in front and stretched out in back. If you are standing in front of the approaching car, the crowded-together waves strike your ears. More than the normal number of waves reach you. This makes it seem as if the pitch of the horn is higher than it really is. As the car passes, the stretched-out waves strike your ears. Now the pitch seems lower than it really is. The sudden drop in pitch happens just as the car passes you. The faster the car is moving, the greater the drop in pitch seems.

This relationship between pitch and motion is called the **Doppler effect.** It is named after Christian Doppler, the Austrian scientist who first explained it. The Doppler effect can also be observed with light waves and radio waves.

For Lesson Questions, turn to page 398.

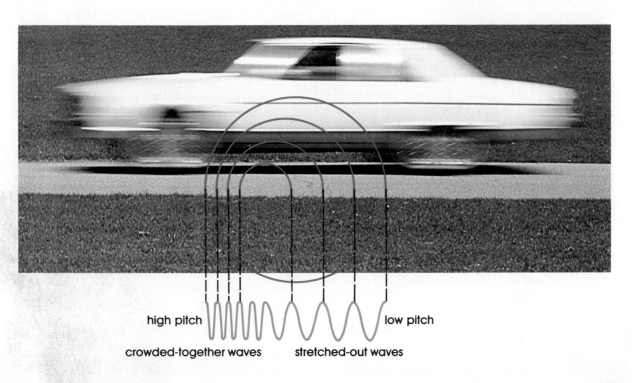

high pitch   low pitch

crowded-together waves   stretched-out waves

Activity

How can you change the pitch of the sound from a vibrating string?

Materials piece of strong thin string about 2 m long / 2 pieces of wood dowel

Procedure
A. Wrap a piece of string once around the top of your desk. Pull the string tight, and tie it with a knot.
B. Place 2 pieces of wood dowel between the string and the desk top. Move the pieces of dowel so that one piece is near each side of the desk.
C. Pluck the string between the pieces of dowel. This is the part of the string that will vibrate to produce sound. Listen to the sound that the string makes.
   1. Describe the sound.
D. Move the pieces of dowel a little closer together. Pluck the string between them, and listen to the sound.
   2. Describe the sound.
E. Repeat step **D** several more times.
   3. Each time, describe the sound that the string makes.

Results
1. When did the string produce the lowest sound?
2. When did the string produce the highest sound?

Conclusion
How is the length of a vibrating string related to the pitch of the sound produced?

Using science ideas
Why do people who play a violin or a guitar change the positions of their fingers on the strings?

Pleasant and Unpleasant Sounds

What are some characteristics of pleasant and unpleasant sounds?

People often use loudness as a means to compare sounds. The loudness of sounds depends on the amount of energy in the sound waves. The amount of energy is shown by the **amplitude** (am′plə tüd), or height, of the wave. The greater the amplitude, the greater the amount of energy in the wave. In the drawings which wave has the greater amplitude?

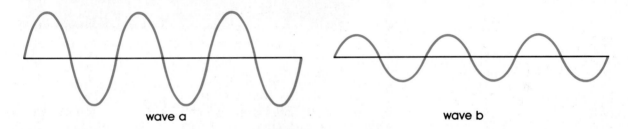

wave a   wave b

If a drum is struck hard, the drum head will vibrate over a greater distance than it would if it were struck lightly. The sound waves formed will have a greater amplitude. Thus, the sound will be loud.

A sound is loudest at its source. The amplitude of the sound wave is greatest there. As a sound wave travels away from its source, the energy in the wave spreads out. The farther a sound wave travels, the less energy it has — so the sound becomes softer.

The cheering at a ball game is a familiar sound. How much energy do you think it takes to make that sound? Scientists estimate that it would take 40,000 people cheering constantly to give off enough energy to keep a 40-watt light bulb glowing! The sound of cheering at a ball game can also be compared with a burning candle. A candle burning wax at the rate of

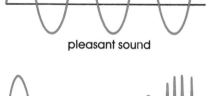

pleasant sound

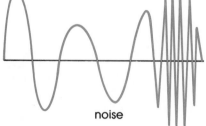

noise

1 g each minute gives off as much energy as the sound of 700,000 people cheering. What forms of energy are given off by the candle?

Compared with other forms of energy, sound is weak. What happens when the energy of a sound wave is increased? If the amplitude is doubled, will a sound seem twice as loud? No, not to a person with normal hearing. The amplitude must be about ten times greater for the sound to be twice as loud.

Some sounds are pleasant to hear but other sounds are not. The sound of a well-played instrument is a pleasant sound. A loud siren may be an unpleasant sound. Unpleasant sounds are called **noise.** You can easily tell the difference between pleasant and unpleasant sounds. But what makes one sound pleasant and another sound unpleasant? Look at the sound waves in the drawings. A pleasant sound has a regular wave pattern. The pattern is repeated over and over. The waves of unpleasant sounds, or noise, are irregular. They do not have a repeated pattern.

For Lesson Questions, turn to page 398.

How Sounds Travel

What determines the speed of sound?

Light travels faster than any other form of energy. It travels fastest through a vacuum. But what about sound? Think of what you learned earlier about how sound travels. You learned that particles of matter vibrate along the path of the wave. Since in a vacuum there is little or no matter, there would be no sound. Sound cannot travel in a vacuum.

The speed of sound varies with the kind of matter through which the sound travels. Look at the table shown below. Compare the speed in gases, in liquids, and in solids. In which state of matter does sound travel the fastest?

SPEED OF SOUND IN DIFFERENT KINDS OF MATTER

Kind of matter	Temperature (°C)	Speed of sound (m/s)
Carbon dioxide (gas)	20	277
Air (gas)	20	344
Alcohol (liquid)	20	1,213
Water (liquid)	20	1,463
Gold (solid)	20	1,743
Copper (solid)	20	3,560
Iron (solid)	20	5,130

Sound travels fastest in solids because in solids the particles of matter are close together. For the same reason, sound travels faster in liquids than in gases.

The speed of sound is also affected by temperature. In general, sound travels faster in matter as the temperature increases. For example, the speed of sound in air increases about 0.6 m/s for each degree Celsius that the temperature rises. Look at the table shown below. What would be the speed of sound in air at 10°C? How does the speed of sound in water change as the temperature increases?

SPEED OF SOUND AT DIFFERENT TEMPERATURES

Kind of matter	Temperature (°C)	Speed of sound (m/s)
Air	0	332
Air	20	344
Air	100	386
Water	0	1,432
Water	20	1,463

Supersonic is a term used to describe speeds greater than the speed of sound. You may have heard the term in relation to the name of an airplane — the SST. SST stands for <u>S</u>uper<u>s</u>onic <u>T</u>ransport. When SSTs fly faster than the speed of sound, they break the sound barrier. This results in a sonic boom. In populated areas, sonic booms can break windows and cause structural damage. A sonic boom is the result of compression waves that build up in front of the plane. When the plane breaks through these compression waves, a shock wave is produced. The shock wave travels across the wings to the rear of the plane. There, some of the wave's energy is released. This produces a loud sound similar to a clap of thunder.

Scientists use a **Mach** (mäk) **number** to compare the speeds of objects that travel faster than sound. The speed of sound is given a Mach number of 1. Objects traveling at twice the speed of sound would have a Mach number of 2, and so on. What would the Mach number be for an object traveling at six times the speed of sound?

Supersonic transport

194

For Lesson Questions, turn to page 398.

Using Sound

What are some ways that sound is used and controlled?

Sounds have a wide range of frequencies. Most people can hear sounds that have a frequency between 20 cycles per second and 20,000 cycles per second. Sounds above and below those frequencies usually cannot be heard.

Those sounds with a frequency above 20,000 cycles per second are called **ultrasonic** (ul trə son′ik). Although out of the range of normal hearing, such sounds have many uses. Ultrasonic sound waves are used in medicine and dentistry to kill bacteria and to clean instruments. Ultrasonic sound is used in certain types of nerve surgery and to find cracks in metal and other materials. It is used to control pests and insects. Ultrasonic sound can even be used to make a sound "picture" of a baby before it is born. From this picture a doctor can tell if the baby is growing normally.

Sonar (sō′när) is another use of high-frequency sound waves. Sonar is used to map the ocean floor and to locate schools of fish and other underwater objects. *Sonar* comes from the phrase SOund NAvigation Ranging. Short bursts of high-frequency sound are sent through the water. If they strike an object in the water, they are reflected back. The distance to the object is found by figuring how long it took the sound waves to reach the object and bounce back.

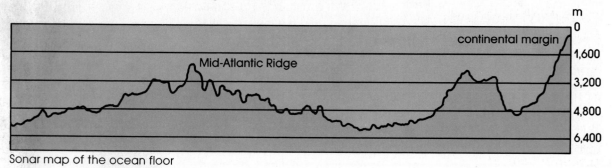

Sonar map of the ocean floor

The loudness of sounds is measured in units called **decibels** (des′ə bels). The symbol for a decibel is dB. Very loud sounds can be harmful. The table shows the decibel levels of different sounds. Sounds above 140 dB may be painful. Over a period of time, sound levels above 90 dB can damage a person's hearing. Often the damage is permanent. Can listening to loud rock bands be harmful to your hearing?

Science & Technology

Ultrasonic sound is used in many areas of medicine. When high-frequency sound waves are directed at a person's body, the waves are reflected in different ways. They create a picture called a sonogram (son′ə gram). Sonograms can show a baby growing inside the mother's body. The images can show the unborn baby's sex. A sonogram can be used to measure the size of the unborn baby's head and bones. It also can show any deformities the baby may have. Ultrasonic sound is used to diagnose and treat illnesses, also. Tumors, gallstones, kidney stones, and heart disorders can be detected with ultrasonic sound waves. In some cases when kidney stones are found, a probe is inserted in the body. Ultrasonic sound waves given off by the probe shatter the stones, which are then passed out of the body. This same kind of sound wave is used for welding certain metals and to clean delicate instruments and watches. Recently, scientists used sonar, or ultrasonic sound, to locate the *Titanic* at the bottom of the Atlantic Ocean.

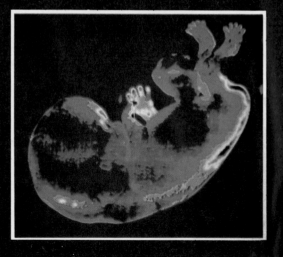

SOME COMMON SOUND LEVELS

Kind of sound	Loudness (dB)
Normal breathing	10
Leaves moving in a breeze	20
Soft whisper	30
Quiet library	40
Quiet restaurant	50
Two people talking	60
Traffic on a busy street	70
Vacuum cleaner	80
Subway train	90
Noisy factory	100
Rock band with amplifiers	110
Riveting machine	120
Jet plane taking off	140
Rocket being launched	180

For Lesson Questions, turn to page 398.

Ideas to Remember

▶ Sound is a form of energy produced by vibrating matter.
▶ Sound travels in all directions from its source.
▶ The energy of a sound wave may be transmitted, absorbed, or reflected by matter.
▶ Pleasant sounds have a regular wave pattern. Unpleasant sounds, called noise, do not have a regular wave pattern.
▶ The speed of sound varies with the kind of matter and its temperature.
▶ Loud sounds can be harmful to your hearing.

Reviewing the Chapter

SCIENCE WORDS

A. Use all the terms below to complete the sentences.

ultrasonic   wave   energy   absorbed   frequency
amplitude   noise   pitch   particles   temperature

Sound is a form of __1__. It travels as a __2__ in all directions from its source. A sound wave is vibrating __3__ of matter that form compressions and rarefactions. More sound energy is __4__ by soft matter than by hard matter. The __5__ of a sound is determined by its __6__. The amount of energy in a sound wave is called the __7__ of the wave. Sounds that do not have a regular wave pattern are called __8__. The speed of sound changes with a change in __9__. Sounds above the normal range of hearing are called __10__.

B. Write the letter of the term that best matches the definition. Not all the terms will be used.

1. How high or low a sound seems
2. A region of crowded particles in a wave
3. The back-and-forth motion of particles of matter
4. Three times the speed of sound
5. A unit of loudness of sound
6. A sound above 20,000 cycles per second
7. The distance from one crest to the next crest in a wave

    a. vibration
    b. Mach 3
    c. decibel
    d. pitch
    e. ultrasonic
    f. amplitude
    g. compression
    h. wavelength

UNDERSTANDING IDEAS

A. Write the correct term for each number in the drawing: wavelength, compression, amplitude, rarefaction.

B. Explain why there cannot be sound in a vacuum.

C. When sound is produced by a vibrating object, which is formed first—a compression or a rarefraction?

D. Which drawing shows a sound wave that is noise? Why?

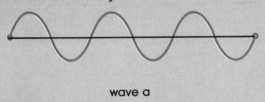

wave a

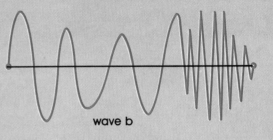

wave b

USING IDEAS

1. Set up and perform an experiment to find out how the pitch is affected by the thickness of a vibrating string.

2. Find out how bats use sound to avoid flying into objects in the dark.

THINKING LIKE A SCIENTIST

Answer the following questions. You may be able to answer some of the questions just by thinking about them. To answer other questions, you may have to do some research.

1. Have you ever noticed how good your voice sounds when you sing in the shower? How can you explain this effect?

2. Some stereo manufacturers like to show how true-to-life their sound systems are by playing a tape of an opera singer. When the opera singer hits a certain note, a glass shatters. Can an opera singer really shatter a glass? If so, explain this effect.

3. Why does it seem that you can hear the sound of the ocean waves when you hold a large seashell close to your ear?

4. Suppose that in a room filled with people of all ages, an experimenter turns on a sound system. She asks everyone to raise their hand as soon as they hear the high-frequency sound coming from the speaker. She observes that almost all of the people under age 16 raise their hand immediately. Almost no one over age 16 raises their hand. Which of the following hypotheses might best explain the observation?

   a. Most people over age 16 have ear damage due to loud rock music and other loud sounds in the environment.

   b. Younger people have more practice in listening, since they spend large amounts of time in school. Therefore, they hear the sound sooner.

   c. The ability to hear high-frequency sounds decreases with age.

   d. As people get older, it takes longer for nerve impulses to travel from their ears to their brain.

CHAPTER 9
Using Electricity

"**T**he Startling Breakthrough That Could Change Our World"
read the headline about a discovery being discussed all over
the globe. What kinds of changes could occur? Picture a world
where trains float above their tracks on a cushion of air. Imagine computers that are smaller and faster than the ones we
know today. Think of a city where all the electric current is
supplied through a handful of cables.

What discovery might make all of this come true? The
superconductor! A superconductor (sü pər kən duk´ tər) is a
substance that can carry electricity with no loss of energy.
You may recall that a conductor is a substance that carries
electricity. But a conductor, such as copper, loses a large
amount of energy in the form of heat.

Scientists have known about superconductors for about
75 years. In the past, superconductors were formed only of

metals. These metals had to be cooled to very, very low temperatures. The cooling process was difficult. But at those temperatures, something happens to the behavior of some metals. These metals can carry electric current without losing energy. At higher temperatures this behavior does not take place.

Scientists have now found other substances that can be made into superconductors. These substances do not need to be cooled to such low temperatures. But they still must be cooled to well below room temperature. What are these amazing substances? They are called ceramics (sə ram´ iks). When you hear the word *ceramics*, you might think of clay bowls and plates. The substances in superconductors are a little like the clay of clay bowls. But scientists have added chemicals to these ceramics to make them different. When cooled, these new ceramics can carry electricity!

Scientists in many parts of the world are in a race to find the best superconductor. They are looking for a substance that carries electricity but does not have to be cooled. Nearly every day, scientists are finding substances that act as superconductors at higher and higher temperatures.

Finding the ideal superconductor is only the first part of the challenge. Scientists must then change this substance into a useful form. They must find a way to change ceramics into wires, tapes, or thin films. Even now superconductors are being formed into very thin wires. They are also being made into rolls of tape. The tape looks a bit like dull dark gray foil.

Scientists may use ceramics in ways never dreamed of before. For example, they may use these wires inside tiny computers. Perhaps they will be able to squeeze all the parts of a computer into a device the size of a watch. Right now, a computer this size is not possible. With substances now used, a lot of heat is produced. The heat forms as current passes through the circuits. With superconductors, scientists could form a tiny computer that does not give off heat.

▲ Computer Chip

Think of yourself as a scientist working with superconductors. For now, aluminum foil will represent the superconductor. You will need a sheet of aluminum foil, a pencil, a metric ruler, scissors, plastic tape, and glue. Using these materials, form the sheet of foil into as many different shapes as possible. For example, you could cut part of the foil into very thin strips. What else can you do with the foil? Share your ideas with the other members of your class.

▲ Preparing superconducting material in the lab (above, left). Superconductor formed into a thin wire (above, right).

◀ A small magnet rises above superconducting material.

In this chapter you will learn how electricity can be used, measured, and controlled. You will learn how it can be changed to other forms of energy.

Electricity and Electrons

How is electricity related to the movement of electrons?

Scientists know much about the world in which we live. However, there are many questions for which they do not yet have answers. For example, scientists cannot explain exactly what gravity is. They also do not know exactly what electricity is.

Not knowing exactly what electricity is has not prevented scientists from learning about electricity. They know it is a form of energy. They can measure it, use it, control it, and change it into other forms of energy. Scientists know that electricity involves the movement of electrons and that it is closely related to magnetism.

Think of what you have learned about the structure of atoms. You know that an atom has a tightly packed central nucleus made of protons and neutrons. You also know that the negatively charged particles called electrons travel in orbits around the nucleus. Do you

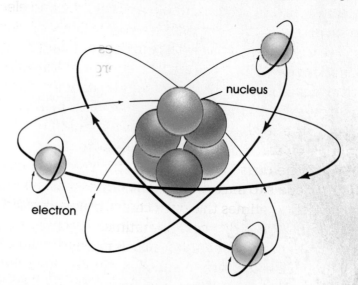

nucleus

electron

recall the definition of energy? Energy is defined as the capacity to do work. How do you think the electrons that help to make up matter can do work? Electrons are always moving. Any body that is moving has kinetic energy. **Kinetic** (ki net′ik) **energy** is active energy — the energy of motion. It is hard to capture the kinetic energy of electrons as they move around the nuclei of atoms. But if the electrons are moved from their orbits, their kinetic energy can be used.

Sometimes, electrons are moved from their orbits by friction. The electrons are rubbed off one object by friction and then pile up on another object. This transfer of electrons from one object to another is called static electricity. There are some uses for static electricity, but for the most part, it is a nuisance. It is not easily controlled. You are probably familiar with these electric charges. They build up on clothes in a dryer, making the clothes cling to each other. Static electricity can build up in your hair when you comb it, causing the hairs to repel each other.

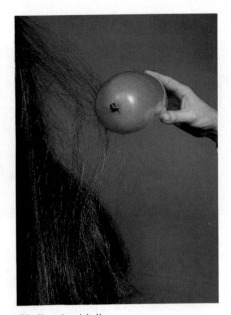

Static electricity

Electrons are much more useful when they are made to move along a conductor. This is called an electric current, or current electricity. When an electric current moves through a wire, trillions of electrons are in motion. One electron does not have much kinetic energy. But together the energy of trillions of electrons is great. Electrons do not *contain* kinetic energy — their kinetic energy is their motion. As with anything else that moves, electrons must be set in motion by some outside form of energy.

A bicycle does not move by itself. You must push on the pedals to make it move. Electrons must also be pushed. Sometimes this push comes from a chemical reaction, as in a dry cell. Sometimes it comes from some other form of energy, such as in a hydroelectric (hī drō i lek′trik) power plant. Here the energy comes from moving water. In other power plants the energy

Photoelectric cell

comes from steam produced by burning a fuel. In other cases the electrons can be moved when they are struck by radiant energy. A device that operates with light energy is called a photoelectric cell. Why does it have this name?

There are two kinds of current electricity—direct current and alternating (ôl′tər nā ting) current. In **direct current (dc)** the electrons always travel in the same direction. This is the kind of current produced when chemical energy is changed to electrical energy in a dry cell or in a car battery. Where is direct current used around your home? In **alternating current (ac)** the electrons move back and forth. First they travel in one direction, then in the opposite direction. Electric power companies produce alternating current. This is the kind of current you use in your home. Alternating current is cheaper to produce than is direct current. It also is easier to transmit over long distances.

Recall that electricity is related to magnetism. They are related in two ways. First, both electricity and magnetism involve the movement of electrons. Second, magnetism can be used to produce electricity, and electricity can be used to produce magnetism. But electricity and magnetism are not the same.

Power plant producing ac

Power lines carrying ac

Appliance using ac

Whenever electrons move through a wire, the wire itself is a magnet. If a wire is wrapped around a nail and then connected to a dry cell, the nail acts as a magnet. Such a magnet is called an electromagnet. Electromagnets are used in telephones, radios, and televisions. Where else are electromagnets used?

SKILL: Making a model

Finding Out

How can you make a telegraph?

One device that uses electromagnets is a telegraph. To make a telegraph, nail to a board a block that measures 3 cm on each side. Nail a metal strip to the block as shown. Hammer a roofing nail to the board so that its head is just below the metal strip. This part of your telegraph is called the sounder. Nail a second metal strip to the board as shown. Bend up the end of this strip. Hammer another nail under the end of this metal strip. This part of your telegraph is called the key. Now wire the telegraph as shown. Press the key to make the sounder click. What part of your telegraph is an electromagnet?

dry cell battery

sounder

key

205

For Lesson Questions, turn to page 400.

Activity

How can you show the relationship between electricity and magnetism?

Materials 45-cm length of insulated wire / dry cell / large file card / scissors / iron filings

Procedure

A. Scrape off about 3 cm of the insulation from each end of the wire. Connect one end of the wire to a terminal of a dry cell. Do not connect the other end.

B. Cut a file card in half to make two cards that are almost square. Pour a small pile of iron filings on one card. Dip the center of the wire into the iron filings. Now lift the wire.
  1. Do the iron filings stick to the wire?
  2. What does this indicate?

C. Connect the loose end of the wire to the other terminal of the dry cell. Again dip the center of the wire into the iron filings. Then lift the wire.
  3. Do the iron filings stick to the wire?
  4. What does this indicate?

D. Disconnect the wire from one terminal of the dry cell. Push the end of the wire through the center of the second card. Reconnect the wire to the dry cell.

E. Hold the card level. Sprinkle some iron filings on it. Then gently tap the edge of the card.
  5. What is the shape of the pattern formed by the iron filings?
  6. Where is the magnetic field around the wire located?

F. Disconnect the wire from both terminals of the dry cell.

Conclusion
How does this activity show the relationship between electricity and magnetism?

Measuring and Controlling Electricity

What are some ways in which electricity can be measured and controlled?

To have an electric current, there must be (1) a material over which electrons can move, (2) a supply of electrons that are free to move, (3) a source of energy to push the electrons, and (4) a complete pathway, or circuit.

The material over which the electrons move is called a conductor. Some materials are good conductors of electrons; others are not. Poor conductors are good insulators. But what causes a material to be either a good conductor or a poor conductor?

Think first of the electrons that move through an electric circuit. These electrons are part of the circuit itself—they are not added to the circuit like water is added to a pipe or a hose. This means that a good conductor must be a material that will release its outer electrons fairly easily. Most metals do this. Therefore, most metals are good conductors. One very good conductor is copper. Aluminum is also a good conductor.

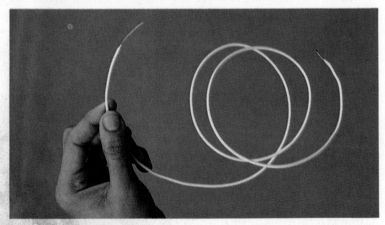

A metal conductor

When you run a race, you can run fast and straight if there is nothing in your way. Similarly, a good conductor must provide a clear path for the movement of electrons. The particles of most metals are more or less separate from one another, as in the drawing of the copper wire. This allows the electrons to move through the metals easily.

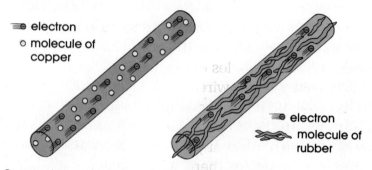

electron
molecule of copper

electron
molecule of rubber

Copper (a conductor) and rubber (an insulator)

Now look at the drawing of rubber, an insulator. Insulators often have large, long, tangled particles. These particles do not allow the electrons to move through the material easily. They stop the electrons or slow them down a great deal. This is why insulators are wrapped around electric wires. They prevent the electrons from leaving their regular path. Rubber, plastic, and cloth are good insulators.

Materials that slow down or stop the movement of electrons may be said to have resistance. The unit of electric resistance is the **ohm** (ōm). The total amount of resistance to the movement of an electric current is measured in ohms.

You know that insulators resist the movement of electrons. Conductors also resist the movement of electrons. Suppose, for example, that you have two wires. One wire is thin and the other is thick. What happens when electrons move through each of the wires? Remember, electrons have a negative charge, and like charges repel each other. The negatively

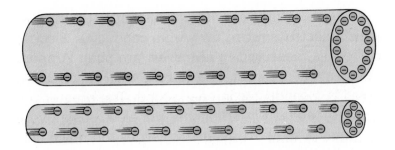

charged electrons in a wire tend to push away from one another. In this way they are similar to the behavior of the like poles of magnets.

Compare the two wires in the drawing. Since electrons repel, they travel near the surface of a conductor. In the thick wire there is plenty of room, so the electrons can move easily. There is little resistance. In the thin wire where there is less room for the electrons to move, the resistance is much greater.

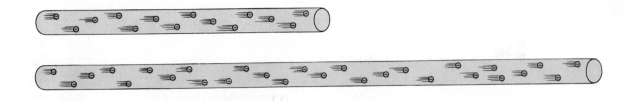

Now look at the wires in this drawing. One is twice as long as the other. Through which wire would it be easiest for the electrons to move? Which wire would have the greater resistance?

The term *voltage* is used to describe the force that moves electrons through a circuit. The force needed to move the electrons is measured in **volts.** It takes more force to move electrons through a wire with high resistance than through a wire with low resistance. The wires in a toaster or in an electric heater have high resistance. Much of the electric energy used to operate these appliances is changed to heat.

The strength of an electric current is the rate at which electrons move through a conductor. Electric current is measured in **amperes** (am'pirs). *Ampere* refers to the number of electrons that move past a point in a conductor in one second. The greater the voltage, the faster and farther the electrons move.

A circuit may overheat if it carries too much current. An overheated circuit can cause a fire. Fuses are used to prevent circuits from overheating. A fuse contains a short length of wire that melts when the current is too great. That breaks the circuit. How much current can the fuse in the picture carry?

The rate, or speed, at which electric energy is used is measured in watts. One ampere of current moving with a force of one volt has one watt of power. This relationship is shown by the following equation.

$$\text{watts} = \text{amperes} \times \text{volts}$$

You have probably seen these terms printed on electric appliances in your home. What is the wattage of the light bulbs shown? What is the voltage?

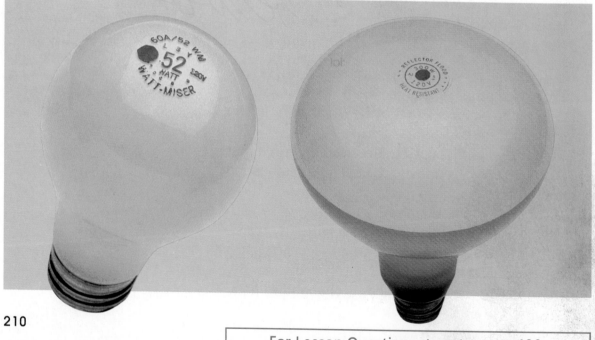

For Lesson Questions, turn to page 400.

Using Electricity

Why is electricity useful, and how is it used?

Perhaps you have heard someone say, "Electricity is our most useful form of energy." But have you ever wondered why? One reason is that electricity can be moved easily. Electricity is much easier to handle than are other sources of energy. It can be produced in one place and then moved long distances over wires. It is easier to move electricity over wires than it is to transport fuel such as coal. Look at the cross section of the electric cable. In one hour, a cable like this can carry as much energy as that in about 55 metric tons of fuel oil.

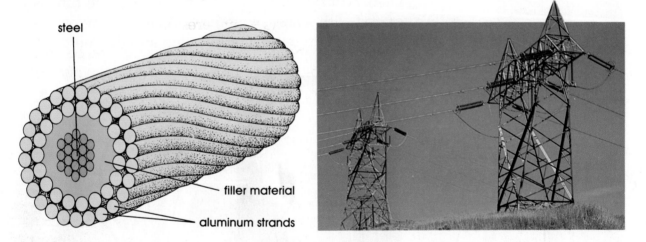

steel

filler material

aluminum strands

No one needs to tell you how important electricity is. Towns come to almost a complete stop when there is a power failure. Every modern business and factory depends almost completely on electricity. So do stores, hospitals, schools, and banks. Without electricity, your home life stops, also. To use electricity, it first must be changed to some other form of energy. Some of those forms are chemical energy, light, heat, and mechanical, or moving, energy.

When you think of electricity, you might think about lights. You may use both incandescent electric lamps and fluorescent electric lamps. The names of these lamps tell something about how they work. Incandescent means "to glow white-hot." Fluorescent means "to give off radiant energy."

There is a long, thin piece of tungsten wire inside an incandescent lamp. The wire is called the filament of the lamp. The filament is coiled or twisted so that the long wire will fit in a small space. You can see the filament in the drawing of the lamp shown here. There is high resistance when electrons move through the filament. This causes much of the electric energy to change to heat. The wire glows white-hot.

A fluorescent lamp is made of a long glass tube filled with mercury vapor. The inside of the tube is coated with a special material. As electricity passes through the tube, electrons bump into the mercury.

electrode

coating inside tube

mercury vapor (gas)

ultraviolet radiation

gas particle

speeding electron

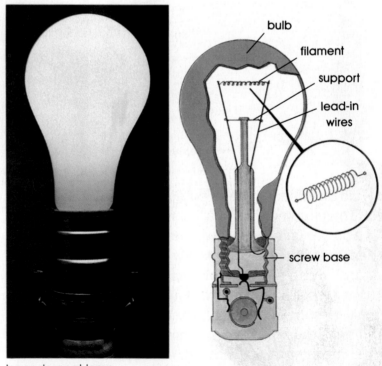

bulb

filament

support

lead-in wires

screw base

Fluorescent lamp

Incandescent lamp

212

This causes ultraviolet radiation to be given off. The radiation strikes the coating of the tube and makes it glow. Fluorescent lamps cost more than incandescent lamps. But they last longer, use less electricity, and do not waste energy as heat.

Motors change electricity to mechanical energy. It is estimated that in an American home there are more than 50 small electric motors. Each of the appliances shown here has a small electric motor. How many of these appliances are in your home? Where are other small electric motors in your home?

Sometimes electricity is used to bring about chemical changes. In such cases, electric energy changes the chemical composition of a material. Often the chemical bonds of the material are broken. This happens with water. When an electric current is passed through water, the water is broken down into hydrogen gas and oxygen gas from which it was formed.

Food processor

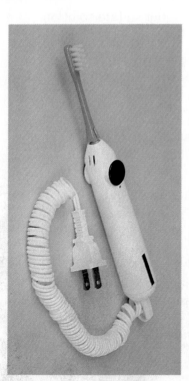

Toothbrush

Hairdryer

Mixer

For Lesson Questions, turn to page 400.

Activity

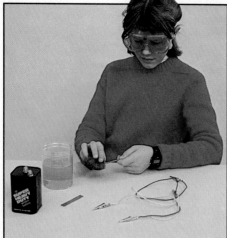

How can electricity be used to bring about a chemical change?

Materials spoon / granular copper sulfate / jar / warm water / large steel nail / steel wool / 2 wire test leads / 6-volt dry cell / safety goggles / copper strip

Procedure

A. Place about 4 spoonsful of copper sulfate in a jar. *Caution Do not get any copper sulfate in your mouth.* Fill the jar with warm water to within about 5 cm of the top. Stir until all the copper sulfate is dissolved.

B. Clean a nail by rubbing it hard with steel wool. Then wash and dry the nail to remove all the grease and dirt.

C. Attach one end of a test lead to the head of the nail. Attach the other end of the test lead to the negative (−) terminal of a dry cell.

D. Suspend the nail in the copper sulfate solution.

E. Wash and dry a copper strip. Attach one end of another test lead to the copper strip. Attach the other end of the test lead to the positive (+) terminal of the dry cell.

F. Suspend the copper strip in the copper sulfate solution. Do this in the same way as you did with the nail. *Caution Be careful not to let the copper strip touch the nail.*

G. Watch the set-up for several minutes.
   1. What do you observe happening to the nail?
   2. What is the source of energy for this reaction?

Conclusion

1. How is the nail being changed?
2. This process is called electroplating. Why is that a good name?
3. How can electricity change the chemical composition of a substance?

Circuits

What is an electric circuit?

As was mentioned earlier, to have an electric current, electrons must move on a complete unbroken pathway. This unbroken pathway is called a complete circuit. If a wire is disconnected or broken, the circuit is broken, and the electrons cannot move. A switch is often used to "break" or "open" a circuit when electric current must be controlled.

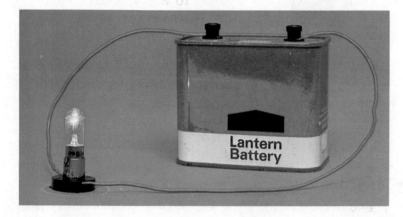

You know that chemists use a form of shorthand to explain chemical reactions. In somewhat the same way, electricians use a type of shorthand to explain electric circuits. The table shows some of the symbols used to explain circuits.

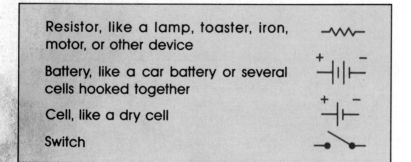

Resistor, like a lamp, toaster, iron, motor, or other device	
Battery, like a car battery or several cells hooked together	
Cell, like a dry cell	
Switch	

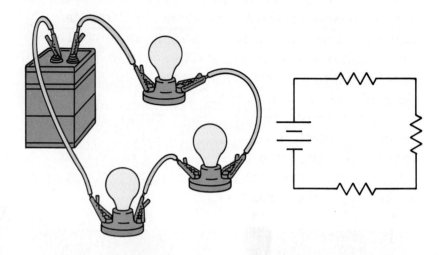

There are two kinds of simple electric circuits—series and parallel. In a **series circuit** there is only one path for electrons. If the path is broken, electrons will not move through any devices in the circuit. In a **parallel circuit** there is more than one path. A break in one path does not stop the movement of electrons through the other paths. Use the information in the table to study the circuits shown. Which is a series circuit? Which is a parallel circuit? Why are most circuits in your home parallel circuits?

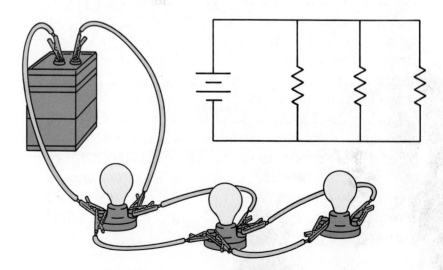

The series and parallel circuits in the drawing are simple. In devices such as televisions and computers, however, there are many complex circuits. The movement of the electrons in these circuits must be controlled if the devices are to work properly. At one time this was done with tubes.

The picture on the left shows a circuit that uses tubes to control current. Until far into the 1950s, radios, television, and other electrical devices contained tubes. Tubes took up much space, produced a lot of heat, and burned out often.

  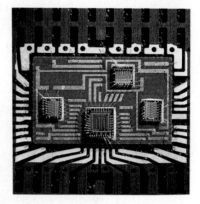

In the late 1950s, tubes were replaced by transistors (tran zis'tərz), shown in the center picture. As you can see, transistors are much smaller than tubes. The transistors are connected to all other parts of the circuit with flat wires. Such a circuit is called a **printed circuit.** The use of transistors greatly reduced the size of a typical circuit. This in turn reduced the size and weight of radios and other such things.

During the 1970s, another advance was made. It allowed a whole circuit, with all the parts needed to control the current, to be put on one silicon chip. A chip, shown on the right, can be smaller than a fingernail. Yet all the parts and connections for the circuit are on the chip. This type of circuit is called an **integrated** (in'tə grā tid) **circuit.**

Thousands of electronic parts can be packed onto a tiny chip. This has further reduced the size of circuits. Handheld calculators and home computers run with circuits contained on tiny silicon chips.

A chip

The use of chips has greatly increased the speed at which computers can store and handle information. A computer stores information in **memory circuits.** These circuits are on chips in many modern computers. As information is put into the computer, the memory circuits become used up. However, the information is lost when the computer is off. To store information permanently, the computer can transfer information to tapes or to memory disks. The tapes or disks put the information back into the computer when needed. A tape or disk can be stored in a safe place or used with another computer someplace else.

Computers also contain circuits that can process information. These circuits calculate, solve problems, and do the jobs the computer was designed to do.

In many computers, the problem-solving circuits are contained on a chip. Such a chip is called a micro-processor (mī krō pros'es ər). A **microprocessor** is a computer on a chip. Computers found in schools and homes contain such chips.

An ant carrying a microprocessor

A computer is given instructions to follow when it is used. Instructions are given in a language that the computer can understand. Many small computers use a language called BASIC. The set of instructions that tells the computer what to do is called a **program.**

The student is using a computer. Refer to the pictures as you read about what is happening.

In the first picture the student has read what the program is about. The student has been told by the computer to press a key to go to the next step.

In the second picture the computer has placed a question on the screen. The question was in the computer's memory circuits. The student has responded by spelling out the answer.

In the third picture the computer has checked the answer. The computer has informed the student that the answer is right. Now the computer will put another question on the screen.

In the flow chart on page 221 trace the path that shows how information may be processed and used immediately. Then trace the path that shows how information may be stored and then recalled later.

Microprocessors are used in other devices besides computers. A calculator is controlled by a microprocessor. It is the microprocessor in a calculator that follows instructions. A person using a calculator enters some numbers and instructions. For example, let us say the person enters 2 + 2 and then presses

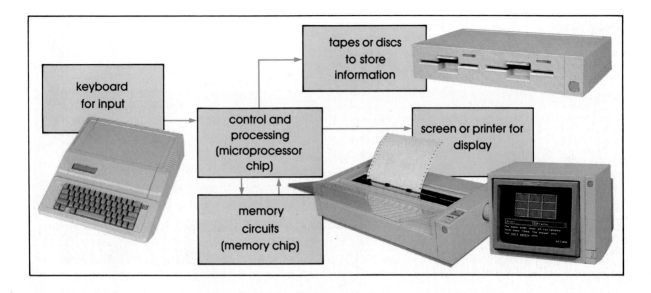

Diagram labels: keyboard for input → control and processing (microprocessor chip) → tapes or discs to store information; screen or printer for display; memory circuits (memory chip)

the equals sign (=). The calculator receives these numbers and the instruction to add them. In a short time, the calculator adds the numbers and shows the answer. The answer may be shown on a display screen, on a paper tape, or on both. What advantage might there be in using a calculator that shows the answer both on a screen and on a tape?

SKILL: Measuring

Finding Out

How fast can a chip calculate?

Test yourself against a chip. Time how long it takes you to write and solve each problem on paper.
a. 3,579 × 46
b. 5.06 + 369.1 + 407.0 + 0.48 + 28.0
c. 10,007 − 123.45
d. 978.3 ÷ 0.16
Now time how long it takes to solve the problems with an electronic calculator. Compare the times. Which problem took the longest to solve on paper? Using the calculator, how long did it take to solve that problem?

Some late-model cars have computerized systems to aid the driver. They are a convenience to the driver and, in some cases, are also a safety factor. A microprocessor is used to keep track of how various systems in the car are operating. This information is displayed on the dashboard of the car. It is continually updated as the car is driven. For example, the fuel computer system calculates how far the car may drive on the fuel still in the gas tank. The distance may be computed both in miles and in kilometers. The microprocessor may monitor, or keep track of, the oil level and oil pressure. The way the engine cooling system performs may also be monitored. A clock on the dashboard can tell the date and the current time. During a trip the clock also computes elapsed time — the time from the beginning to the end of the trip. Other computerized systems include a speed alarm and an odometer that computes the distance traveled on a trip.

Microprocessors are used in many other ways. They are used in cars and electronic games. In cars they may tell drivers about such conditions as fuel level, oil level, and even whether the door is closed. In electronic games they make different sound and light patterns. As you play such a game, the microprocessor reacts to your actions by changing the patterns.

Computers and microprocessors have changed our lives. Computers help us store and recall large amounts of information. Computers also help us use this information to solve problems. New uses for computers and microprocessors will be found every year. They will continue to play an important role in our lives.

For Lesson Questions, turn to page 400.

Ideas to Remember

▶ Electricity is a form of energy that involves the movement of electrons.

▶ Electricity can be measured in terms of amperes, volts, watts, and ohms.

▶ Electricity is useful because it can be produced in one place and transmitted rapidly to another place.

▶ Electricity can be changed to other forms of energy.

▶ Electrons move only when there is a complete unbroken path called a circuit.

▶ Computers are important in storing, processing, and using information.

Reviewing the Chapter

SCIENCE WORDS

A. Write the letter of the term that best matches the definition. Not all the terms will be used.

1. The kind of chip that contains problem-solving circuits
2. A measure of the resistance to the movement of electrons
3. A circuit containing transistors that are attached by flat wires
4. Current in which the electrons always move in one direction
5. A set of instructions that tells a computer what to do
6. A device that consists of a conductor wrapped around an iron core
7. A circuit in which all parts and connections are contained on a chip
8. Current in which the electrons move first in one direction and then in the opposite direction
9. The force needed to move electrons through a circuit
10. A measure of the number of electrons that move past a point in a conductor in one second
11. A computer circuit in which information is stored
12. A measure of the rate at which electric energy is used

a. watts
b. printed circuit
c. electro-magnet
d. memory circuit
e. amperes
f. micropro-cessor
g. program
h. short circuit
i. alternating current
j. ohms
k. volts
l. direct current
m. integrated circuit
n. computer

UNDERSTANDING IDEAS

A. A cause makes things happen. An effect is what happens. For each pair of sentences, write which is the cause and which is the effect.

1. a. A conductor gets hot.
   b. A conductor offers resistance to the movement of electrons.

2. **a.** A wire is disconnected from a dry cell.
   b. There is no movement of electrons.
3. **a.** Memory circuits become used up.
   b. The keyboard is used to put data into a computer.

B. Describe how electronic circuits have changed.

C. Study the computer flow chart shown. Match the letters in the chart with the correct part and function listed below.

1. Memory circuits (memory chip)
2. Tapes or disks to store information
3. Control and processing (microprocessor chip)
4. Screen or printer for display
5. Keyboard for input

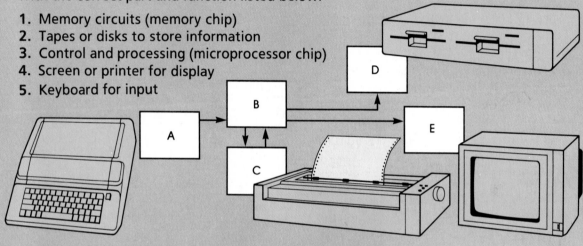

USING IDEAS

1. Find out some of the terms used in the computer language known as BASIC. What will a computer do when it receives each instruction?

2. Find out how an electric motor changes electric energy to mechanical energy.

THINKING LIKE A SCIENTIST

Answer the following questions. You may be able to answer some of the questions just by thinking about them. To answer other questions, you may have to do some research.

1. When the electricity in your home goes off during a storm, you can often pick up the phone and report the problem to the electric company. How can the phone work without any electricity?

2. Why does a television antenna on the roof work better than the one on the television set?

3. How does a satellite dish antenna receive so many more channels than an ordinary antenna?

Science in Careers

The study of matter and energy falls under two general areas in science. These are *chemistry* and *physics*. Both the **chemist** and the **physicist** are interested in the nature and behavior of matter. Both study the relationships between energy and matter, but they may investigate different aspects.

Chemists are usually more concerned with the physical and chemical properties of elements and compounds. **Analytical chemists** determine the kinds of matter present in particular samples. They may also determine the amount of each element or compound in a sample. **Organic chemists** study the compounds of carbon. Areas of their work often overlap areas of biology. **Physical chemists** study the energy changes that occur in chemical reactions.

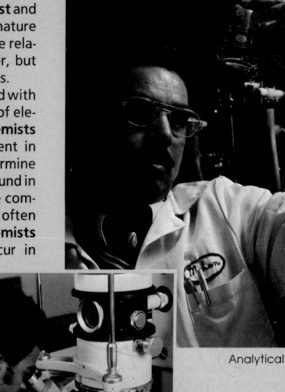

Analytical chemist

Biochemist

Physicists may be interested in matter on a very large or very small scale. Some physicists study the nature of light and electricity. Others investigate the structure and behavior of particles that are smaller than atoms. And many physicists study the relationships between energy and matter. Perhaps this type of work would interest you.

226

People in Science

DOLPHUS E. MILLIGAN
(1928 – 1973)

Dr. Milligan was a chemist. He studied what happens to molecules as they break apart during chemical reactions. Using an instrument called a spectroscope, Dr. Milligan was able to identify a number of short-lived chemical units called reaction intermediates. The reaction intermediates exist only for a brief period of time during chemical reactions. However, they play important roles in how matter rearranges during chemical reactions.

A spectrometer being used to investigate chemical reactions

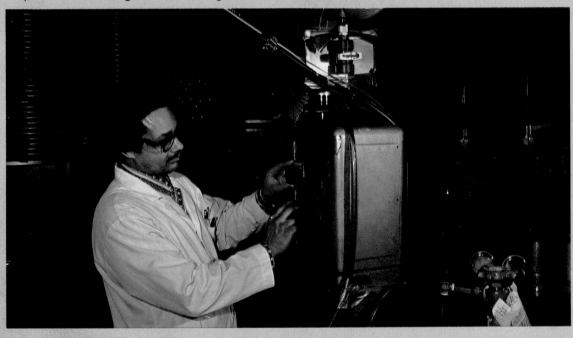

Developing Skills

WORD SKILLS

Prefixes and suffixes are word parts that change the meanings of the base words to which they are added. A prefix is added to the beginning of a base word. A suffix is added to the end of a base word. The tables show how prefixes and suffixes are used to change the meanings of words.

Use the tables for help in determining the meaning of each of the following words. If you do not know the meaning of the base word, look it up in a dictionary.

1. ato<u>mic</u>
2. poison<u>ous</u>
3. element<u>al</u>
4. <u>non</u>acid
5. <u>un</u>reactive
6. compres<u>sion</u>
7. <u>ultra</u>violet
8. <u>super</u>conductor
9. fission<u>able</u>
10. <u>extra</u>terrestrial

Prefix	Meaning	Example
extra-	beyond	extraordinary
non-	not	nontoxic
super-	above, most	superabundant
ultra-	beyond	ultrasonic
un-	not, opposite of	unfair

Suffix	Meaning	Example
-able	that can be	obtainable
-al	of, having the nature of	ornamental
-ic	having to do with	metallic
-ion	act or process of	expression
-ous	full of	joyous

READING AN ENERGY LABEL

Most new large appliances now come with an energy label like the ones shown on the next page. These labels can be used to help compare the amount of energy different types of the same appliance will use. Study the labels shown here. Use the labels to answer the following questions.

1. Which of the appliances will use the least amount of energy in one year?
2. Which will use the most energy in one year?
3. Suppose you pay 6 cents per kilowatt-hour. How much will it cost to use appliance **A** for 3,000 hours of use?
4. At the same rate, how much more will it cost to use appliance **B**?
5. Suppose appliance **B** costs $200 less than appliance **C**. Which appliance will have cost you less after 3,000 hours of use? (To determine the total cost of an appliance, add the cost to purchase it to the cost of energy to run it.)

228

Appliance A

7.5

Least efficient model 5.5 — Most efficient model 8.7 — ▼ THIS MODEL

Energy Efficiency Rating (EER)

This energy rating is based on U.S. Government standard tests.

How much will this model cost you to run yearly?

Yearly hours of use		250	750	1000	2000	3000
		Estimated yearly $ cost shown below				
Cost per kilowatt hour	2¢	$4	$12	$16	$32	$48
	4¢	$8	$24	$32	$64	$95
	6¢	$12	$36	$48	$95	$143
	8¢	$16	$48	$64	$127	$191
	10¢	$20	$60	$80	$159	$239
	12¢	$24	$72			

Ask your salesperson or local utility for the energy rate (cost per kilowatt hour) in your area. Your cost will vary depending and how you use the product.

Important Removal of this label before consumer pur... (42 U.S.C. 6302)

▲ **Appliance A**
Price: $425.00

▶ **Appliance B**
Price: $360.00

Appliance C

9.5

Least efficient model 5.5 — Most efficient model 8.7

Energy Efficiency Rating (EER)

THE ENERGY EFFICIENCY RATING OF THIS MODEL WAS NOT AVAILABLE AT THE TIME THE RANGE WAS PUBLISHED.

How much will this model cost you to run yearly?

Yearly hours of use		250	750	1000	2000	3000
		Estimated yearly $ cost shown below				
Cost per kilowatt hour	2¢	$3	$10	$13	$26	$38
	4¢	$6	$19	$26	$51	$77
	6¢	$10	$29	$38	$77	$115
	8¢	$13	$38	$51	$102	$154
	10¢	$16	$48	$64	$128	$192
	12¢	$19	$58	$77	$154	$230

Ask your salesperson or local utility for the energy rate (cost per kilowatt hour) in your area. Your cost will vary depending on your local energy rate and how you use the product.

...f this label before consumer purchase is a violation of federal

▲ **Appliance C**
Price: $560.00

Appliance B

9.0

Least efficient model 5.8 — Most efficient model 9.0 — THIS MODEL ▼

Energy Efficiency Rating (EER)

This energy rating is based on U.S. Government standard tests.

How much will this model cost you to run yearly?

Yearly hours of use		250	750	1000	2000	3000
		Estimated yearly $ cost shown below				
Cost per kilowatt hour	2¢	$7	$22	$29	$58	$87
	4¢	$15	$44	$58	$116	$174
	6¢	$22	$65	$87	$174	$261
	8¢	$29	$87	$116	$232	$348
	10¢	$36	$109	$145	$290	$435
	12¢	$44	$131	$174	$348	$522

Ask your salesperson or local utility for the energy rate (cost per kilowatt hour) in your area. Your cost will vary depending on your local energy rate and how you use the product.

Important Removal of this label before consumer purchase is a violation of federal law (42 U.S.C. 6302)

USING THINKING SKILLS

We were first made aware of our limited energy resources in the 1970s, when we had our first "energy crisis." Since then, some people have tried to change their life-styles to use as little energy as possible. Think about this as you answer the following questions.

1. Should people always purchase the appliance or automobile that uses the least amount of energy? Explain your answer.
2. Should there be laws to make companies produce appliances and automobiles that use little energy? Explain your answer.

229

UNIT THREE

Investigating the Earth and Space

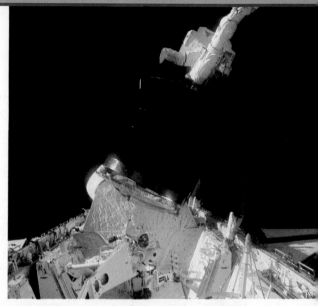

Chapter 13—Exploring Space Recently, a disabled satellite was recovered in space and repaired. In Chapter 13 you will learn about the past accomplishments and the future expectations for exploring space.

Chapter 12—Forecasting the Weather Both living and nonliving things are affected by the weather. Would knowing in advance how and when the weather will change have prevented ice crystals from forming on this plant? Chapter 12 deals with the kinds of data meteorologists use to forecast the weather.

230

Chapter 10 — The Earth's Resources This oil drilling rig and platform shows one way in which a valuable resource is obtained from the oceans. In the future we may depend more and more on the oceans for food, fuel, minerals, and other resources. In this chapter you will find out how resources are used and abused.

Chapter 11 — Changes in the Earth's Crust Volcanic activity changes the earth's crust. How is that shown in this ground surface temperature map of Miyako Island, Japan? In Chapter 11 you will find out how the earth's crust is changed in other ways.

Mt.Jinanyama

Ako

| 15. | 16. | 17. | 18. | 19. | 20. | 21. | 22. | 25. | 30. | 35. | 40. | 45. | 50. | (°C) |

CHAPTER 10
The Earth's Resources

What was it like on the earth 5,000 years ago? Scientists have many ways to piece together how things once were. For example, they can study fossils or look at paintings on cave walls. They can look at layers of rocks or study mummies. Most of the things that scientists study have changed a great deal over the years.

Suppose scientists could study something that has not changed in thousands of years. Think of what a chance that would be! It would be almost as good as moving back through time in a time machine.

Scientists had a chance to study something that might not have changed in thousands of years. They studied air that had been buried for 4,600 years! Where was this air? How could scientists study it?

The air was contained in a huge pit in Giza, Egypt. This pit is near the Great Pyramid in which King Khufu is buried. Experts on ancient Egypt believed that the pit contained a large wooden boat. When an Egyptian ruler was buried, a boat was buried nearby. This boat was thought to carry the ruler to his or her final resting place in heaven.

The scientists who studied both the boat and the air are from the United States and from Egypt. They knew that the pit was sealed with limestone slabs. No living thing had entered the pit in thousands of years. So the scientists believed that the air was unchanged. They thought the air could be exactly the way it was 4,600 years ago! The team of scientists wondered how the old air compared with modern air. Did they both contain the same gases? Was the ratio of gases in the old air the same as the ratio in modern air?

Egyptian burial boat

232a

Site of burial boat discovered in 1954. This boat is about 3½ meters from the pit now being studied.

How could scientists study this old air? Could they just reach in and grab a sample of the air? How could they pull out air that was trapped behind a huge slab of stone? Could studying the air change its nature?

These are some of the questions that the scientists were asking themselves. One answer came in the form of a special drill. A similar drill had been used for taking samples from the moon. The drill was sealed to the roof of the pit holding the boat. As the drill entered the stone slab, bits of stone were removed with a vacuum device. Samples of air from different levels of the pit were removed and placed in bottles. Tests were done on these samples.

Now try this

Obtain a "mystery bag" from your teacher. This bag contains a familiar object. It is something you can find in your classroom. Your task is to find out what is in the bag. But you cannot open the bag!

Gather as much data as you can about the contents of the bag. Then list all other methods you can use to find out about the object. You can even list those methods not available in your classroom. For example, you may know of a device for studying hidden objects. List this device and explain how it may be used. Identify the contents of the bag. Give reasons for your answer.

Robert Moores, an engineer, operates a drill like the one used at the pyramid

What were the scientists' goals? They wanted to find out how air has changed over thousands of years. But they did not want to change the air by the method used to study it.

The scientists wanted to disturb the pit as little as possible. So, they did not walk inside it. Instead, they viewed the inside of the pit with two cameras. They lit up the inside of the pit with a light that did not add any heat to the air.

One thing the researchers wanted to study was the amount of carbon dioxide in the air. Why were they interested in this gas? Some scientists believe that carbon dioxide has been building up over time. This build-up may be causing an increase in the temperature of the earth. A study of the air in the pit could help to show whether this gas has been increasing around the earth.

Scientists also wanted to look for pollen grains and other once-living things in the air samples. Such organisms could tell something about life on the earth thousands of years ago.

After the contents of the pit were observed and studied, the pit was resealed. What do you think the scientists found out about the wooden boat and the ancient air?

Air is one of the earth's most valuable resources. In this chapter you will learn about the earth's natural resources and how some of these resources may be reused.

233

Living Renewable Resources

How are living resources renewed?

Forested land

Cutting trees for lumber

The materials we use that come from the earth are called natural resources (ri sôr′siz). A **natural resource** is a valuable material that is found in nature and used by people to meet their needs. Some natural resources are air, water, plants and animals, metals, and soil. What are some others?

Some resources are renewable (ri nü′ə bəl). A **renewable resource** is one that is replaced naturally. Plants are renewable because they grow and reproduce. But this does not mean that the supply of plants will never run out. Some plants may be used faster than they can be replaced. Trees are a good example. At one time, trees were abundant in the United States. It is estimated that over 40 percent of the land was once covered by forests.

Many trees were cut for fuel and for lumber. Trees were also cut to clear the land for farming and other uses. People thought that there would always be

Area cleared of trees

Area replanted with young trees

A wildlife refuge

enough trees because they are a renewable resource. But trees were being cut down faster than new trees could grow. As a result, trees became scarce in many places. Today large numbers of trees are grown on tree farms. Special methods are used so that the trees will grow faster. Now, trees that are used up can be replaced faster with new trees.

Animals are also renewable resources. They replace themselves by reproducing. Animals are widely used by people for food, for their hides, and for other materials that they contain. People once thought that the supply of wild animals would never run out. Now, because of overhunting, some kinds of animals no longer exist. How can this be prevented in the future? Many kinds of animals are now raised on farms and ranches. Some wild animals are protected in refuges (ref'yüj iz). The numbers of many such protected animals are now increasing.

Over a period of time, living resources can be renewed. But as the earth's population increases, the resources are used faster. So they must be renewed even faster. In addition the living resources that we now have must be used more carefully.

For Lesson Questions, turn to page 402.

Nonliving Renewable Resources

How are nonliving resources renewed?

Nonliving things do not grow or reproduce. Yet some nonliving resources are renewable. Three of these nonliving resources are water, air, and soil.

Water is needed by all living things. Water is found in lakes, ponds, streams, rivers, and oceans. It is also found under the ground and in the air.

The supply of water is renewed in a natural cycle called the water cycle. Trace the path of water in the drawing. (1) Water evaporates from the surfaces of ponds, lakes, and oceans. The water vapor rises into the air. (2) As it rises the water vapor cools and changes into liquid water. (3) Water falls back to the earth, in the form of rain, snow, sleet, or hail. Some of this water falls into bodies of water. Other water soaks into the ground. Water that seeps deep into the ground is called ground water. Most of the earth's fresh water is stored in the ground as ground water. The stored water is available again for use by plants

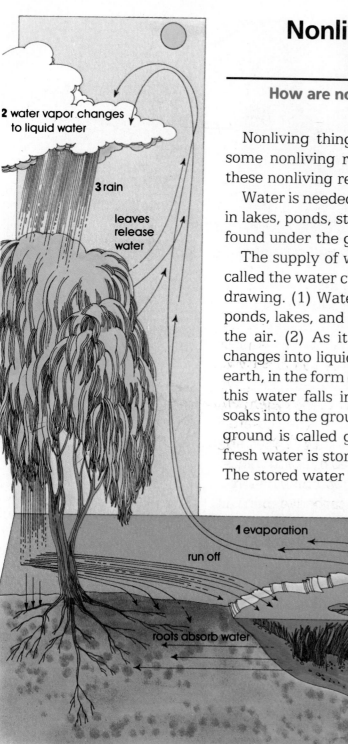

2 water vapor changes to liquid water

3 rain

leaves release water

1 evaporation

run off

roots absorb water

The water cycle

236

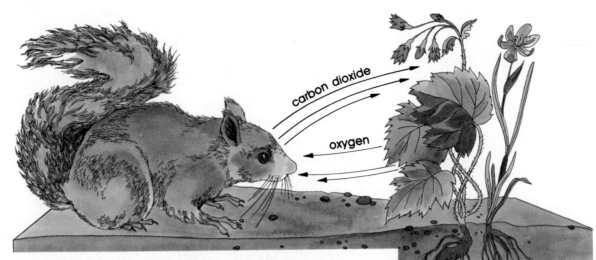

How oxygen and carbon dioxide are renewed

and animals. It is important that supplies of ground water are not allowed to become polluted.

It would be difficult to say which resource is the most important. But certainly, air is one of the most important. Almost all living things need air to survive. Air, a mixture of gases, is a renewable resource. Two of the most important gases in air are oxygen and carbon dioxide. How are these gases renewed after they are used? The drawing shows that oxygen and carbon dioxide in the air are renewed by living things.

Most living things use oxygen to obtain energy from food. During this process, carbon dioxide is given off as a waste product. Green plants use carbon dioxide and give off oxygen when they make food. If there were no green plants the carbon dioxide in the air would build up to a very high level. Also, the amount of oxygen would decrease greatly.

Soil is another renewable resource. Soil provides minerals that plants need to grow. When soil is rich in these minerals, it is said to be **fertile.** As plants grow, they remove these minerals from the soil. Then as plants die and decay, the minerals are returned to the soil. In this way, soil can remain fertile. Often dead plants are used to make compost to mix in the soil.

A compost pile

For Lesson Questions, turn to page 402.

237

Nonrenewable Resources

What resources cannot be renewed?

Certain resources can be renewed. But this is not true of all resources. Some of our most important resources are nonrenewable (non ri nü′ə bəl). A **nonrenewable resource** is one that exists in a limited amount. Sometimes, nonrenewable resources are called irreplaceable resources. Once used, these materials cannot be replaced in a reasonable amount of time. Rocks from the earth's crust are nonrenewable resources. Limestone, sandstone, granite, and slate are important building materials. Minerals are also examples of nonrenewable resources.

Granite building

Granite quarry

A **mineral** is any pure, hard material that is found in the earth's crust. Examples of some useful minerals are quartz, mica, salt, and sulfur. Quartz is used to make glass. Mica is used in electronic equipment, toasters, paints, and inks. Salt, as you know, has many uses. It is mined in many places on the earth. Salt is also collected by evaporation from seawater.

Sulfur is used in matches, fertilizers, medicines, and paper pulp. It is also used in products such as bleaching agents, dyes, and paints. Much sulfur is found in Texas and Louisiana and under the Gulf of Mexico. Sulfur is mined by pumping hot water deep into the mines. The hot water melts the sulfur. The melted sulfur is then forced to the surface.

Metals are among the most useful of the nonrenewable resources. Metals must be separated from the materials they are found with in the ground. These materials are called ores. An **ore** is rock or mineral from which useful metal can be obtained.

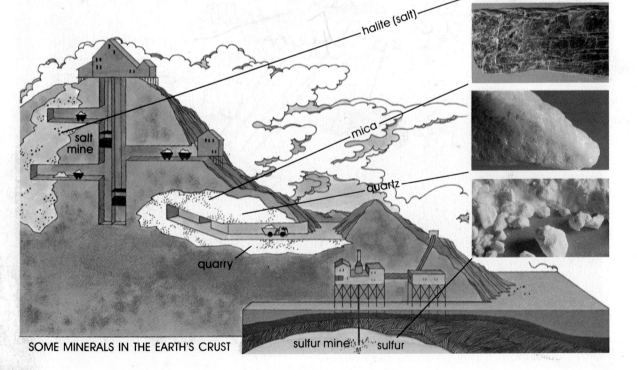

SOME MINERALS IN THE EARTH'S CRUST

halite (salt)

salt mine

mica

quartz

quarry

sulfur mine   sulfur

Finding Out

Where are some deposits of nonrenewable resources found?

POTENTIAL RESOURCE DEPOSITS		
Resource	Longitude	Latitude
1. coal	76 W	41 N
2. iron ore	93 W	47 N
3. uranium	108 W	34 N
4. copper	24 E	8 S
5. nickel	100 W	56 N
6. gold	84 W	48 N
7. natural gas	116 W	34 N
8. uranium	2 E	46 N
9. silver	112 W	32 N
10. oil	102 W	32 N

Pretend that you are an international miner. You have been given a list of places in the world where deposits of certain nonrenewable resources might be found. But before you can do anything, you must determine where each deposit is located. Use an atlas or a globe to do this. Then make a list that shows each deposit and the country it is found in. If the deposit is found in the United States or Canada, indicate the state, territory, or province in which it is found. Then plan a trip with the shortest possible route that will let you visit each deposit.

Ores are obtained by mining. Some ores are mined from open pits, such as the one in the picture. Others are taken from mines deep under the ground. In some ores the metals are not chemically combined with other materials. These metals are in pure form. Such

Iron mine

Iron ore

240

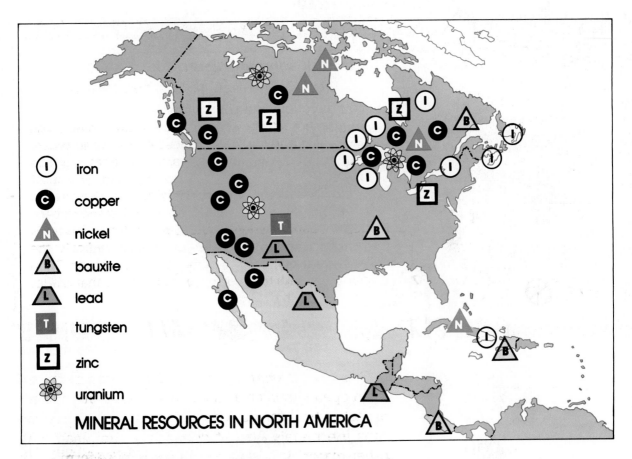

MINERAL RESOURCES IN NORTH AMERICA

Legend:
- Ⓘ iron
- Ⓒ copper
- N nickel
- B bauxite
- L lead
- T tungsten
- Z zinc
- ⚛ uranium

metals are called **native metals.** Gold, silver, and copper are often found as native metals.

Some ores are called high-grade ores. These ores contain much metal. Low-grade ores have small amounts of metal. Supplies of high-grade ores have decreased. So now, low-grade ores must be mined.

Iron is the fourth most plentiful element in the earth's crust. However, only a small amount of the element can be obtained as iron ore. Iron is our most important metal. About 100 million metric tons of iron are used in the United States each year.

The map shows some places where certain minerals and metals are found in North America. Which of these resources can be found nearest to where you live?

For Lesson Questions, turn to page 402.

Recycling

You have learned that many resources are nonrenewable. But some of these resources can be used again if they are recycled. **Recycling** (rē sī′kling) is the collecting and re-treating of materials so that they can be reused. Metals and paper have been recycled for many years. But since the 1960s, people have become more aware of the need for recycling.

Junked cars are a good source of iron and steel. These metals are melted down and formed into useful items again. Aluminum cans are recycled to make new cans. Other products, such as those in the pictures, may be made from recycled aluminum.

Glass can be recycled, too. Glass bottles may be cleaned and used again. Items made of glass can also be ground up and melted to make new glass items.

Recycled paper is often used in making new paper products. It is also used in insulation and plasterboard. Items such as those in the pictures on page 243 may be made from recycled paper. What materials in this house are made from recycled aluminum?

Bales of crushed aluminum cans for recycling

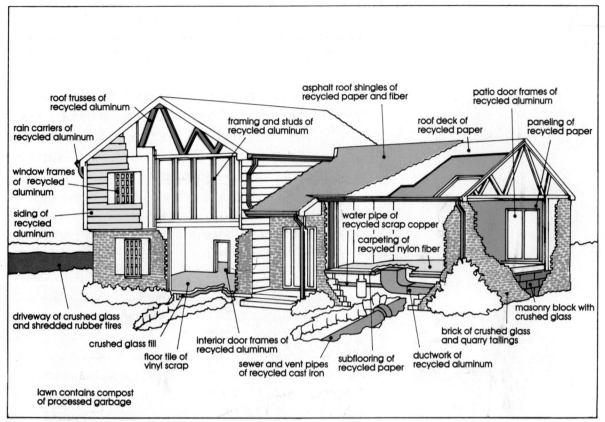

House made almost entirely from recycled materials

Labels on the diagram:
- roof trusses of recycled aluminum
- rain carriers of recycled aluminum
- window frames of recycled aluminum
- siding of recycled aluminum
- framing and studs of recycled aluminum
- asphalt roof shingles of recycled paper and fiber
- roof deck of recycled paper
- patio door frames of recycled aluminum
- paneling of recycled paper
- water pipe of recycled scrap copper
- carpeting of recycled nylon fiber
- masonry block with crushed glass
- driveway of crushed glass and shredded rubber tires
- crushed glass fill
- floor tile of vinyl scrap
- interior door frames of recycled aluminum
- sewer and vent pipes of recycled cast iron
- subflooring of recycled paper
- ductwork of recycled aluminum
- brick of crushed glass and quarry tailings
- lawn contains compost of processed garbage

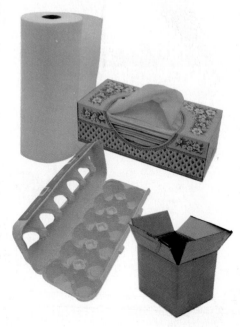

Many towns have set up centers to collect waste materials. In such centers, glass, metal, and paper are separated. These materials are then sold to companies that recycle them. The small recycling centers are important. But they collect only a small amount of the materials that can be recycled. Today less than one tenth of the materials that can be reused are being recycled.

There is another reason why recycling is important. If waste materials are not recycled, they are often dumped in landfills. A **landfill** is a place where wastes are dumped and then covered with soil. Landfill sites are no longer readily available in many states. Recycling not only saves natural resources, but it also saves valuable land.

For Lesson Questions, turn to page 402.

Activity

How do acids in soil help break down metal wastes?

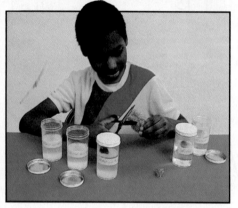

Materials 5 small jars with lids / measuring cup / water / 9 aspirin tablets / plastic spoon / steel wool / copper pot-scrubber / scissors

Procedure

A. Rotting leaves and bark in the soil often give off an acid called salicylic (sal ə sil'ik) acid. This is the same acid found in aspirin.

Pour a half-cup of water into each of 5 small jars. Put 3 aspirin tablets in each of three of the jars. Stir the water in the jars that contain the aspirin tablets. The tablets should break apart, but they will not completely dissolve. *Caution Do not taste the aspirin or aspirin and water.*

B. Make two balls of steel wool about the size of a cherry. Put one ball in a jar with water and aspirin. Put the other in a jar of plain water. Label each jar.

C. Cut two balls about the size of a cherry from the copper pot-scrubber. Put one ball in a jar with water and aspirin. Put the other in a jar of plain water. Label each jar.

D. Leave the last jar of water with aspirin as it is. Label this jar.
  1. What is the purpose of this jar?
  2. Write your prediction of what will happen to the contents of each jar after 2 days.

E. Screw a lid on each jar. Place the jars where they will not be disturbed. At the end of 2 days, observe the contents of each jar.
  3. What did you observe?

Conclusion

1. Do acids help to break down metal wastes?
2. Do acids break down different metals in the same way?

Fossil Fuel Resources

How are fossil fuels used?

Other important resources from the earth are the fossil fuels. **Fossil fuels** are fuels such as coal, oil, and natural gas, which were formed from the bodies of dead plants and animals. This process occurred millions of years ago.

Fossil fuels are used in two main ways. They are burned for the heat energy they contain, and they are used as feedstocks. A **feedstock** is a raw material from which other materials are made. These photos show some of the products made from fossil-fuel feedstocks.

Many of the plastic packages and containers that people use are used only once. Then they are thrown away. It is estimated that to make each item, an amount of petroleum equal to three times the item's mass is needed. Think of the amount of petroleum that is wasted in this way.

Strip mining for coal

Fossil fuels have many uses. But they must first be removed from the earth. Coal is taken from the earth in two ways. One way is by strip mining. In a strip mine the earth is pushed away to expose the coal, which is close to the surface. The coal is then removed by huge machines. Coal is obtained also from shaft mines, which extend deep into the earth.

In the past, strip mining often ruined the land. Today, however, most mining companies make efforts to reclaim the mined land. Many states require this. Trees may be planted, or lakes and recreational areas may be developed. In this way the reclaimed coal strip-mining region becomes a valuable resource of a different kind.

Oil and gas are removed from the earth through wells. Wells are drilled deep into the earth's crust. Once the oil or gas has been reached, pumps are used to bring it to the surface. Oil removed from the earth is called crude oil. To be made into useful products, crude oil must be refined. The products made from crude oil include gasoline, jet fuel, and heating oil.

The crust beneath the oceans is also a rich source of fossil fuels, especially oil. There is oil beneath every

Offshore oil wells

ocean of the world. It is found in shallow areas near the shores.

Offshore wells provide more than 20 percent of the oil used in the world. The drawing shows how an offshore well is drilled from a platform on the surface of the water. In the United States there are several offshore wells. They are in the Gulf of Mexico and off the coast of southern California. There are new wells being drilled along the East Coast.

The ocean floor may also be a rich source of natural gas. It is believed that certain areas off the East Coast of the United States may hold much natural gas. Finding out exactly where this gas is located is costly. Once it has been found, it could increase our supplies of fossil fuels. What may be some problems with drilling for oil and gas offshore?

oil

No one knows the amounts of fossil fuels that are still in the earth. The amounts may be much greater than what scientists currently think they are. But they also could be much less. The map shows where coal, oil, and natural gas are now found in North America. It also shows oil and gas wells off the coasts. What fossil fuels can be found nearest you?

Fossil fuels are rapidly being used up. Some fossil fuels may be forming today. But the process takes millions of years. In addition the conditions of the earth are no longer what they were when the fossil fuels first formed. Since these fuels cannot be replaced, they are nonrenewable resources. What can be done to conserve, or avoid wasting, fossil fuels?

For Lesson Questions, turn to page 402.

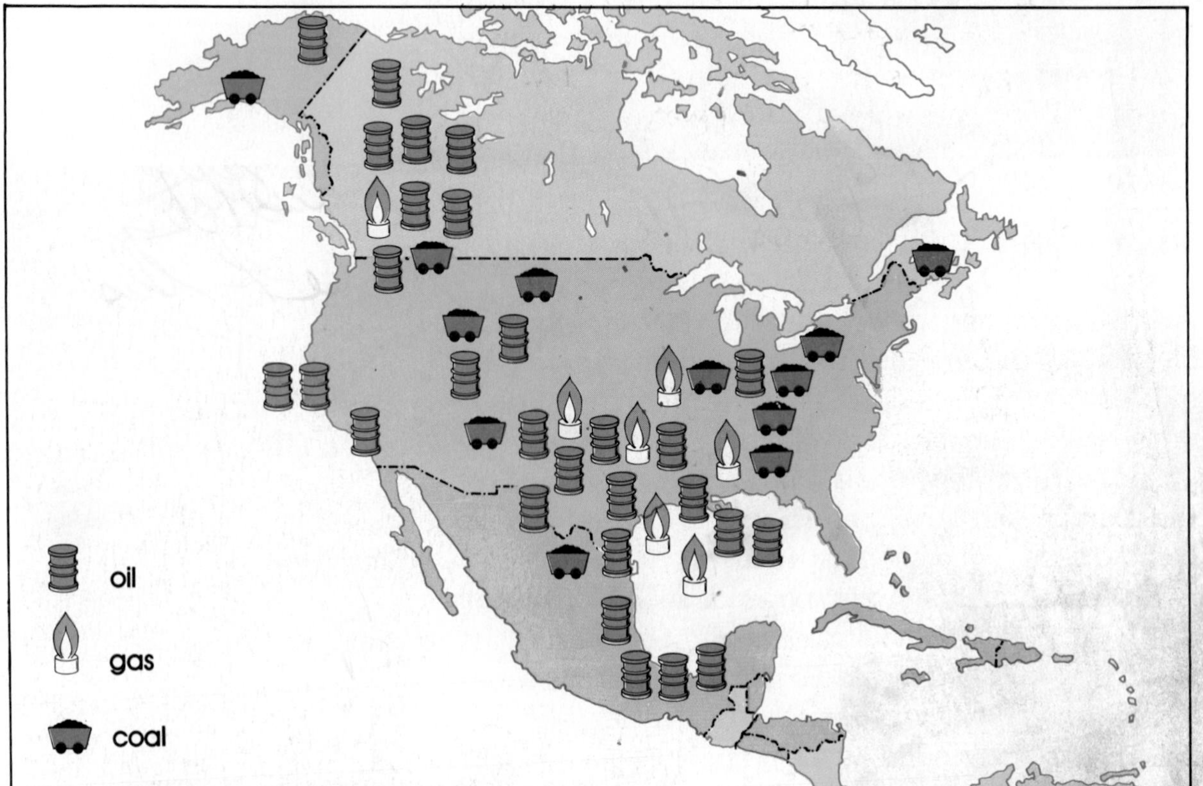

oil

gas

coal

FOSSIL FUELS IN NORTH AMERICA

Resources from the Oceans

What resources do we get from the oceans?

Oceans cover more than 70 percent of the earth's surface. The earth is the only planet in the solar system with large amounts of liquid water. The oceans contain valuable resources. The water in the oceans is salt water. The salt in the oceans is mostly sodium chloride. Seawater also contains salts made of bromine, magnesium, sulfur, and calcium. In fact, seawater contains at least traces of all the elements that make up the earth's crust.

Salt can be separated from seawater. This is done in a process called **desalination** (dē sal ə nā′shən). This process is useful for two reasons. First, it removes salt from seawater. The salt may then be used for different purposes. Second, it makes fresh water, which is used for drinking and for watering crops.

Desalination plant

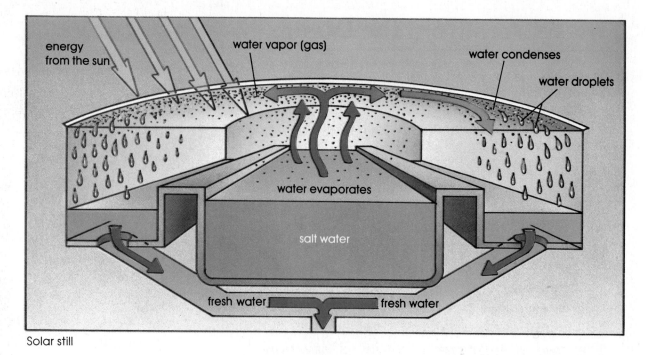

energy from the sun

water vapor (gas)

water condenses

water droplets

water evaporates

salt water

fresh water   fresh water

Solar still

One device that is used to separate salt from seawater is a **solar still.** Look at the drawing of the solar still. Energy from the sun evaporates the seawater. The water changes to water vapor, and the salt remains. The water vapor can be cooled to form liquid water again. This water is fresh water, free of salt, that could be used for drinking.

As the number of people in the world increases and water supplies become polluted, greater supplies of fresh water are needed. Many cities that need water are near oceans. These cities can benefit most from the desalination of seawater. They may also be able to supply fresh water to cities not near the oceans. But the desalination process is quite costly.

In addition to providing fresh water, desalination provides about 29 percent of all the salt used in the world. Other minerals, such as bromine and magnesium, are taken from the salt. Bromine is used in making medicines. Magnesium is often mixed with aluminum to make a light, strong metal.

How does a solar still work?

Activity

Materials jar or paper cup / warm water / plastic spoon / table salt / saucer / metric ruler / large clear bowl / large plate

Procedure

A. Half fill a jar with warm water. Add two spoonfuls of salt. Stir well.

B. Put a saucer on top of a large plate. Place them where sunlight will fall on them.

C. Pour salt water from the jar into the saucer until the water is about 3 mm deep.

D. Place a large clear bowl upside down over the saucer and plate.

E. Observe your solar still the next day.
   1. What do you observe in the large plate and on the bowl?

Results

1. What happened to the water in the saucer?

2. Do you think the water in the large plate is fresh water or salt water? Give reasons for your answer.

3. Where did the energy come from to operate the solar still?

Conclusion

In a brief statement, describe how a solar still works.

Using science ideas

Imagine that you are stranded on a desert island with no source of fresh water. All you have is a parachute, a few metal containers, and plastic bags holding food supplies. Describe how you would obtain fresh water.

Most of the high-grade ores from the solid earth have been used up. But some important ores have been found on the ocean floor. Mining the oceans will probably become more important in the future. The ores in the oceans are often found in lumps called **nodules** (noj′ülz). Nodules contain large amounts of valuable minerals. Many are made up of black manganese (mang′gə nēs) ore. Manganese is added to steel to make it easier to form and shape.

Nodules have also been found to contain small amounts of copper, nickel, and cobalt. Copper is used to make electric wiring and plumbing pipe. Nickel is used in making stainless steel. Cobalt is added to certain materials to give them strength. The pictures show nodules from the ocean floor. Scientists are trying to find ways to collect nodules without upsetting the balance of life in the oceans.

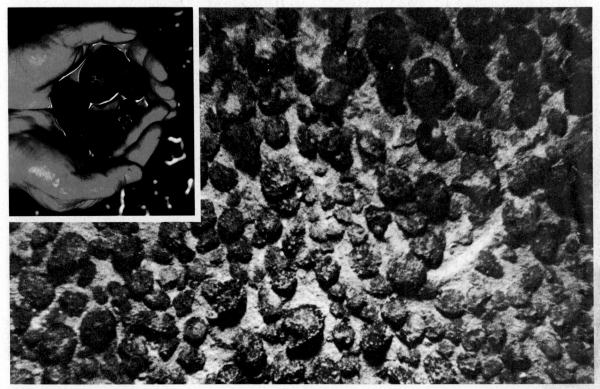

Nodules from the ocean floor

Food is another resource obtained from the oceans. The oceans have been a source of food for thousands of years. But fishing cannot supply all the food needed by the growing number of people. In the future, fishing may be replaced by mariculture (mar′ə kul chər). **Mariculture** is the farming of the oceans for food.

& TECHNOLOGY

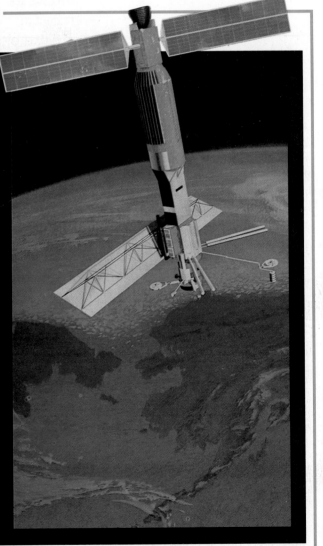

Special sensors on some satellites aid in locating natural resources. One kind of sensor picks up radiant energy reflected by things on and near the earth's surface. Everything reflects radiant energy in its own special way. It is like a signature that aids in the identification of the resource. The signatures for different resources show up as certain colors on the image produced by the satellite. One application of this technique helps fishermen find schools of fish. Many fish eat organisms called plankton. Plankton have their own radiant energy signature. Where there are large quantities of plankton, there are likely to be large quantities of fish. Fish may also be located by mapping water temperatures and ocean currents. Buoys are used to regularly measure ocean temperature and currents. This information is relayed to satellites, which then beam it to computers on land. The computers analyze this information and identify regions where fish are likely to be found. This enables fishermen to locate favorable fishing grounds faster and easier than otherwise would be possible.

Today, scientists are testing different ways of farming the oceans. One way is to raise fish and shell-fish in bays and inlets. In these places the fish are protected from strong waves and from natural enemies. Large amounts of fish can be grown in this way.

Japan is far ahead of other countries in farming the oceans. They have been doing so for many years. Recently, Japanese scientists have succeeded in hatching and growing female-only saltwater fish. The female fish grow to be about four times larger than male fish.

Another product being farmed in the oceans is algae. In some countries, such as China and Japan, algae are used as food for people and animals. In addition, algae can be dried and made into a powder.

Drying algae

This powder can be added to other foods. It is a good source of protein.

The oceans will probably be used more and more as a source of food in the future. But they cannot be used as garbage dumps at the same time. Many people believe that sewage and other wastes dumped into the oceans will be diluted and made harmless. But these wastes enter ocean food webs. Valuable food is destroyed by this pollution. Pollution must be prevented if the oceans are to be farmed successfully.

For Lesson Questions, turn to page 402.

Ideas to Remember

▶ A natural resource is a valuable material that is found in nature and used by people to meet their needs.

▶ Living resources and some nonliving resources — such as air, water, and soil — are renewable resources.

▶ Some resources, such as minerals and metals, are nonrenewable resources.

▶ A mineral is any useful material that is found in the earth's crust.

▶ An ore is rock or mineral that contains useful metal.

▶ Recycling is the collecting and re-treating of materials so that they can be reused.

▶ Fossil fuels are fuels such as coal, oil, and natural gas, which were formed from the bodies of dead plants and animals.

▶ Fossil fuels are used as sources of heat energy and also as feedstocks.

▶ A feedstock is a raw material from which other materials are made.

▶ The oceans are rich in resources, such as minerals and foods.

Reviewing the Chapter

SCIENCE WORDS

A. Write the letter of the term that best matches the definition. Not all the terms will be used.

1. Any useful material that is found in the earth's crust
2. Any resource that exists in a limited amount
3. The collecting and re-treating of materials so that they can be reused
4. The separation of salt from seawater
5. A raw material from fossil fuels, from which other materials are made
6. Lumps taken from the ocean floor that contain valuable materials
7. Rock or mineral from which useful metal can be obtained
8. Any resource that is replaced naturally
9. A resource such as coal, oil, or natural gas
10. Farming the oceans

a. feedstock
b. fossil fuel
c. mineral
d. fertile
e. ore
f. hematite
g. nonrenewable resource
h. mariculture
i. nodules
j. recycling
k. desalination
l. renewable resource

B. Unscramble each group of letters to find a science term from the chapter. Write a sentence using each term.

1. tieelrf   2. reo   3. dlseuon
4. lsat   5. olca   6. mlairne

UNDERSTANDING IDEAS

A. Do the following.

1. Explain the difference between a renewable natural resource and a nonrenewable natural resource. Give two examples of each.
2. Write the page number of each picture in this chapter that shows a natural resource or a method of obtaining a natural resource. Write **M** by the page number for each natural resource picture that shows a mineral. Write **O** by the page number of each mineral picture that shows an ore.

B. The graph shows the composition of solid waste disposed of by an average town. Suppose that the town is producing 1 million kg of solid waste a year.

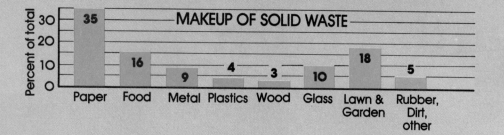

1. Determine the amount of paper, the amount of metal, and the amount of glass that is thrown out each year.
2. Suppose the town recycles 30 percent of its waste paper. How much paper is recycled yearly?

3. Suppose the town recycles 10 percent of its waste metal and receives $0.10/kg. How much does the town earn yearly?

USING IDEAS

The map on page 241 shows where some metals and minerals are mined in North America. What are some important minerals and metals that North American countries import?

THINKING LIKE A SCIENTIST

Answer the following questions. You may be able to answer some of the questions just by thinking about them. To answer other questions, you may have to do some research.

1. In his book *Cry the Beloved Country*, novelist Alan Paton said, "Keep it, guard it, care for it, for it keeps man, guards man, cares for man. Destroy it and man is destroyed." What do you think Alan Paton was describing? State your reasoning.
2. People have been using minerals ever since the first flint arrowhead was used for cutting. Today we use minerals in thousands of ways each day. What minerals are used in (a) chalk, (b) a mirror, (c) camera film, (d) a flash bulb, (e) a pencil, (f) a car battery, (g) car headlights, (h) fertilizer for plants?

CHAPTER 11

Changes in the Earth's Crust

People in the village of Nyos (nē'ōs) were just finishing their evening meal when disaster struck. A strange odor filled their huts. The smell was like that of rotten eggs or burned gunpowder. Then the people began to feel dizzy. Some began to vomit. Many villagers began running into the street to escape the bad odor and sickness. But there was no escape. Within a short time the villagers fell down dead. They were killed by a strange cloud of gas.

Where and when did this tragedy occur? What caused it? The sudden death of the villagers happened in Cameroon, a country in central Africa. A large cloud of gas rose suddenly from nearby Lake Nyos. The cloud floated quickly and silently, killing people and livestock. More than 1,700 people died within a few hours. Uncounted numbers of animals perished. The date was August 21, 1986.

Teams of scientists came in from many parts of the world to study the disaster. One of these scientists was Joseph Devine of Brown University. Why was Devine called to the scene? He is an expert on volcanoes. Two years earlier there had been a similar incident in a nearby village. Then, too, a gas cloud had floated over the village from a lake. Thirty-seven people had died. Devine and other scientists had studied the waters of that

AFRICA

Lake
Nyos

Cameroon

lake, looking for clues to the disaster. Many of these scientists returned to Cameroon in 1986 to study this greater tragedy.

What had caused the death of so many people and animals? Lake Nyos is a crater lake. That is, it is found at the opening of an old volcano. The opening, or crater, is filled with water. Scientists believe that carbon dioxide gas collects at the bottom of the lake. Most of the time this gas just stays at the lake bottom, dissolved in the water there. It is usually under the pressure of all the water above it.

Scientists think there might have been a slight earthquake on August 21, 1986. This quake could have disturbed the layers of water in Lake Nyos. With the water stirred up, the carbon dioxide could rise higher up in the lake and escape into the air. Carbon dioxide is heavier than the air above the lake. So this cloud of heavy gas could then just float out over the village. Villagers died because they could not breathe in enough oxygen.

▲ Sample of water showing carbon dioxide gas.

You need four small bottles of a carbonated drink. Such a drink contains carbon dioxide under pressure. Place two of the bottles in a refrigerator for 24 hours. Leave the other two bottles out at room temperature for 24 hours. Record what happens in each of the following cases. **Caution:** *Open all bottles over a sink.* **(1)** Open one refrigerated bottle. **(2)** Shake the second refrigerated bottle and then open it. **(3)** Open one of the bottles that stayed at room temperature. **(4)** Shake the other bottle that stayed at room temperature and then open it.

Describe what occurred in each bottle. What gas was released? Which of these four bottles is most like Lake Nyos on August 21, 1986?

◀ **Dr. Devine, holding the umbrella, talks with another scientist.**

Could something like this ever happen again? There are still large amounts of carbon dioxide gas in the waters of Lake Nyos. So there is still the danger of another deadly cloud one day rising from the lake. Scientists are still studying the region. They are hoping another tragedy never occurs.

In this chapter you will learn how movements of the top layers of the earth can cause earthquakes. You will also learn about other kinds of changes in the earth's crust.

◀ **Scientists study the water of Lake Nyos.**

The Floating Crust

How does the crust of the earth move?

For hundreds of years, scientists have observed changes in the earth's crust. They have questioned how mountains formed. They have asked why fossils of water animals, such as the fossils shown here, have been found on mountains. They have wondered why certain continents, like Africa and South America, fit together so well.

Over the years many theories about the earth's crust have been suggested. A **theory** is an idea that is used to explain observed facts. One theory stated that changes in the crust were caused by the cooling and shrinking of the earth. According to this theory there was once only one large continent on the crust of the earth. As the inside of the earth cooled, it began to shrink. This caused the crust to become wrinkled, much like the skin on a baked apple. As a result, parts of the single continent collapsed, forming ocean basins and several smaller continents.

In 1908 a geologist named Frank B. Taylor suggested that the earth had not shrunk. He said that the

A marine fossil found in mountains

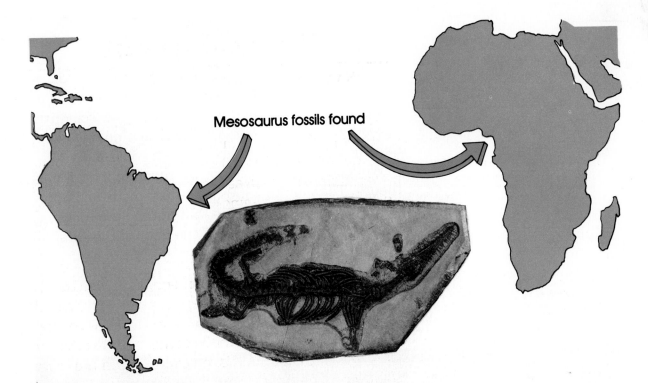

Mesosaurus fossils found

continents formed from two large continents, one located over each pole. These continents broke apart. The smaller continents that resulted from this breakup moved apart in a "creeping" motion. Most scientists just ignored Taylor's idea.

About 3 years later another scientist, Alfred Wegener (vā′gə ner), suggested a similar idea. Wegener was a teacher of astronomy and the study of weather. He read about how the same kinds of fossils had been found in South America and Africa. Most scientists believed this could be explained by a bridge of land between the two continents. They believed the bridge had sunk with the cooling of the earth. Wegener did not agree. He decided that the continents were once joined in a single land mass. He stated that the land mass broke apart and that the continents drifted, much like icebergs. According to Wegener's theory the continents are still drifting today. Wegener's theory is called **continental drift.**

One piece of evidence that Wegener used to support his theory is the way South America fits with Africa. More evidence was that the same kinds of fossils and similar plants and animals were found in both places. Despite this evidence, few scientists agreed with him. One reason was that no one could explain why or how the continents could move.

Wegener died without getting much support for his theory. Then in the 1960s, scientists made an important discovery. They found that hot molten rock was flowing up through cracks in the floor of the Atlantic Ocean. They also discovered a huge ridge of high mountains under the ocean. The ridge curved halfway between South America and Africa, and its shape matched that of the two continents.

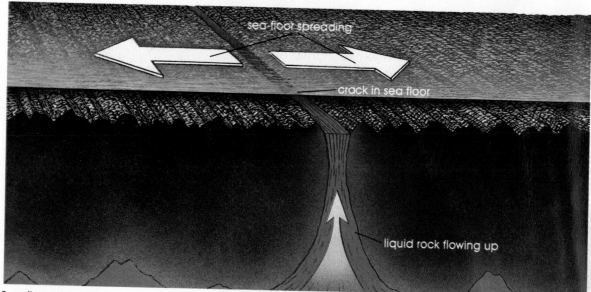

Sea-floor spreading

Scientists suggest that the ridge formed from a huge crack in the earth's crust. Molten rock flowing from the crack formed the mountains. As the molten rock hardened, it pushed the older ocean floor apart. This is called **sea-floor spreading.**

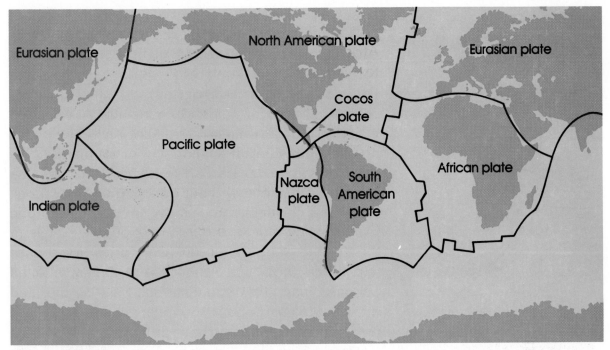

Major earth plates

Look at the drawing that shows sea-floor spreading. You can see where hot liquid rock rises to the ocean floor. Notice how the rock spreads out in both directions after it reaches the ocean floor. This is what pushes the older ocean-floor material outward.

The theory of sea-floor spreading explained how and why continents could move. Wegener's theory was accepted at last. Sea-floor spreading and other evidence have been used to support a new theory. This theory is called the plate tectonic (tek ton'ik) theory. The word *tectonic* comes from a Greek word that means "builder."

The **plate tectonic theory** suggests that the crust of the earth is made of a number of large rigid plates and a number of smaller ones. The major plates are shown here. Most of the plates are named for the continents that rest on them. What are the names of the major plates? Plates with continents move relatively slowly, about 2 cm each year. Those without continents can move faster, about as much as 12 cm each year. According to the theory, the continents rest on top of these plates. The layer of the earth under the crust is the **mantle** (man′təl). The upper mantle is made of hot rock, somewhat like melted plastic. The plates float on this hot rock. The plates are moved by the hot flowing rock of the mantle. The whole system of plates is like a jigsaw puzzle. One plate cannot move without affecting all the others. The plates collide in some places. In other places, one plate slips over or under another plate.

Scientists suggest that the continents were once joined in a single land mass. That land mass is called Pangaea (pan jē′ə). Scientists believe that the land mass broke apart about 150 million years ago. Since that time the continents have drifted to their present positions. Where will they be years from now? The drawing shows one way the continents may appear in the future. Compare the positions of the continents today with their possible positions in the future. What changes can you point out?

Pangaea

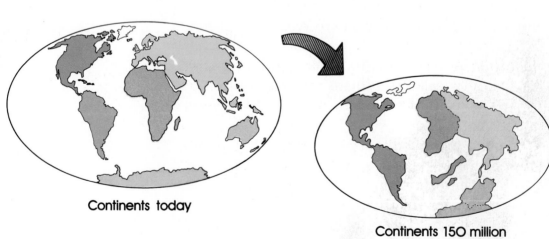

Continents today

Continents 150 million
years from now

For Lesson Questions, turn to page 404.

Activity

Were the continents once joined in a single land mass?

Materials tracing paper or sheet of continent shapes / scissors / cardboard / glue

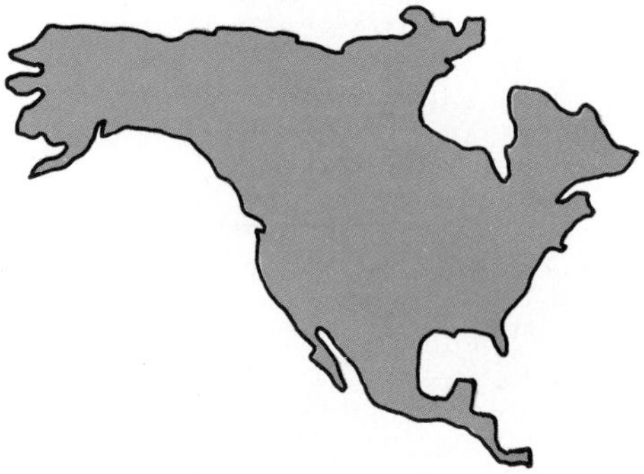

Procedure

A. Trace the continents shown in this activity, and cut them out. Or cut the shapes of the continents from the sheet provided by your teacher.

B. Fit the east coast of South America next to the west coast of Africa.

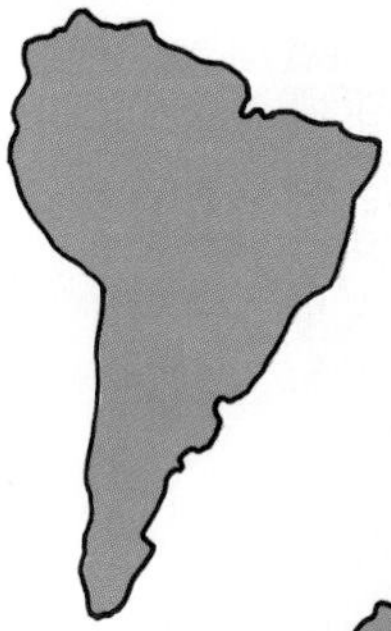

C. Fit the other continents next to South America and Africa to form a single land mass.

    1. Do the continents fit together well to form a single land mass?

D. When you have made your land mass, glue it to a piece of cardboard.

    2. Which continents seem to fit together well?

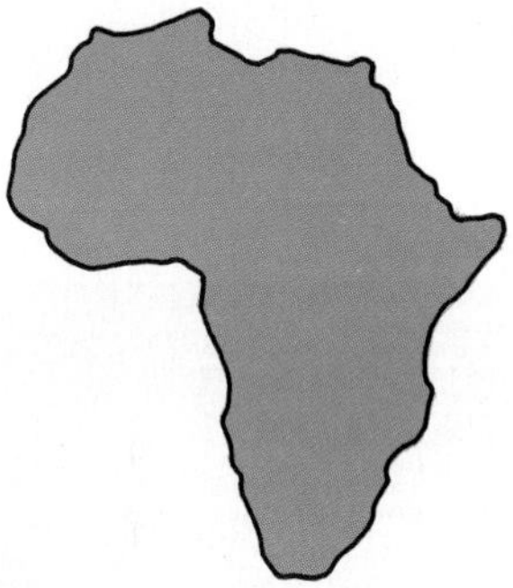

Conclusion

What evidence is there that the continents were once joined in a single land mass?

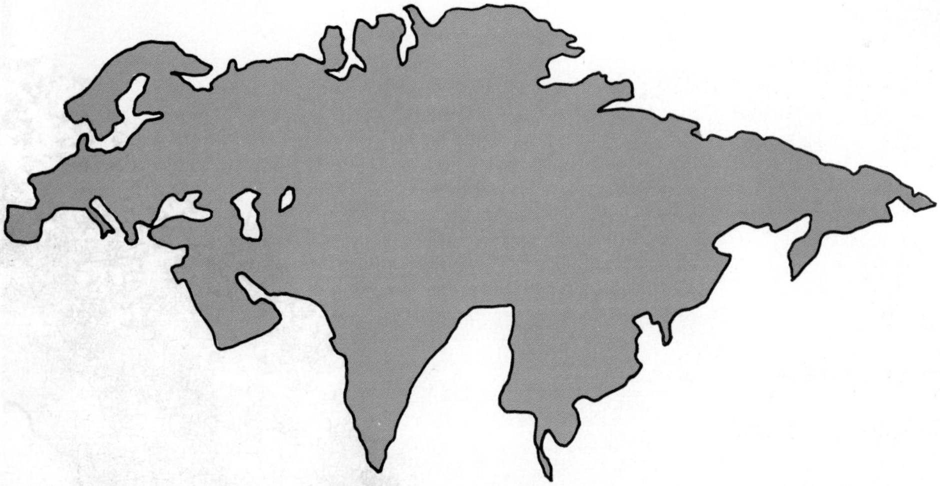

Earthquakes

What causes earthquakes?

Have you ever heard anyone say "solid as a rock" or "as firm as the ground under your feet"? People who have been through an earthquake know that the earth is not always solid or firm! But how are earthquakes related to plate tectonics?

To understand something about earthquakes, do this: Press the palms of your hands tightly together. As you continue to press them tightly, try to rub one palm over the other. Your palms will probably slip suddenly past each other.

Scientists have learned that earthquakes are closely related to the movement of the earth's plates. As the earth's plates move, they press against each other. As with the palms of your hands, the pressure builds until one plate slips past another. This produces an earthquake. An **earthquake** is a sudden movement of the earth's crust. The map on page 267 indicates where most earthquakes on the earth occur.

Earthquake damage

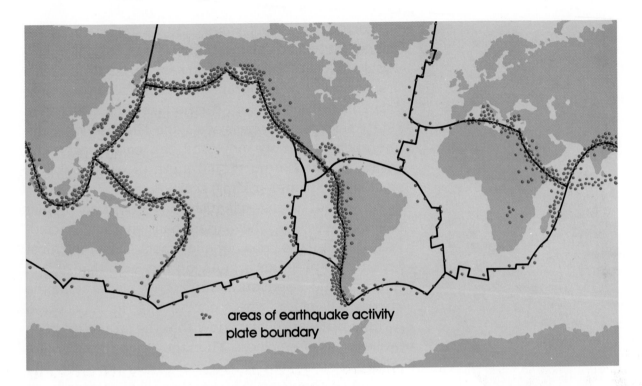

areas of earthquake activity

— plate boundary

The crust has cracks caused by the movement of the plates. These cracks are called **faults.** The San Andreas Fault in California is one example.

Earthquakes relieve pressures in the earth's crust. The point where the pressure is relieved is called the **focus** of the earthquake. Find the focus in the drawing. Vibrations, or shock waves, are sent out in all directions from the focus. Smaller waves, called aftershocks, are often sent out after the earthquake.

focus

fault

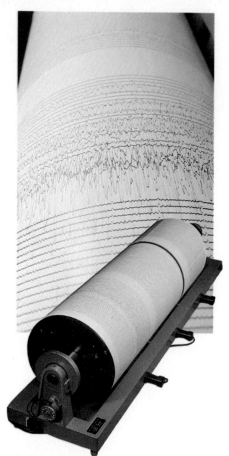
Seismograph

Earthquake shock waves can be recorded by instruments called **seismographs** (sīz′mə grafs). Scientists can locate the focus of an earthquake from such a recording. A seismograph also helps scientists measure the strength of an earthquake. The strength is stated as a number between 1 and 10. The higher the number, the more powerful the earthquake. The scale for measuring the strength of earthquakes is called the Richter (rik′tər) scale.

In recent years, scientists have tried to predict earthquakes. They have used many methods, including studying the behavior of animals. One of the most promising methods is applying the "gap theory." In this method, scientists identify those places along the borders of plates where earthquakes have occurred within 30 years. They know that the strain has been relieved in these places. Then they map places where there is strain but where there have not been any recent earthquakes. Why are these likely places for an earthquake? The "gap" map shown here was drawn before the 1985 Mexican earthquake. Was the prediction made with this map accurate?

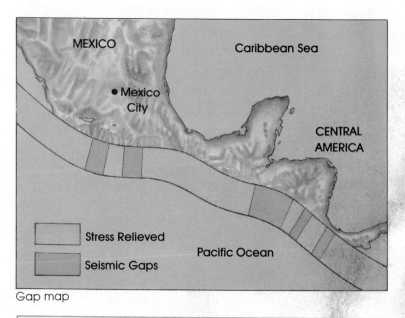
Gap map

268

For Lesson Questions, turn to page 404.

Activity

Can you find the location of an earthquake?

Materials   tracing paper / drawing compass

Procedure

A. The seismographs at three different stations re-corded an earthquake. The data about the location of the earthquake is as follows: (1) It was 1,275 km from San Francisco. (2) It was 1,500 km from El Paso. (3) It was 960 km from Seattle.

B. Trace the map of the United States. Mark and label on the map the three cities listed.

C. On a piece of paper, mark the distance that repre-sents 1,275 km. Set your compass to this distance. Draw a circle on your map, with San Francisco at the center.

D. Repeat step **C**, first for El Paso, then for Seattle.

Conclusion
In what state did the earthquake occur?

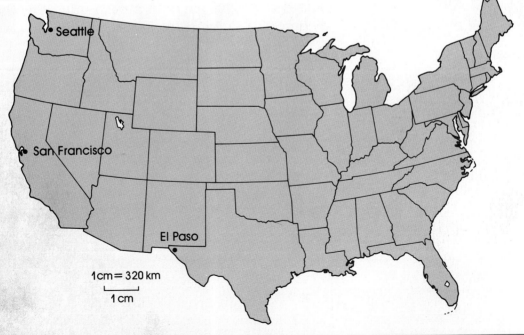

1cm = 320 km

1 cm

Volcanoes

What causes volcanoes?

Can you name something that destroys old things but at the same time creates new things? A volcano fits this description. A **volcano** is an opening in the earth's crust through which hot molten rock moves from deep inside the earth. Sometimes the movement of molten rock is sudden, explosive, and violent. Other times the movement is slow and steady.

Volcanoes destroy land and living things. When Mount St. Helens in Washington State erupted in 1980, more than 3 cubic km of rock were lost. The eruption knocked down trees up to 24 km from the volcano. Land around the volcano was buried in ash as deep as 150 m. But volcanoes also form new land. For example, the ocean floor has been formed from volcanoes. Volcanoes also produce fertile soil.

Mount St. Helens, Washington, eruption and damage

Scientists do not understand volcanoes completely. One reason for this is that it is impossible to get instruments inside an active volcano. It is also impossible to study the inside of the earth, where the hot molten rock is formed.

To help understand volcanoes, look at this map. It shows where most of the world's volcanoes are located. Compare it with the one on page 267. Why are they so much alike? One reason is that, like earthquakes, volcanoes can be explained by plate tectonics.

As you know, the earth's crust is made of plates. There are several things that can happen where two plates meet. For example, two plates can move away from each other. This is what is happening along the floor of the Atlantic Ocean. Here, **magma** (mag′mə), the melted rock inside the earth, flows up through cracks. This causes the ocean floor to spread. This type of volcanic activity does not produce mountain-like volcanoes. Therefore it is not usually noticed.

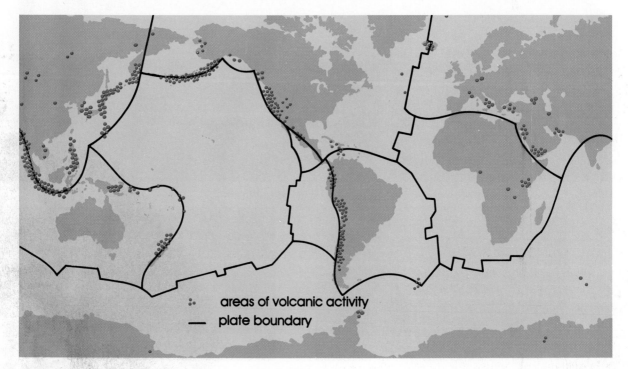

∴ areas of volcanic activity
— plate boundary

In some places, two plates collide. When this happens, magma is forced up through cracks in the crust. Magma that reaches the surface is called **lava.** If the pressure inside the earth is great enough, lava, ash, and rocks will be blown from the volcano. This is what happened at Mount St. Helens.

Where two ocean-carrying plates collide, one may sink under the other. Melting of parts of the sinking plate occurs. Some of the melted rock is forced to the surface. Chains of volcanic islands, such as the Aleutian Islands of Alaska, are formed in this way.

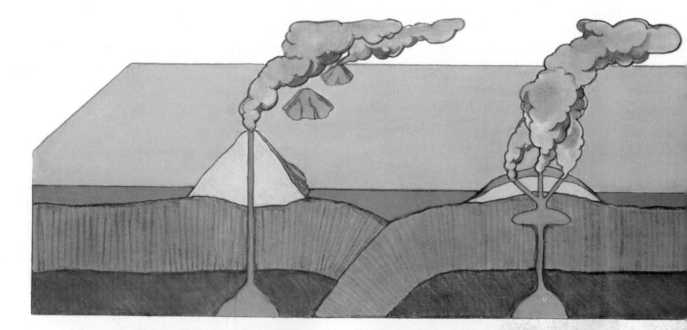

Island volcano

Hot-spot volcano

As a plate carrying an ocean sinks under a plate carrying a continent, parts of the ocean plate melt. Volcanoes are produced along the edge of the continent in places where magma is pushed toward the surface. Mount St. Helens was formed in this way.

Some volcanoes occur in the middle of plates. In this type of volcano, a chamber of magma forms deep under the ground. A volcano builds as the magma moves toward the surface. Such a volcano is called a hot-spot volcano. The volcanoes that formed the Hawaiian Islands are hot-spot volcanoes.

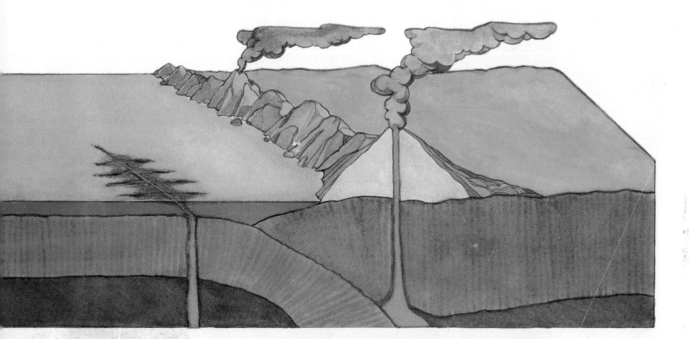

Continent volcano

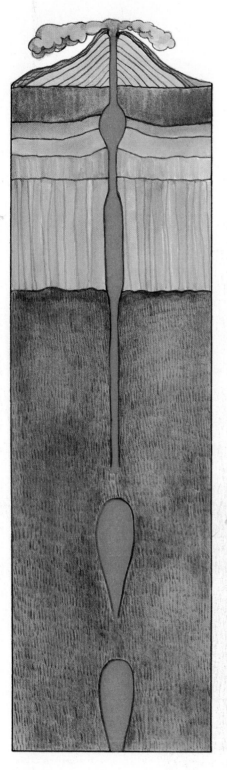

A volcano begins in the earth's mantle. Magma from this region floats upward in tadpole-shaped blobs. As the magma blobs reach the upper mantle and crust, they slow down. The magma wedges through cracks in the crust until it reaches a **magma pool.** This is a chamber in which the magma collects. There materials in the magma slowly mix. Pressure builds as they mix. Finally the magma shoots up through a crack and escapes in a volcanic eruption.

Often just before a volcano erupts, a cloud of water vapor may escape. Scientists are trying to find other ways to predict volcanic eruptions. At the present time, one of the best ways is to study historical records. Old volcanoes often erupt again and again. Another way to predict eruptions is to use seismographs. Earthquakes often indicate that a volcano is about to erupt.

Two other methods can be used to predict volcanic eruptions. One method involves the use of an instrument called a tiltmeter. A tiltmeter measures changes in the tilt of land. It works like a carpenter's level that has both ends anchored in the ground.

Tiltmeter

A second method involves the use of a laser. In this method, a laser beam is aimed at a volcanic mountain from a spot several kilometers away. Changes in the size of the mountain can be measured by timing how long it takes for the beam to be reflected.

Both of these methods detect tiny shifts that occur in the land around a volcano before an eruption. This shifting is caused by the buildup of magma.

For Lesson Questions, turn to page 404.

Science & Technology

▶ Laser beams are used to measure movements of the earth's crust along fault lines. The laser beams (seen in the picture inset) are aimed across the fault line to a target several kilometers away. The target reflects the beam back across the fault line. Since light travels at a constant speed, the beam should always be reflected in the same amount of time. Any change in the amount of time indicates that the crust has shifted. Movements of only a few millimeters over a period of 10 days have been measured by this method.

◀ A satellite that looks like a cosmic golfball is being prepared to aid scientists in predicting earthquakes. It will provide a fixed point in space from which pulses of laser light can be reflected. The laser pulses will be beamed to the satellite from opposite sides of a fault line. The satellite's 426 special reflectors are designed to return the laser pulses to their exact point of origin. Any change in the time it takes the pulses to be reflected will indicate that the crust has shifted along the fault line.

275

Mountain Building

How are mountains formed?

Huge mountain ranges are found in a number of places on the earth. The Himalayas in Asia rise more than 8,000 m above sea level. The Rocky Mountains in the western United States and Canada rise more than 6,000 m. How are mountain ranges formed?

Scientists think that mountain ranges form when plates collide. When two plates carrying continents collide, the crust of each plate folds. As the plates push each other, their crusts are forced higher and higher. Large mountain ranges are formed in this way. The Alps were formed when the African plate rammed into the Eurasian plate. The Himalayas were formed when the plate carrying India rammed into the plate carrying Asia. Since these plates are still

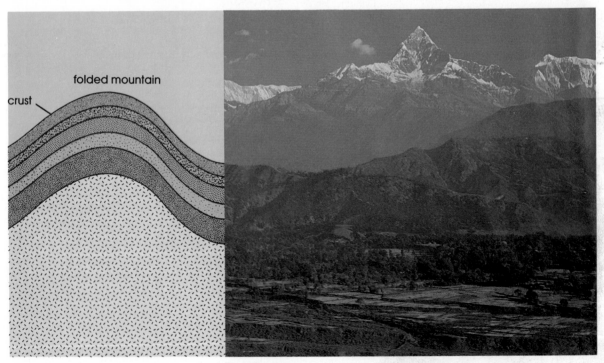

The Himalayas

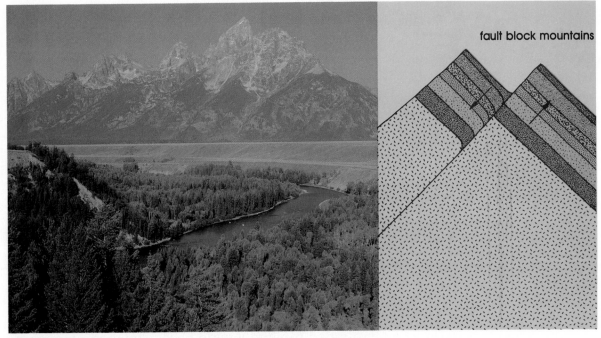

fault block mountains

The Teton Range

moving, the Himalayas are still being pushed up. They are pushed up about 5 cm each year. However, they are eroded at the same rate. Therefore, there is no overall increase in their height.

A mountain range is also formed when an ocean plate sinks beneath a plate carrying a continent. When this happens, the ocean plate pushes against the crust of the plate carrying the continent. The land is forced up, and mountains form. Mountains that form through collisions between plates are called **folded mountains.**

Not all mountains form directly from collisions between plates. Sometimes, mountains form along faults in the crust. Blocks of crust on one side of a fault move up while blocks of crust on the other side move down. Mountains formed in this way are called **fault-block mountains.** The Tetons of western North America are fault-block mountains. Scientists are not sure what forces the blocks of crust to move.

Finding Out

How can you demonstrate the formation of folded mountains?

Get three or four hand towels or bath towels. Make two piles of towels. Each pile represents a plate carrying continents. Slowly push the two "plates" into each other. Continue pushing them together until mountains form. Why, do you think, are these mountains called folded mountains?

Sometimes, magma is forced up under the crust but does not break through the surface. Instead the magma pushes the crust up, forming a mountain with a rounded top and a wide base. The magma eventually hardens under the crust. This type of mountain is called a **dome mountain.**

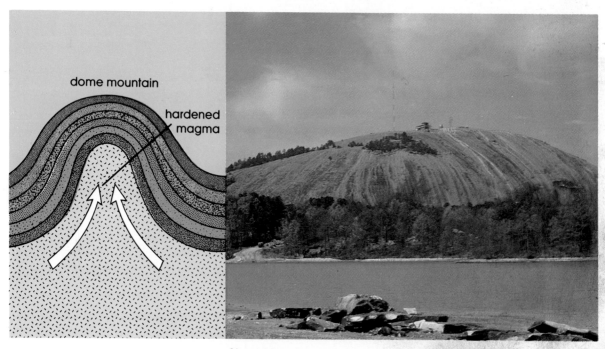

Stone Mountain

Mountains change slowly over the years. Much of this change is due to weathering by wind and rain. Because of this weathering, older mountain ranges are lower and have more rounded tops than do younger ranges. Which mountain range shown here is older?

For Lesson Questions, turn to page 404.

The Rocky Mountains

The Blue Ridge Mountains

Ideas to Remember

▶ The earth's crust is made up of plates that move over the mantle.
▶ Earthquakes can occur when plates collide with, pull away from, or slip past each other.
▶ Volcanoes are produced when magma pushes up through cracks in the crust. Most volcanoes occur near plate boundaries.
▶ Most mountain ranges form from collisions between plates. Fault-block mountains and dome mountains seem to form in other ways.

Reviewing the Chapter

SCIENCE WORDS

A. Use all the terms below to complete the sentences.

folded mountains   seismographs   faults   dome mountain
plate tectonic theory   earthquake   plate   volcanoes

    The __1__ states that the crust of the earth is made of a number of large rigid sections. Each section is called a/an __2__. When sections of the crust suddenly slip past each other, a/an __3__ occurs. Cracks in the crust along which rocks have moved are called __4__. When sections of the crust slip, waves moving out from the focus can be recorded by __5__.

    Magma sometimes pushes through the surface along plate boundaries, forming __6__. If magma pushes the surface up and then hardens underneath, a/an __7__ forms. When two plates collide, the crust may be forced up, forming __8__.

B. Copy the sentences below. Use science terms from the chapter to complete the sentences.

1. The process in which hot liquid rock flows up and hardens to form new ocean floor is called _____.
2. The place where rocks slip is called the _____ of an earthquake.
3. Magma that reaches the surface is called _____.
4. When blocks of rock on opposite sides of a fault move vertically, _____ form.
5. The theory of _____ was an early idea that the continents move.

UNDERSTANDING IDEAS

A. Look at the following diagrams. Which one shows folded mountains? Which shows fault-block mountains? Which shows dome mountains?

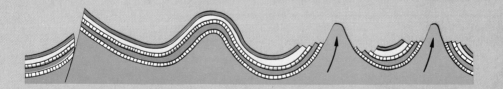

B. Earthquakes and volcanoes usually occur in the same kind of region of the earth. Explain why this is so.

C. A cause makes things happen. An effect is what happens. For each pair of sentences, write which is the cause and which is the effect.

1. **a.** Folded mountains form.
   b. Two plates collide.
2. **a.** Part of a plate sinks and melts.
   b. Volcanoes are produced.
3. **a.** Sections of rock slip past each other.
   b. Shock waves move out from the focus.

4. **a.** Low mountains with rounded tops occur.
   b. Wind and rain erode the land.
5. **a.** Certain facts are observed.
   b. A theory is proposed.

USING IDEAS

1. Collect pictures of various mountain ranges. Find out how each was formed. Locate the mountain ranges on a globe.

2. Find out about the New Madrid, Missouri, earthquake of 1811. How do scientists explain this earthquake?

THINKING LIKE A SCIENTIST

Answer the following questions. You may be able to answer some of the questions just by thinking about them. To answer other questions, you may have to do some research.

1. In the November 1985 volcanic eruption in Colombia, South America, thousands of people were buried by mud. Where could the mud have come from?

2. Is there a limit to the height of mountains on planets? The peak of the highest mountain on Earth, Mt. Everest, is 8.8 km above sea level. The highest mountain in the solar system is Olympus Mons, a volcanic mountain on Mars. This mountain is over 24 km high. What hypothesis can you form about what limits the height of a mountain?

3. Other scientists before Alfred Wegener had noticed how the continents seem to fit together like pieces in a jigsaw puzzle. However, not many scientists supported Wegener's theory of continental drift. What do you think most scientists look for in a theory before they support it?

CHAPTER 12
Forecasting the Weather

September 8th, 1900, my birthday! . . . A peculiar light hung over the island. Papa walked in the front door. He had been away all night. He said it was reported that the Gulf was inland seven blocks and that there was a bad storm raging all through the Gulf. We lived on 35th Avenue, a road leading straight through to the Gulf. It wasn't long after Papa's arrival that the Gulf came roaring down the road, great big breakers dashing. The Gulf then seemed to come in all at once with a loud roar. The water was four feet deep in our yard.

Papa called my brothers, Richard and Norman. All three worked frantically, packing Papa's books up the stairs to the second story, as the water was then just coming into the house. Grandma was heartbroken, thinking of all our lovely furniture, silver, and imported carpets being ruined. One heavy, high breaker dashed against our home. It seemed as though the house would collapse. Papa said, "Come, we must get out of here immediately." Although we had a big home, it was in a direct . . . path for the water to come through.

. . . Papa, Richard, and Norman, my grown brothers Arthur and Harold, . . . Grandma and I all dashed for the front door. The house was rocking. Papa said it would go to pieces any minute . . . So we started on, the three men struggling down the middle of the street, the men swimming, and struggling to keep in the center of the road, as Papa said this was the safest course. Everything looked so strange, all the island [under] . . . water.

This story is part of an account by Edith C. Munger. Edith was a young girl living in Galveston, Texas, at the turn of the century. Galveston was built on an island in the Gulf of Mexico. Edith wrote this account just after a terrible hurricane hit her home.

The family swam down the road to a house on higher ground. They made their way into a room at the center of the house. Everyone crawled under a heavy table for shelter. They all stayed under the table for what seemed like hours. The winds tore at the house, pulling away one room after another. Then all that was left was this center room. But finally the waters began to go down. This very lucky family survived the worst hurricane that ever hit the United States!

Courtesy Rosenberg Library, Galveston, Texas

Galveston before the hurricane

Courtesy Rosenberg Library, Galveston, Texas

Courtesy Rosenberg Library, Galveston, Texas

Galveston just after the hurricane

Courtesy Rosenberg Library, Galveston, Texas

Galveston sea wall in 1905

The hurricane that struck Galveston on September 8, 1900, left behind death and destruction. More than 4,500 m of beachfront were washed away. The total number of houses lost was 3,636. About 6,000 people, or 18 percent of the people of Galveston, died during this disaster.

Help poured in from many parts of the world. Private citizens from all over the United States sent money to help. Businesses began reopening soon after the storm. Homeowners began digging out from under the wreckage. The mighty town of Galveston would not die.

The most important rebuilding was in the form of a sea wall. This structure was meant to hold back the waters of any future storm. Work began on October 27, 1902. The material for rebuilding was brought in by freight car. Thousands of carloads were brought in from the mainland—5,200 carloads of crushed stone, 1,800 of sand, 1,000 of

Galveston sea wall in recent times (below); map of Galveston (right)

To make an accurate forecast, a weather watcher must know the direction of the wind. You can make a device for telling the wind direction. This device is called a wind sock. You will need a pair of pliers, a wire coat hanger, a plastic garbage bag, scissors, masking tape, an empty metal can, sand, a straw, and a felt-tip marker.

Use the pliers to snip off the hook of the hanger. Bend the hanger into the shape shown. Cut a plastic garbage bag into two pieces of the shape shown to the right. Tape the sides closed with masking tape. Tape the wide end of the bag over the wire circle as shown. Set aside the wire and the plastic bag.

Place a straw upright in the center of an empty metal can. Pour sand into the can to hold the straw up. Insert the straight part of the hanger into the straw. Make sure the wire and bag can swing around freely. Write *N* on a piece of tape. Attach this tape to the outside of the can.

Set the device outdoors in an open area. Make sure it is a windy day. Turn the can so that *N* faces north. Note how the wind causes the device to spin around. How can you use the wind sock to tell wind direction? To tell wind speed?

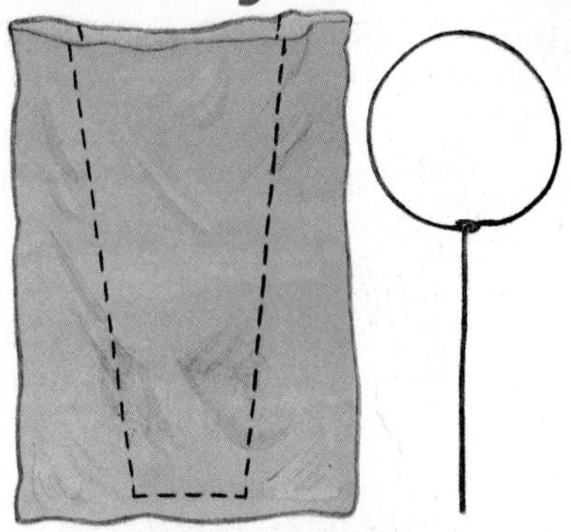

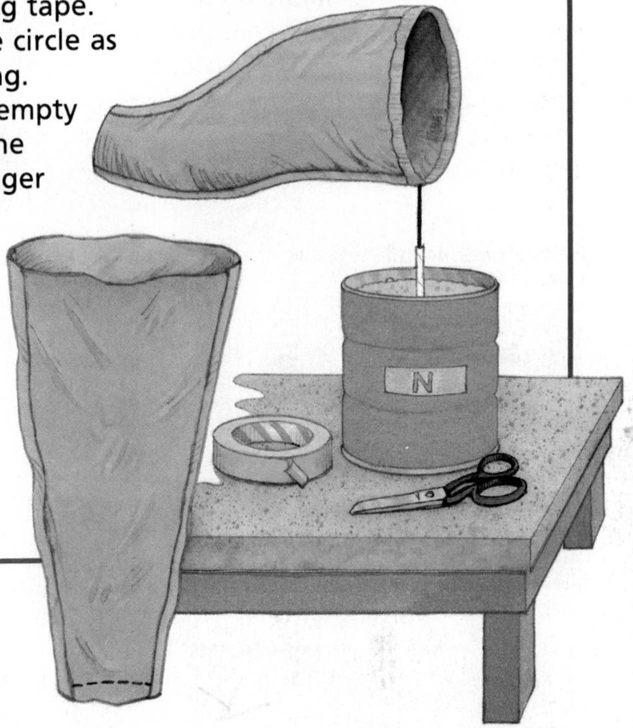

cement. On July 29, 1904, the job was completed. A huge concrete wall had been built to hold back the waters. The wall was 5.1 m high. The sea wall extended along the beach for 5,278 m.

The first real test of the sea wall came on August 16, 1915. Winds of 147 km per hour were measured. Survivors of the terrible storm of 1900 held their breath. Would the wall protect their town? Yes! Galveston was safe!

In this chapter you will learn how information about the weather is gathered. You will find out how weather changes are predicted.

Weather Instruments

How do we get information about the weather?

Weather affects our lives in many ways. Many of our activities depend on the weather. What activities can you think of that are affected by weather? The weather helps you decide what type of clothes to wear. A baseball game may be canceled because of rain. School may be closed because of a snowstorm. You may decide to go to the beach because the day is sunny and warm. How have the people in these pictures adapted to different kinds of weather?

The study of weather is called **meteorology** (mē tē ə rol′ə jē). The word *meteorology* comes from two Greek words that mean "high in the air" and "study." You can see why this is a good name for the study of weather. A scientist who studies weather is called a **meteorologist** (mē tē ə rol′ə jist). Meteorologists make weather forecasts. A **forecast** is a statement of what the weather will probably be like in the future. The forecast tells what is most likely to happen. Why are weather forecasts important?

To make forecasts, meteorologists carefully observe weather conditions. They use special instruments to measure temperature, air pressure, wind speed and direction, and other conditions. The picture and drawing show some of these instruments. What weather instruments do you use at home?

Winds are caused by the movements of air masses. Wind speed and direction may affect the weather. A **wind vane** shows wind direction. Winds are named for the direction from which they blow. For example, a north wind blows *from* the north and toward the south. An **anemometer** (an ə mom′ə tər) tells wind speed. Look at the picture. The cups catch the wind, making the arms spin. As the arms spin, the wind speed can be measured. The stronger the wind blows, the faster the arms spin.

A **wind sock** can show both the wind speed and the wind direction. The wind sock rotates on a pole, showing the wind direction. If the sock is blowing straight out, it shows that the wind is strong. If the sock is limp, there is very little wind. Wind socks are often found at small airports. They are used to find the direction in which planes should take off or land.

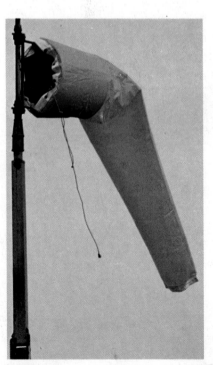

Wind sock

Anemometer and wind vane

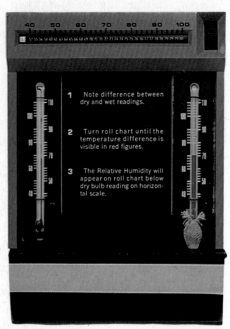

Wet-and-dry-bulb thermometer

Humidity refers to any moisture in the air. There is always some humidity. But relative humidity refers to the *amount* of moisture in the air. **Relative humidity** is the amount of water vapor in the air compared with the greatest amount of water vapor the air can hold at that temperature. Warm air can hold more water vapor than cool air can hold. Would the relative humidity be higher on a warm, cloudy day or on a clear, cool day?

Relative humidity is stated as a percent. A relative humidity of 50 percent means that the air has half the total amount of water vapor that it can hold. Explain "relative humidity of 25 percent."

Relative humidity is measured with a **wet-and-dry-bulb thermometer.** This instrument has two thermometers. One has a wet bulb, and one has a dry bulb. The difference between the temperatures is found. Then a table is used to determine the relative humidity. For example, suppose that the dry-bulb temperature is 25°C. There is a 5° difference between the dry-bulb temperature and the wet-bulb temperature. Use the table on page 287 to determine the relative humidity.

People feel uncomfortable when the relative humidity and the temperature are high. What is the weather like for the people in the pictures?

Activity

How can you measure relative humidity?

Materials 2 Celsius thermometers / cardboard / rubber bands / wide cotton shoelace / scissors / water / clock or watch

Procedure

A. Put two Celsius thermometers side by side on a piece of cardboard. Use rubber bands to hold them in place.

B. Cut a small length of cotton shoelace. Cut one end open.

C. Soak the piece of shoelace in water, Slip the opened end over the bulb of one of the thermometers. You have made a wet-and-dry-bulb thermometer.

D. Fan the thermometers for 2 minutes. Record the temperature reading of each thermometer.
   1. Find the difference between the two temperatures. Use that number and the dry-bulb temperature to find the relative humidity in the table.
   2. Determine the relative humidity each day at the same time for a week. (Be sure to wet the shoelace each time.)

E. Make a table showing the 7 days, the dry-bulb reading for each day, and the relative humidity for each day. Then draw a graph showing the change in relative humidity for the days shown in your table.

Conclusion

1. What two conditions of the air determine relative humidity?

2. Why did you need to take a dry-bulb reading as well as a wet-bulb reading to determine relative humidity?

Using science ideas

Why do you feel more uncomfortable on a hot day with high relative humidity than on a hot day with low relative humidity?

RELATIVE HUMIDITY
(percent)

Dry-bulb temp. (°C)	Difference between wet-bulb and dry-bulb temp. (°C)								
	1	2	3	4	5	6	7	8	9
15	90	81	71	61	53	44	36	27	20
16	90	81	71	63	54	46	38	30	23
17	90	81	72	64	55	47	40	32	25
18	91	82	73	65	57	49	41	34	27
19	91	82	74	65	58	50	43	36	29
20	91	83	74	66	59	51	44	37	31
21	91	83	75	67	60	53	46	39	32
22	92	83	76	68	61	54	47	40	34
23	92	84	76	69	62	55	48	42	36
24	92	84	77	69	62	56	49	43	37
25	92	84	77	70	63	57	50	44	39
26	92	85	78	71	64	58	51	46	40
27	92	85	78	71	65	58	52	47	41

Relative humidity

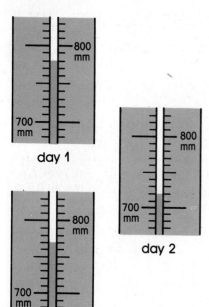

day 1

day 2

day 3

Air pushes on all surfaces that it touches. This push is called **air pressure.** Warm air presses down on the surface of the earth with less pressure than cold air does. For this reason, warm air masses have lower air pressure than cold air masses have. Warm air can hold more moisture than cold air can. Because of this, low-pressure air masses often bring cloudy weather. High-pressure air masses often bring fair weather.

Air pressure is measured with a **barometer** (bə rom′ə tər). Barometric (bar ə met′rik) readings are usually given in millimeters or in inches. A "falling barometer" usually means that warm, moist low-pressure air is moving in. A "rising barometer" usually means that cool, dry high-pressure air is moving in. Look at the barometric readings in the drawing. What weather changes probably took place?

Finding Out

SKILLS: Measuring, Communicating, Inferring

What conditions affect the dew point?

The temperature at which the water vapor in air begins to condense is called the dew point. You can determine the dew point of the air in your classroom. You will need a shiny metal can, a thermometer, and some ice. Half-fill the can with water. Add one or two ice cubes to the water. Stir the water with a stirring rod. As you stir, watch for water to condense on the outside of the can. As soon as condensation begins, measure the temperature of the water. This temperature is the dew point. Measure and record the dew point at the same time each day for one week. A rise in the dew point means that the amount of water vapor in the air has increased. If there is a decrease in the dew point, what does this indicate about the amount of water vapor in the air?

For Lesson Questions, turn to page 406.

Collecting Weather Data

How are weather data gathered?

As you have learned, many kinds of instruments are used to measure weather conditions. Where and how is weather information gathered? Data are collected from land weather stations, high-altitude balloons, ships, airplanes, and spacecraft. In fact the National Meteorological Center in Maryland receives the following information every day.

50,000 reports from land weather stations
2,500 reports from balloons in the upper air
3,000 reports from ships all over the world
3,200 reports from airplanes
1,300 reports from spacecraft, in addition to
100 photographs from spacecraft
3,000 reports from radar stations

These reports include information on air temperature, air pressure, wind speed, wind direction, and relative humidity. The reports provide data on the amounts of rain, snow, and hail. Other weather data include cloud cover, ocean currents, and the locations and movements of storms. It would take people a long time to analyze all this information. But the data about the atmosphere are fed into computers. One type of weather computer can analyze tens of millions of pieces of information every second.

Most weather data are gathered from weather stations on land. Ships also provide weather data for the oceans. There are several thousand weather stations around the world sending data to weather centers. There, weather forecasts are prepared.

Weather balloons are another source of weather data. These balloons carry instruments that measure air temperature, air pressure, and humidity at differ-

weather satellite

weather balloon

weather plane

ship

buoy

weather station

ent levels of the atmosphere. Weather data are also collected by ships and planes. In ocean regions, ships transmit data to land weather stations.

Some weather stations use radar to gather weather information. Radar can detect storms. A storm appears as a cloudy region on a screen like the one shown in the picture. The speed and direction of a moving storm can be detected by radar. How would these data help a meteorologist to forecast weather?

Weather stations on the land measure only the weather on or near land. Information provided by ships is usually limited to normal shipping routes. So, together these two types of weather stations only provide information about part of the earth.

Weather **satellites** (sat′ə līts) have become very important in meteorology. Satellites orbit the earth and send back weather data. In this way, weather in all parts of the earth can be observed. Weather satellites circle the earth at different altitudes and exam-

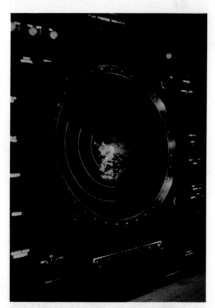

Weather radar

Weather satellite

Weather plane

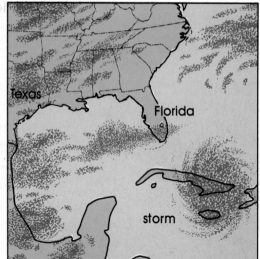

Weather satellite picture

ine different parts of the atmosphere. One weather satellite is called TIROS, or Television Infra-Red Observation Satellite. Another satellite is known as GOES, or Geostationary Operational Environmental Satellite. Today much weather information is collected by two TIROS and two GOES satellites.

Weather satellites send back signals that are changed into pictures by computers. Such pictures show cloud cover and areas of ice and snow. Satellite pictures are helpful in following the paths of storms. You have probably seen a weather satellite picture on your television. Compare the satellite picture with the drawing. Where is a major storm located? What is the weather like over southern Florida? What is the weather like over southern Texas?

Meteorologist plotting data

Computers are useful tools in weather forecasting. Data from satellites, radar, and other sources are processed by a computer. Using this data, the computer can predict changes in the atmosphere. The short-term forecasts are often more accurate than the long-term ones. The photo shows a meteorologist plotting computer data to forecast weather.

For Lesson Questions, turn to page 406.

Weather Forecasts

How are weather forecasts made?

Meteorologists carefully study weather data. They use the data to predict patterns and changes in the weather. Meteorologists use observations to make weather forecasts. They observe clouds and changes in clouds. They observe the movements of air masses. An **air mass** is a large body of air with the same amount of moisture and humidity throughout. The air mass over a certain area of land determines the kind of weather for that region. For example, a warm, wet air mass will mean hot, humid weather.

Changes in the weather take place when air masses move. The weather changes occur at a **front,** the border between two unlike air masses. For example, suppose a cold air mass moves into a warmer air mass. The place where these two air masses meet is called a cold front. How would you describe a warm front? The picture below shows a meteorologist with a map that shows a cold front.

jet
stream
paths

Usually, meteorologists can predict the weather by keeping track of the speed and direction of moving air masses. But sometimes, unusual weather changes take place. In recent years, meteorologists have realized that high-speed winds, called **jet streams,** may influence how air masses move. One way to describe a jet stream is to think of it as a very fast-moving "ribbon" of air that is high above the earth. At times a jet stream may move at more than 320 km/h. A jet stream moves from west to east. It also moves north and south, in a wavelike motion.

Scientists know that jet streams are related to severe weather. They believe that violent storms may be related to jet streams. Sometimes a jet stream does not follow its normal path. This is when unusual weather may occur. In the winter of 1976 – 1977, the path of the jet stream moved farther north and farther south than usual. The result was an extremely cold winter in the United States. Find the normal jet stream path and the "off course" jet stream path in the drawing. How are the two paths different?

Meteorologists use their own weather observations and the data collected by instruments to help make forecasts. Computers are also used to help make forecasts. Weather forecasters base short-range forecasts

on this data. The more data available, the more accurate the forecast. Short-range forecasts are those made for not more than 3 days in advance. These forecasts are usually accurate.

Weather is the day-to-day change in conditions of the atmosphere. But climate is the average weather for a large region over a long period of time. A scientist who studies climate is called a climatologist (klī mə tol′ə jist). A **climatologist** studies worldwide weather conditions over a long period of time. What type of climate is shown in the picture?

Climatologists use records of past weather to make long-range weather forecasts. A long-range forecast is really a scientific estimate. Long-range forecasts are not very accurate. Usually, forecasts are made for no more than 30 days at a time. Look at the drawing below. It shows a 30-day precipitation forecast. What is the precipitation forecast for your area?

Long-range forecasts are made by studying past weather patterns. As better and more-complete records of weather are kept, better long-range forecasts will probably result. At present, however, it is difficult to forecast weather far into the future.

For Lesson Questions,
turn to page 406.

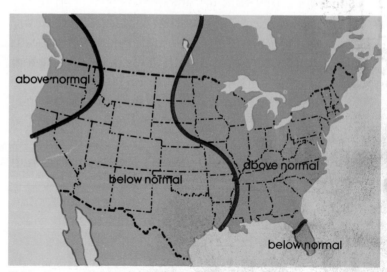

Thirty-day precipitation outlook

Activity

How are some weather predictions made?

Procedure
Study the table. Then use information from the table to make weather predictions for the four situations below.
1. South winds; air pressure 755.22, falling fast
2. Northwest winds; air pressure 764.87, rising fast
3. Southwest winds; air pressure 767.32, steady
4. East to north winds; air pressure 756.81, falling fast

Wind direction	Air pressure at sea level (mm)	Kind of weather to be expected
SW to NW	764.54 to 767.08, steady	Fair, with little temperature change for one or two days
SW to NW	764.54 to 767.08, rising fast	Fair, followed by rain within two days
SW to NW	767.08 or above, steady	Continued fair, with little temperature change
E to NE	764.54 or above, falling fast	Rain probable in summer within 24 hours; in winter, rain or snow and windy
SE to NE	762.00 or below, falling slowly	Steady rain for one or two days
SE to NE	762.00 or below, falling fast	Rain and high wind, clearing within 36 hours
S to SW	762.00 or below, rising slowly	Clearing within a few hours, fair for several days
S to E	756.92 or below, falling fast	Severe storm soon, clearing within 24 hours; colder in winter
Going to W	745.00 or below, rising fast	Clearing and colder
E to N	756.92 or below, falling fast	Severe northeast gale, heavy rain; in winter, heavy snow and cold wave

Conclusion
1. What two instruments would be needed to make weather predictions with this table?
2. What kind of weather can be expected with rising air pressure? With falling air pressure?
3. What are some ways to predict weather?

Weather Maps

What is a weather map, and how is it used?

Meteorologists use weather maps to help them predict weather changes for different regions. A **weather map** is a map on which the weather conditions over a large area are recorded. These maps are prepared by computers at the National Weather Service, a government agency. You saw one kind of weather map on page 292. You may have seen other types of weather maps in newspapers.

There are several types of weather maps. A weather map may show the temperature in different areas. Sometimes, lines are drawn to connect areas that have the same temperature. These lines are called **isotherms** (ī'sə thėrmz). What are the temperature readings for the isotherms shown on the map?

Lines are used to connect places on a weather map that have the same air pressure. Each line is called an **isobar** (ī'sə bär). The air pressure is shown at the ends of each isobar. The air pressure is usually given in units called millibars. What air-pressure readings are shown at the ends of the isobars on the map on page 297? Based on this map, what would the air pressure be near Chicago? What would it be like near Miami?

You have probably seen the symbols *H* and *L* on a weather map. These symbols indicate a high-pressure area and a low-pressure area. Remember, an area of high pressure usually brings fair weather. An area of low pressure usually brings cloudy weather. Find the highs and lows on the map. Meteorologists study the movements of these pressure areas. The information helps them predict weather changes.

A weather map usually shows the locations of air masses, cold fronts, and warm fronts. Wind speed and direction, rain or snow, cloud cover, and fog conditions may also be shown.

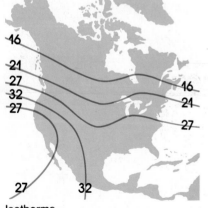

Isotherms

Study the symbols used on a weather map. Then study the map in the drawing. What type of front is moving up the East Coast of the United States? What is the temperature near Galveston, Texas? What is the weather like in Seattle, Washington?

For Lesson Questions, turn to page 406.

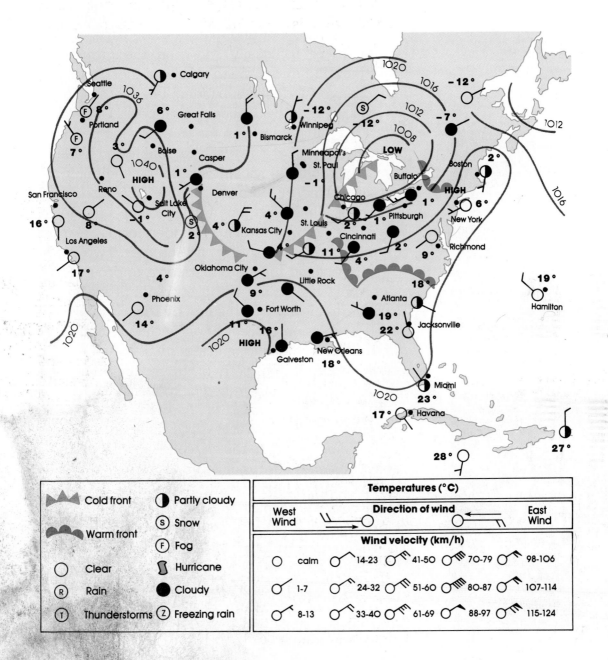

	Temperatures (°C)		
	Direction of wind		
West Wind			East Wind

Cold front ◑ Partly cloudy
Warm front ⓢ Snow
○ **Clear** Ⓕ Fog
Ⓡ **Rain** Hurricane
Ⓣ **Thunderstorms** ● Cloudy Ⓩ Freezing rain

Wind velocity (km/h)

○ calm	14-23	41-50	70-79	98-106
1-7	24-32	51-60	80-87	107-114
8-13	33-40	61-69	88-97	115-124

297

Storms

What are some violent changes in weather?

The weather for a region usually follows a regular pattern. For example, in the southwestern states the weather is often hot and dry. In some parts of Minnesota, there is usually snow on the ground by Christmas. But from time to time, weather conditions may change suddenly. A sudden, unexpected storm may occur and then quickly disappear. Or a large storm may affect a region for an extended period of time. Such changes in weather are often violent. Some examples of violent weather conditions are thunderstorms, blizzards, tornadoes, and hurricanes.

Perhaps the most common violent change in weather is a **thunderstorm.** Thunderstorms are most common during late spring and summer. Two conditions are needed for a thunderstorm to occur. First, there must be rapidly rising currents of warm air. Usually this air has been heated by the warm ground below it. A rising current of air is called an **updraft** (up'draft). Second, the updrafts must contain much water vapor. When both of these conditions are present, a thunderstorm begins to form.

Air cools rapidly as it rises. As the rising air cools, condensation occurs. Water vapor changes from a gas to a liquid or a solid. In the air, condensation of water vapor causes tiny drops of liquid water or ice crystals to form. These drops of water or ice form a cloud. As the air currents keep rising, the cloud builds up higher. A huge dark cloud called a thunderhead forms. The thunderstorm forms inside the thunderhead.

As rising air currents inside the cloud continue to cool, more water vapor condenses. A typical cloud has billions of tiny water droplets that collide and grow larger. Finally the water drops fall as rain.

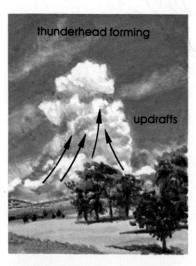

thunderhead forming

updrafts

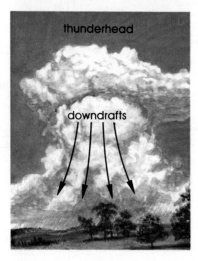

thunderhead

downdrafts

Sometimes drops of water are lifted back into the cloud by an updraft. If the air in the cloud is below freezing, the water changes to ice. The ice particles collect more layers. As the layers build up, the balls of ice become larger. Finally the balls of ice fall to the earth as hailstones. A current of cool air comes down with the rain or hail. A falling air current, called a **downdraft** (doun'draft), is shown on page 298.

Rapidly rising air causes electrical charges to build up inside the cloud. These charges can jump from one cloud to another. They can also jump between a cloud and the earth. Lightning is the movement of these charges. Lightning heats the air and causes it to expand rapidly. After a lightning flash, the air cools and contracts. The expansion and contraction of the air cause the vibrations heard as thunder. Lightning from thunderstorms can be very dangerous.

Hailstones

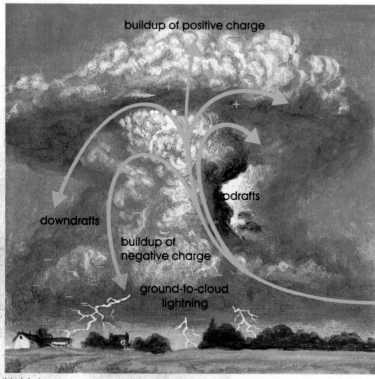

buildup of positive charge

updrafts

downdrafts

buildup of negative charge

ground-to-cloud lightning

Lightning

A **tornado** is a very violent windstorm. Tornadoes usually last only a short time. Some may last only 20 minutes. But longer-lasting tornadoes also occur. An average tornado travels 25 km. The width of its path is about 0.5 km. Winds may be as high as 500 km/h.

Over 400 tornadoes are reported in the United States each year. Tornadoes occur in every state in the nation. But they occur most often in the Midwest and in the South Central States.

Tornadoes are most likely to occur in late spring and early summer. They form within thunderheads but only under certain conditions. First there must be a layer of warm, humid air close to the ground. Above that there must be a layer of cold, dry air. The layer of cold air keeps the warm air from rising. Then a rapidly moving cold front must move into the region. It acts like a wedge, lifting the warm, humid air. The warm air becomes trapped between the two layers of colder air. Some of the warm air breaks through the cold air above and rushes upward. More air follows, forming the twisting mass of air that is a tornado funnel. The funnel is usually dark in color because of the dirt that is carried by the rising air.

Many tornadoes never touch the ground. But serious damage results where a tornado does touch the earth's surface. A tornado may tear roofs off buildings and uproot trees. Cars and people have been swept up by tornadoes. The damage caused is severe. But the area that is damaged is usually limited.

Forecasters issue a tornado watch if conditions are likely for a tornado to form. They issue a tornado warning if a tornado has been sighted and people need to seek shelter.

Tornado damage

Science & Technology

◀ New kinds of data, obtained by satellites, aid in forecasting the weather. The map shows the total ozone (ō'zōn) content of the atmosphere. Ozone is a form of oxygen. Each color on the map represents a different amount of ozone. Certain weather disturbances not evident from other data can be detected by noting how the amount and distribution of ozone changes from day to day.

▶ Weather satellites may also be equipped with instruments to measure temperature and moisture in the atmosphere. The successive orbits of these satellites provide nearly global coverage. The data obtained is translated by computers into a temperature/moisture profile. The profile aids in making forecasts of weather patterns. What region of the world can be identified in the profile shown?

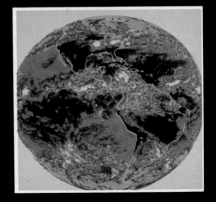

A **hurricane** (hėr′ə kān) is a violent storm that develops over the ocean in a tropical area. A hurricane is a large mass of warm, moist air.

Hurricanes form more slowly than tornadoes. Like a tornado, a hurricane is a rotating mass of air. In both cases, air in the center is low pressure. But a hurricane affects a much larger area than a tornado. The width of a hurricane is usually about 650 km. The winds are at least 119 km/h. In the center is a calm region about 30 km wide. This region is called the eye of the storm. The strongest winds of a hurricane whirl or rotate around the eye. The rotation of the winds is the result of the earth's rotation on its axis. These winds may be 200 to 240 km/h. Hurricanes move more slowly than do tornadoes. But they last longer, and the high winds and rain can do much damage.

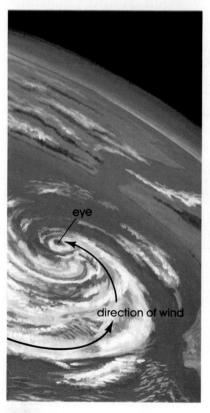

eye

direction of wind

Hurricane

A hurricane's strong winds and rain can also cause huge ocean waves to form. These waves, called storm surges, can flood land areas and cause deaths and damage.

People can avoid a hurricane more easily than they can avoid a tornado. Meteorologists use instruments, satellite pictures, and radar to track hurricanes. Forecasters issue warnings of an approaching hurricane so that people can leave the areas that are most likely to be affected hardest by the storm. Many lives can be saved in this way.

For Lesson Questions, turn to page 406.

Ideas to Remember

▶ The study of weather is called meteorology.

▶ A weather forecast is a statement of what the weather will probably be like in the future.

▶ Weather forecasts are based on measurements of conditions such as wind speed and direction, relative humidity, and air pressure.

▶ Weather data are gathered at land weather stations and from weather balloons, satellites, ships, and planes.

▶ Meteorologists study the movements of air masses to predict weather changes.

▶ A weather map is a map on which weather conditions over a large area are recorded; meteorologists study weather maps to make forecasts.

▶ Short-range weather forecasts are generally accurate; long-range forecasts are less accurate.

▶ Storms such as thunderstorms, tornadoes, and hurricanes are examples of violent weather conditions.

Reviewing the Chapter

SCIENCE WORDS

A. Copy the sentences below. Use science terms from the chapter to complete the sentences.

1. A scientist who studies weather is called a/an _____.
2. A/An _____ is used to measure wind speed.
3. A/An _____ is used to determine wind direction.
4. Air pressure is measured with a/an _____.
5. Relative humidity is measured with a/an _____.
6. The border between air masses along which weather changes occur is called a/an _____.
7. Weather conditions over a large area are recorded on a/an _____.
8. Rising currents of air containing much water vapor can result in the formation of a/an _____.
9. A violent storm that forms within a thunderhead is called a/an _____.
10. A large storm that forms over the ocean in a tropical area is called a/an _____.
11. A scientist who studies worldwide weather conditions over a long period of time is called a/an _____.

B. Identify each of the following.

1. It sends back information about weather from outer space. What is it?
2. It is a rapidly rising current of air often associated with a thunderstorm. What is it?
3. It is a statement about what the weather will be like in the future. What is it?
4. It is an instrument that shows both wind speed and wind direction. What is it?
5. It is a high-speed wind that is related to the movement of air masses. What is it?

UNDERSTANDING IDEAS

A. Explain the Difference between the terms.

1. meteorologist, climatologist
2. isobar, isotherm
3. hurricane, tornado
4. updraft, downdraft

B. Study the map below. Answer the questions that follow. Use the weather map on page 297 to review the symbols.

1. What are the temperature and cloud cover near Centerville?
2. What type of front is approaching Springfield?
3. What is the air pressure near Oakdale?
4. What are the wind speed and air pressure near Clayton?
5. What type of front is approaching Hilltop?

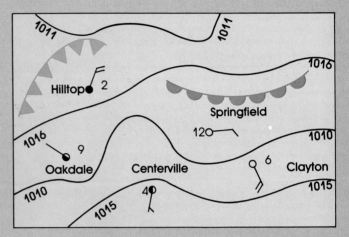

USING IDEAS

1. How can people prepare for a weather emergency?
2. Find out what the precipitation or temperature forecast is for the next 30-day period. Keep a record of the actual weather conditions, and compare it with the 30-day forecast.

THINKING LIKE A SCIENTIST

Answer the following questions. You may be able to answer some of the questions just by thinking about them. To answer other questions, you may have do to some research.

1. In 1960 a pilot named William Rankin was forced to bail out of his airplane. As he fell, he dropped into a thunderhead. He faced heavy rain, high winds, and lightning. When he finally fell from the thunderhead, his parachute opened and he landed safely. He had been in the cloud about 40 minutes. Why, do you think, did it take so long for him to fall through the cloud?

2. You have learned that the sun's rays shine on the earth longer on June 21 than on any other day of the year. If that is so, why isn't June 21 the hottest day of the year?

305

CHAPTER 13
Exploring Space

You belong to the first generation that will see frequent travel in space. You and your classmates may be living in space stations. You may be solving problems that have puzzled humans for centuries.

If you want space travel to be in your future, you must begin to prepare now. Would you like to know how it feels to be weightless? Would you like to learn about rocketry? Would you like to take part in a mock space mission? All of these goals can be met in one place—U.S. Space Camp.

The U.S. Space Camp, in Huntsville, Alabama, will sweep you right into the future. This exciting place provides a training program for students in the fifth through the twelfth grades. Campers launch their own rockets. Each rocket carries two live bees. The campers experience *g*-forces, or the feeling of extra weight as a spacecraft pulls away from the earth. To campers the *g*-forces feel like a soft weight pressing against the body. Campers experience weightlessness, also known as zero gravity. They enter a special tank of water that allows them to feel weightless. While in the tank, they perform certain simple tasks. These tasks are like some that might be done on a real mission.

Campers wear the same type of clothing that is worn by mission specialists on a space mission. Campers wear training suits worn by astronauts on prior space travels. Students at Space Camp prepare and eat meals that astronauts would eat. Each camper uses a tray with devices for holding the food and utensils.

Campers learn about the structure of the space shuttle. They find out about its design and what it can do. Students train in a copy of the space shuttle orbiter. The shuttle orbiter carries the crew and payload into space. It is the main part of the shuttle. This orbiter is an almost exact copy of an orbiter that has been used for prior space missions. Campers also learn about the history of space travel. They may even get a chance to talk with astronauts, who visit the camp from time to time.

The highlight of the stay at Space Camp is a mock mission aboard the space shuttle. Campers go through launch, orbit, reentry, and landing. During their trip they must respond to an "emergency" in flight. Campers' training and problem-solving skills are put

You are going to construct a *g*-detector from a paddleball toy. (One *g* is the force you feel on the surface of the earth. If you are in a spacecraft, you will feel different *g*-forces. For example, as you lift off, you will feel two or three times as heavy as you do on earth. You then feel 2 or 3 *g*'s. There are times when you can feel lighter than 1 *g*. For example, you can feel lighter than 1 *g* when you are on a roller coaster or when you go down in an elevator.)

To make your *g*-detector you will need a paddleball, a thumbtack, scissors, glue, and a paper pattern. You can either enlarge the pattern shown here or use a pattern given to you by your teacher. Cut out the pattern and glue it to your paddleboard, as shown. Attach the string and ball to the thumbtack. Adjust the length of the string so that the ball hangs in front of the *1 g* circle.

Use the *g*-detector to measure the *g*-forces in different places. Take the *g*-detector into an elevator. Prepare a chart for recording your results. Record the position of the ball as the elevator goes up, during the ride, and when the elevator stops. Take three rides. Record the data for each of the rides. Compute the average of these three figures.

Take the *g*-detector to several other places. You could use it on a slide, a swing, and a merry-go-round. You could also use it on a ferris wheel.

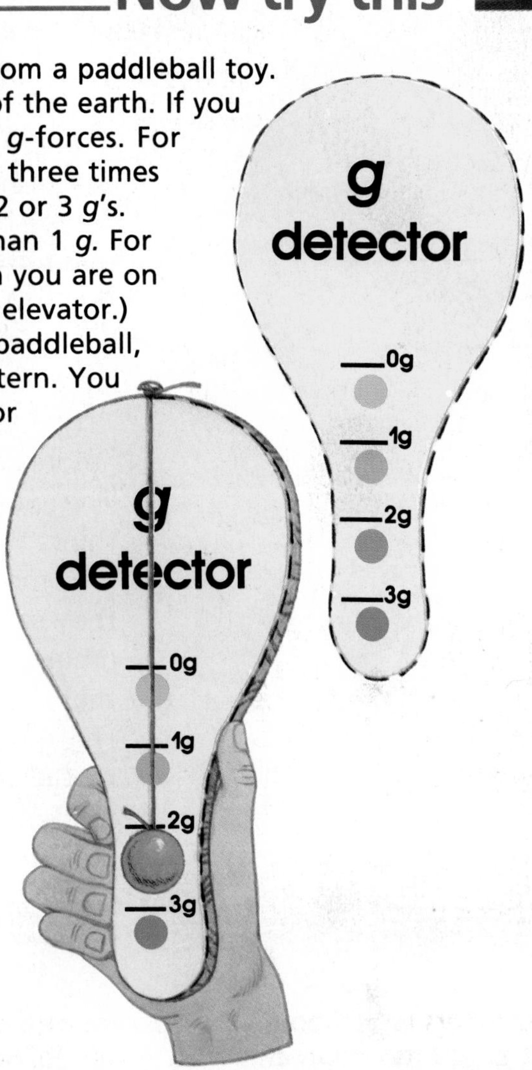

g detector

—0g
—1g
—2g
—3g

to the test. A week of Space Camp is an experience not soon forgotten. For some people it may be the beginning of a lifetime career—that of astronaut. Is space travel in your future?

In this chapter you will follow the exploration of space from early times to the present. You will also learn about future plans for using and exploring space.

Exploring from Earth

How do people on Earth gather information about space?

Astronomy (ə stron'ə mē) is the study of space and the many things it contains. Astronomy began when people first looked at the sky. Early people discovered many things about the sky. For example, they found that a star's location with respect to other stars does not seem to change. They also found that certain stars were seen during certain seasons.

People noticed that a few objects seemed to move among the stars. They called these objects planets. The word *planet* means "wanderer." Why, do you think, was this name used?

Some people developed models to explain what they saw. Ptolemy (tol'ə mē), an early Greek astronomer, developed one of the first models. He taught that the sun, stars, and planets moved around Earth. His model was accepted for many centuries. This model was replaced in the 1500s by a sun-centered model. This model was developed by Copernicus (kə pėr'nə kəs).

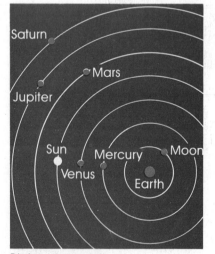

Ptolemy's model

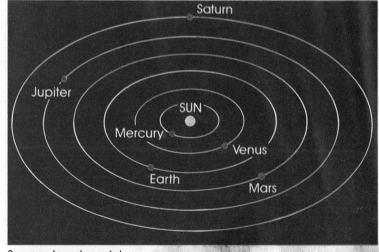

Sun-centered model

The first astronomers did not have special tools to help them study the sky. They had only their eyes to use in gathering information. Over the years, however, many tools have been developed to study the sky. One of the most useful of these tools is the telescope. Galileo (gal ə lā′ō) was the first person to use a telescope to study the sky.

The most common telescope is the optical telescope. This telescope collects light from distant objects. The light forms an image, which is then magnified. There are two kinds of optical telescope. One kind uses a glass lens to gather light. It is called a **refracting telescope.** This was the type of telescope used by Galileo. The other kind uses a curved mirror to gather light. It is called a **reflecting telescope.** Each kind uses a lens to magnify the image. Compare the refracting telescope and reflecting telescope shown here.

Reflecting telescope

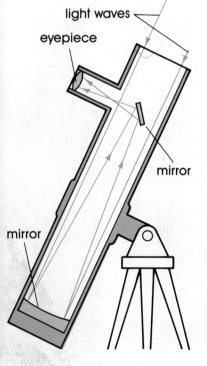

Refracting telescope

309

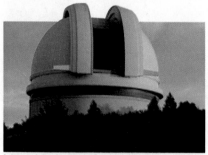

Mount Palomar Observatory

Observatory telescope

Modern telescopes are housed inside large domes that have sliding panels in the roof. These buildings are called **observatories** (əb zër′və tôr ēz). Most modern telescopes are computer-controlled. They can be focused on any part of the sky and then follow an object for several hours. Modern telescopes may also have camera attachments. Photographs taken provide permanent records for the astronomers.

All the telescopes discussed so far are optical telescopes. One problem with an optical telescope is that clouds, dust, and air pollution can prevent scientists from using them.

Another type of telescope is the **radio telescope.** A radio telescope "listens" to outer space. It can probe farther into space than an optical telescope can. Another advantage is that a radio telescope can be used even when clouds, dust, or air pollution are present.

Radio telescopes collect radio waves that are given off by objects in space. Scientists have learned that many objects in space give off both light and radio waves. Some objects give off only radio waves.

Linear array telescope

Dish radio telescope

There are two main types of radio telescopes. A dish radio telescope is named for its shape. It may be pointed in one direction or steered to observe any part of the sky. A second type of radio telescope is called a linear array telescope. This type of telescope consists of a long line of antennas.

Science & Technology

Various wavelengths of electromagnetic radiation are given off by objects in the universe. Many of these wavelengths are absorbed or distorted by the earth's atmosphere. This limits what can be learned about the universe by using telescopes on the earth. Scientists have found that the best place to study space is from space itself. Some telescopes already in orbit can sense gamma rays, X rays, and ultraviolet and infrared radiation, as well as the wavelengths of visible light. Observations made in these wavelengths of the electromagnetic spectrum have provided data on the structure of stars, galaxies, and the cosmos. One of a new generation of space telescopes is shown in the drawing. It will be the most powerful optical telescope ever built. When placed into orbit, this telescope will give astronomers a new eye on the universe. It is designed to explore the universe in the wavelengths of visible and ultraviolet light. With this telescope, astronomers expect to see 7 times farther into space than was previously possible. Perhaps they may be able to see to the edge of the visible universe. They expect to see quasars and galaxies. Stars may be seen that are 50 times fainter than those seen by the most powerful telescope on the earth. From the data they get, scientists hope to learn how the universe is changing. More importantly, they hope to learn how those changes will affect the earth.

For Lesson Questions, turn to page 408.

Activity

How does a radio telescope work?

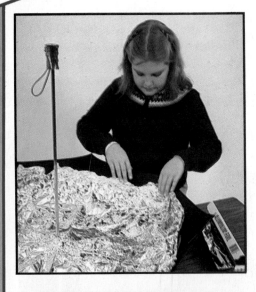

Materials umbrella / heavy-duty aluminum foil / transistor radio

Procedure

A. Open an umbrella, and line the inside with aluminum foil.

B. Place a transistor radio on your desk. Find a station that comes in weakly on the radio. Turn the radio until you get the best possible reception from this station.

C. Hold the umbrella behind the radio. The foil should face the incoming radio waves.

D. Move the umbrella to find the best reception.
  1. Why, do you think, did the radio reception improve?

E. Now find a strong station on the radio.

F. Hold the umbrella between the radio and the incoming waves. The foil should face the waves.
  2. What happened to the reception?

Conclusion

1. Why does a radio telescope have a large dish shape?
2. What is the function of the aluminum foil in this activity?

Using science ideas

Why are radio telescopes usually located away from large cities?

Exploring from Space

How is space explored using rockets and satellites?

Scientists continue to study space from Earth's surface. But the earth's atmosphere prevents scientists from getting a completely clear view of distant bodies. Because of this, scientists also send objects out into space to gather data.

Rockets are used to launch objects into space. A rocket must have enough power to overcome Earth's gravity. A rocket overcomes this force by burning a large amount of fuel. The fuel is burned in a **combustion chamber.** This is an enclosed chamber with an opening at the bottom. As the fuel burns, hot gas is produced. The gas pushes on the sides of the chamber, as shown in the drawing.

Gas pushes on the top of the chamber but not on the bottom. This is because the bottom end is open, allowing the gas to escape. The force against the top of the chamber is not opposed by a force against the bottom. So the rocket moves up.

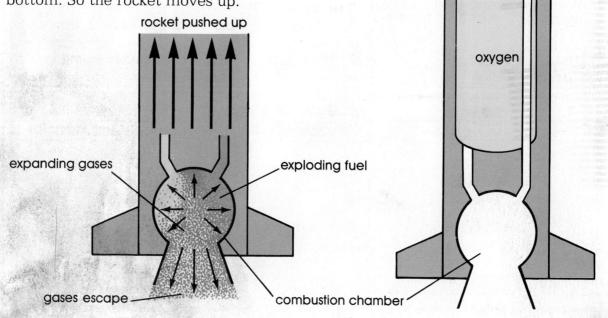

rocket pushed up

expanding gases

exploding fuel

gases escape

combustion chamber

control systems

fuel

oxygen

Sputnik 1 (model)

Satellites were among the first objects launched into space by rockets. A **satellite** is an object that travels in an orbit around another object in space. In order for a satellite to go into orbit, it must travel fast enough to escape the earth's gravity. A rocket enables the satellite to do this. A rocket must go faster than 40,000 km/h to escape Earth's gravity. After releasing the satellite, the rocket usually falls back to Earth. To stay in an earth orbit, a satellite must travel at a speed of about 28,000 km/h.

The first satellite to be placed in orbit was Sputnik I, which was launched in 1957 by the Soviet Union. Explorer I was the first United States satellite. It was sent into space in 1958.

Both of these satellites provided scientists with valuable information. Sputnik I sent back data on the temperature of space. Explorer I discovered that Earth is surrounded by radiation belts. Later satellites studied Earth's magnetic field, took pictures of the sun, and gathered data on meteorites.

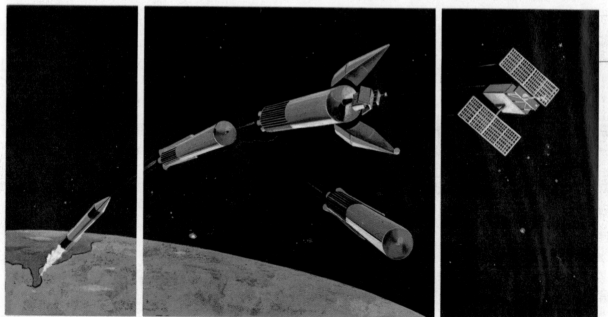

Rocket launch   Rocket falls back to Earth   Satellite enters orbit

Activity

How does a rocket move?

Materials fishing line / meterstick or metric tape / scissors / drinking straw / masking tape / balloon / twist tie

Procedure

A. Do this activity with a partner. Cut a 5-m length of fishing line. Attach one end of the fishing line to a door handle or an object of similar height.

B. Blow up a balloon. Attach a twist tie to the end so that air will not escape.

C. Tape a drinking straw to the balloon. The balloon and straw make up your rocket.

   1. Which part represents the combustion chamber?

D. Slide the loose end of the fishing line through the drinking straw.

E. Hold the string tight and in a straight line. Remove the twist tie. Observe how your rocket moves.

   2. How far did your rocket travel?
   3. How can you make your rocket travel farther?

F. Repeat the activity. Try to make your rocket travel farther.

   4. How far did it travel?

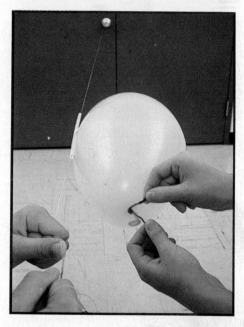

Conclusion

1. What makes your rocket move?
2. Why did your rocket move farther the second time it was launched?

Using science ideas

Make a rocket-powered car or boat. Test your rocket-powered vehicle.

Satellites are also used for purposes other than exploring space. For example, Landsat satellites are used to give scientists information about Earth. Each Landsat contains special cameras. The cameras can detect areas of pollution on Earth. They can also show where minerals may be found. Landsat pictures can even help farmers estimate how large their harvests will be. The Landsat picture on the left shows the area around Phoenix, Arizona. The red in the picture on the right shows cornfields in Nebraska and Iowa.

Landsat picture of Arizona

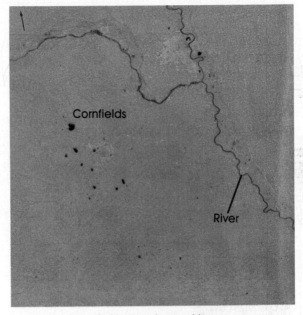

Landsat picture of Nebraska and Iowa

Some satellites are used to study weather. Weather satellites take pictures of Earth. Such pictures show where storms are located and how they are moving. These data help scientists forecast the weather for several days. Weather satellites keep watch on the weather all around the world.

Satellites are also used to send signals. One kind of satellite just reflects radio signals from one place on Earth to another. For example, such a satellite might

IRAS

Communications satellite

reflect telephone signals. These satellites are placed in orbit at the same speed as the rotating earth. By traveling at this speed, they always remain above the same location on Earth.

Another kind of satellite receives radio waves and strengthens them. The waves can then be beamed to Earth or recorded for later use. One of the most famous satellites of this kind is Telstar. Telstar made possible the first TV broadcast across the Atlantic Ocean. Today, satellites can transmit live TV broadcasts almost anywhere in the world.

One of the most successful satellites was the Infrared Astronomical Satellite, or IRAS. Before it stopped working in November 1983, IRAS discovered five new comets, three rings of dust in the solar system, thousands of new asteroids, and hundreds of thousands of new stars. One of the more interesting things IRAS discovered was what is believed to be a new solar system, around the star Vega. Once scientists have finished studying information gathered by IRAS, scientists believe that 50 other new solar systems may be found.

Rockets are also used to launch spacecraft that do not go into Earth orbit. Instead these craft are sent out to gather data on the moon and the planets. Such spacecraft are called **space probes.**

American probes sent to Venus sent back data about that planet's atmosphere. Two Viking probes launched by the United States tested the air and soil of Mars. In addition the Viking probes conducted experiments to search for life in the soil of Mars.

Two Voyager probes have been launched by the United States. The path of Voyager 2 is shown here. Both probes took close-up pictures of Jupiter and Saturn. The pictures showed moons that had never before been seen around these planets. The Voyagers also sent back close-up pictures of Saturn's rings.

In 1986, Voyager 2 passed Uranus. It located at least 10 new moons and several new rings. From data the probe sent to Earth, scientists found that the magnetic field around Uranus wobbles. They also found that Uranus gives off an ultraviolet glow.

Voyager 2 will reach Neptune in 1989. Toward the end of this century, both probes will leave our solar system. Each Voyager spacecraft contains recordings of sounds on Earth, messages in different languages, and pictures of Earth scenes. These are messages to whatever living beings find the probes.

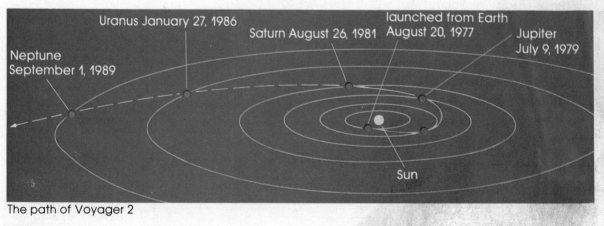

The path of Voyager 2

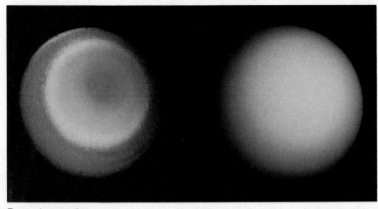

Two views of Uranus

An interesting and unique use of space probes involved Halley's Comet. Several space probes from many countries studied the comet. One space probe, called Giotto, was launched by the European Space Agency. This probe came within 500 km of the comet's head. Information from all of the space probes was shared by the various countries. This international effort provided scientists around the world with an enormous amount of information about comets.

SKILLS: Communicating, Interpreting data

Finding Out

What did we learn about comets from space probes?

Scientists learned a great deal of new information about comets by studying Halley's Comet. Much of this information came from the space probes that were sent by different countries. Use magazines and newspapers from late 1985 and 1986 to find out about this international space program. Which countries took part in the program? What space probes were used? How close did each space probe come to Halley's Comet? What did scientists learn from the space probes?

319

For Lesson Questions, turn to page 408.

People in Space

What kinds of activities are performed by people in space?

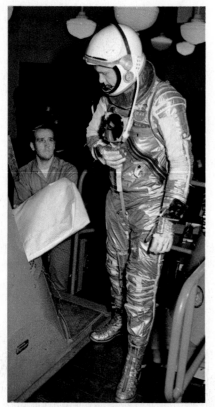
John Glenn

The first person in space was Yuri Gagarin, a Soviet astronaut. The first American in space was Alan Shepard, in 1961. He flew in the space capsule *Freedom 7* as part of the Mercury space program. The first American to orbit Earth was John Glenn, in 1962. Glenn orbited Earth three times during his flight.

One of the goals of the American space program was to find out if people could live in space. Scientists wondered how weightlessness would affect the astronauts' muscles and bones. So far, it seems that calcium is lost from the bones during time spent in space. Astronauts who remain in space for long periods may lose some strength in their muscles. Special exercise programs help to correct these problems.

An early goal of the American space program was to send astronauts to the surface of the moon. This program was called Project Apollo. A new rocket, the Saturn V, was developed for the Apollo project. The Saturn V was the largest rocket ever built. With the Apollo spacecraft on top, the rocket stood almost 120 m high and weighed about 3 million kg.

The first landing on the moon was in 1969. A Saturn rocket launched on Apollo spacecraft carrying three astronauts into Earth orbit. The spacecraft then carried the astronauts to the moon, a three-day journey. Two of the astronauts landed on the moon, in a vehicle called the lunar module. The third remained in the Apollo spacecraft orbiting the moon. The astronauts on the moon's surface gathered samples and took measurements. They then returned to the Apollo spacecraft to journey home. In all, the United States has sent 12 astronauts to the moon's surface.

Astronaut in weightless state

Skylab

In the 1970s the United States launched Skylab. Skylab was an orbiting space laboratory. Astronauts traveled to and from Skylab in an Apollo spacecraft. Three astronauts could occupy Skylab for as long as 3 months. The Skylab astronauts performed many experiments, including observing and taking measurements of Earth and the sun. Three teams of astronauts worked aboard Skylab during its lifetime.

America's space shuttle flights began in 1981. The space shuttle is the first reusable space vehicle. Twin rockets help to boost the shuttle into space. The rockets then parachute to Earth and are recovered to be used again. The shuttle can remain in orbit for as long as 2 weeks. It can carry a crew of seven. After completing its mission, the shuttle returns to Earth. Since its has wings, it lands much like an airplane. The shuttle can then be flown again. Why is a reusable space vehicle helpful in the exploration of space?

The shuttle can carry satellites into space. The crew members can then launch the satellites into separate orbits. With the shuttle, the cost of launching satellites has been reduced.

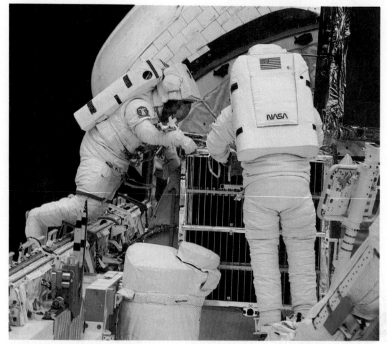

Solar Max being repaired

The shuttle can also retrieve satellites from orbit. These can then be repaired and placed back into orbit. In 1984 the satellite Solar Max was spinning uselessly in orbit. Astronauts were able to leave the shuttle and fix the satellite. To do this, they first had to "capture" the satellite. After the satellite is retrieved, it is put in the cargo bay of the shuttle. There it can be repaired or carried back to Earth to be repaired.

On January 28, 1986, the twenty-fifth mission of the space shuttle was launched. The spacecraft, known as Challenger, had a crew of seven men and women. One minute and 15 seconds after the launch the spacecraft exploded. All seven crew members were killed. This was the first time since 1967 that astronauts had died in the U.S. space program.

The Challenger tragedy reminded everyone that space travel can be dangerous. A study of the rocket boosters showed that there was a leak in the seal joining the boosters. The effect of this accident will be felt by the American space program for many years.

322

For Lesson Questions, turn to page 408.

The Future of Space

How will space be explored and used in the future?

It is likely that people will increase their activities in space in the future. For example, space stations will allow people to work in space for many months. Some scientists aboard the stations will gather data about space. Others might experiment with new alloys or find ways to make new products. The space stations might serve as launching pads for other spacecraft.

Space colonies may also be developed in orbit. A colony might be made up of several large space stations. Some of the people living in the colony might run factories to produce goods in space. Others might be involved in mining on the moon or on asteroids. The minerals could be sent to Earth or used in the space factories to produce goods.

Mining in space

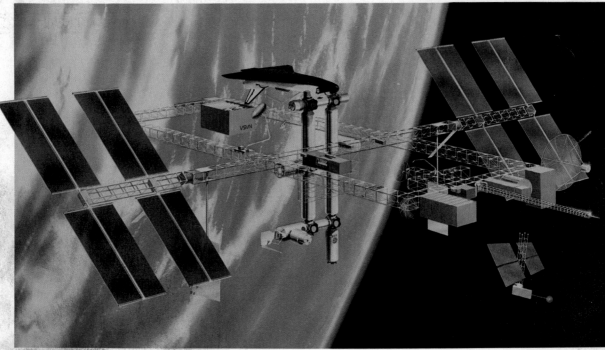

Space station

Space shuttles could also be used to build power plants in space. Such power plants would collect solar energy. The energy would then be beamed to Earth, in the form of waves. These waves would be changed to electricity.

Hospitals may be built in space in the future. Some doctors believe that such hospitals could provide special care for patients with certain illnesses. In space there is no feeling of weight. Heart patients could benefit from this because their hearts would not have to work as hard. Patients with burns would not have to lie in bed on their injuries. They could float freely in their weightless condition. Some doctors feel that this would help burns heal faster.

At some time, people may move beyond the orbit of Earth to live and work. Colonies might be set up on the moon or on Mars. These colonies would be like cities beyond Earth. Such a city might grow up around an observatory or a laboratory on another planet. In the future, people may live not only on the planet Earth but also elsewhere in the solar system.

Power plant in space

Lunar city

For Lesson Questions, turn to page 408.

How Space Exploration Affects You

How has the exploration of space changed people's lives on Earth?

It is possible that you will be a space traveler. However, whether or not you travel in space, the space age is affecting your life in many ways. For instance, materials that were developed for the space program are now used in many products here on Earth. These products are called "spin-offs" of space research.

Some clothlike fabrics that were developed for the space program have proved useful on Earth. For example, a lightweight fabric that reflects light and heat was used in the construction of a satellite. This material is now used to make emergency blankets.

Fabrics used in space suits are also being used for other purposes. Fabric roofs have been built over sports stadiums and department stores. A fabric roof is light in weight and can help to keep the enclosed area cool. In addition, fabric roofs are low in cost.

Space-suit fabric has also been used in new types of fire-fighting outfits. The new outfits will not burn or melt. They are waterproof, yet allow body heat and body moisture to pass out.

Much of the early work on tiny circuits was done for the space program. Computers and other electronic devices aboard a spacecraft must be small and light in weight. So miniature circuits were developed for these devices. Today such tiny circuits are used in microcomputers, calculators, electronic games, and many other products that you learned about earlier.

The food industry now uses some of the methods that were developed to keep food fresh during space flights. These methods produce good-tasting food that does not spoil at room temperature. The powdered and freeze-dried foods available today are produced by these methods.

Special materials for cooking food have also come from the space program. These materials do not crack when heated or frozen. Therefore they make very sturdy dishes for cooking and freezing food. Food can be stored in these dishes in the freezer. The dishes can then be put into a hot oven, right from the freezer.

A unit that purifies water on the space shuttle has been adapted for use on Earth. The new water filter can be attached to a faucet. It can kill bacteria in the

Freeze-dried foods

water. It can also remove chemicals that cause water to taste bad.

The space program has even produced recreation products. For example, have you ever seen someone hang gliding? Hang gliders were developed from a special wing that was first made to recover space-craft.

Paramedics

The space program has led to new medical products. One of these is a medical unit in a briefcase. The unit is designed for use by a paramedic. It can be used to check a person's vital signs, such as pulse and blood pressure. It can also be used to restore normal heart-beat in a person whose heart is not beating properly. The unit contains a two-way radio. So a paramedic treating a patient can contact a doctor for instructions. This new medical unit was developed from one that is used to check the health of astronauts.

Many other products have resulted from research in the space program. These include a new welding tool, a new forestry vehicle, and a new camera. New products will continue to be developed in the future.

Ideas to Remember

▶ Telescopes on Earth are used to gather data about space.
▶ Satellites are used to study both space and our own planet.
▶ Space probes have been sent to gather data about the moon and the planets.
▶ People travel in space. Some have explored the moon. Others perform experiments, test products, and gather data while in space.
▶ People may live and work in space in the future.
▶ Many products now in use on Earth were developed as a result of the space program.

For Lesson Questions, turn to page 408.

Reviewing the Chapter

SCIENCE WORDS

A. Copy the sentences below. Use science words from the chapter to complete the sentences.

1. The study of space and the things it contains is called _____.
2. A/An _____ is a telescope that uses a glass lens.
3. A/An _____ is a telescope that uses a curved mirror.
4. A building that contains a telescope and that is set up to study space is called a/an _____.
5. Objects called _____ are placed into orbit to study the earth.
6. Rockets are used to launch _____ from the earth to gather data about the moon and the planets.
7. A rocket overcomes gravity by burning fuel in a/an _____.
8. In the future, people might live and work in space for months at a time while staying in _____.

B. Identify each of the following.

1. What is the name of the first device used to send satellites into space?
2. What is the name of the spacecraft that can be recovered and reused?
3. What is any object that orbits another object in space called?
4. What is the name of the space probe that landed on Mars?
5. What is the name of the spacecraft that carried people to the moon?

UNDERSTANDING IDEAS

A. Describe ways in which the exploration of space has changed people's lives on Earth.

B. Explain the difference between the terms.

1. space probe, satellite
2. space station, space colony
3. rocket, combustion chamber
4. optical telescope, radio telescope
5. dish radio telescopes, linear array telescope

C. Describe ways in which people may use space in the future.

D. Describe three everyday materials or products that are spin-offs from space research.

E. Drawings of four kinds of telescopes are shown. Identify the refracting telescope, the reflecting telescope, the linear array radio telescope and the dish radio telescope.

USING IDEAS

1. Collect newspaper articles about space exploration. Place them in a scrapbook. Include a short summary about the content of each article.

2. Using scientific information and your imagination, create a detailed drawing or write a short story about a space colony of your own design.

THINKING LIKE A SCIENTIST

Answer the following questions. You may be able to answer some of the questions just by thinking about them. To answer other questions, you may have to do some research.

1. NASA scientists try to anticipate problems in space exploration. One of the problems they try to avoid involves sleeping. In space there is no day or night. However, astronauts maintain the same sleep schedule they had on the earth. Why is this important?

2. Scientists consider as much information as possible before making a decision. Why, do you think, did scientists choose Florida as a site for launching spacecraft?

3. One problem with living in the weightless environment of outer space is eating. Food floats off dishes and spoons and liquids float out of cups. How can these problems be solved? Design a device, such as a container for a liquid or a spoon, that can be used in space.

Science in Careers

There are many careers in the fields of earth science and space science. Most of the jobs are highly technical and require advanced training. But some jobs require only on-the-job training.

Geologists study the structure of the earth itself. Some geologists study patterns of earthquake or volcanic activity. Others are involved in locating deposits of fossil fuels.

Many **meteorologists** work for the government. The National Oceanic and Atmospheric Administration (NOAA) employs meteorologists at weather stations all across the United States. The meteorologists take weather measurements and then prepare weather forecasts. Commercial airlines also employ meteorologists.

Petroleum geologist

Astronomers often combine research at observatories with teaching astronomy at the college level. Some astronomers work for the National Aeronautics and Space Administration (NASA). They may be involved in the study of the solar system. Their work some-

Meteorologist

times includes analyzing data sent back by space probes. Other astronomers are interested in the study of objects deep in space, such as distant galaxies. Such astronomers do much of their work at observatories located around the country. As you can see, earth science and space science offer a variety of opportunities.

People in Science

JAKOB BJERKNES
(1897 – 1975)

Jakob was born in Stockholm, Sweden. His father, Vilhelm, was a famous meteorologist. Vilhelm identified air masses and fronts as causes of changes in weather. Jakob became a meteorologist, too. He went on to study the conditions and movements of air masses and fronts. Jakob and Vilhelm worked out the idea of polar fronts. Jakob was the first person to suggest the existence of jet streams.

The movement of a hurricane can be predicted

Developing Skills

WORD SKILLS

Many English words come from Latin, Greek, and other languages. If you know the meanings of words in other languages, you can often understand the meanings of English words. The tables list word parts that come from other languages and give their meanings.

Use the tables for help in writing a definition for each of the following words. You can do this by breaking each word into parts. For example, the word *lithosphere* is made of these parts: *litho- + sphere*. Check your definitions by finding the meanings of the words in a dictionary.

1. lithosphere   2. asteroid
3. cosmology   4. agronomy
5. paleontology 6. luminous

Word part	Meaning
agro-	of fields, soil
aster-	star
cosmo-	universe
litho-	stone
lumin-	light
pale-	old, ancient
-onto-	organism

Word part	Meaning
sphere	ball, globe
-logy	science of
-nomy	knowledge of
-oid	like
-ous	full of
-scope	for seeing

READING A PICTOGRAPH

A pictograph uses symbols to show information. The pictograph on the next page shows the effects of acidity on different kinds of water animals. The graph indicates in what range of acidity different kinds of animals can survive. Use the pictograph to answer the following questions.

1. In what range of acidity can smallmouth bass survive?

2. Which of the animals has the greatest survival range?

3. Which of the animals has the smallest range?

4. Which animal has the greater range, lake trout or brown trout?

5. Which animals can survive in water with a pH of 4.5?

6. What is the range of acidity in which yellow perch can survive?

7. Write down how many hours you have done homework each day for the past seven days. Use this data to make a pictograph. What symbol did you use for your pictograph?

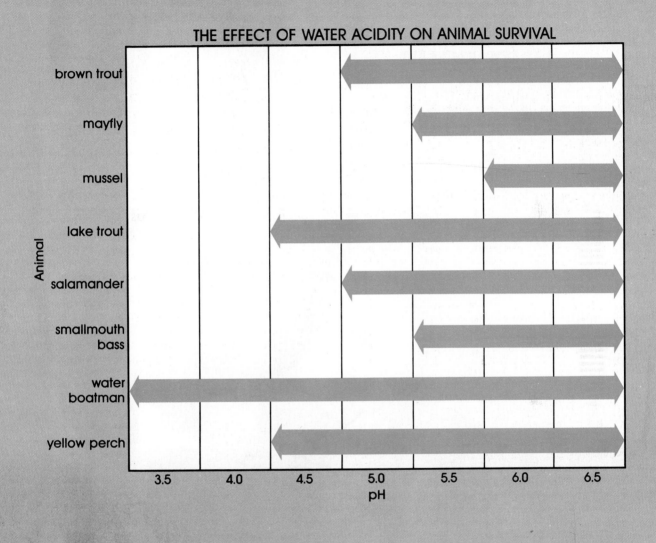

THE EFFECT OF WATER ACIDITY ON ANIMAL SURVIVAL

USING THINKING SKILLS

Acid rain may be one of the biggest pollution problems today. Acid rain results from the addition of certain chemicals to the air. These chemicals change to acids and fall to the ground as rain and snow. In most eastern states the rain has a pH of about 4.5. Some scientists think that acid rain is causing many eastern lakes to become too acidic. Think about this as you do the following.

1. Use a reference book to find out some possible causes of acid rain.
2. What, if anything, should be done about acid rain? Explain your answer.

UNIT FOUR

Investigating the Human Body

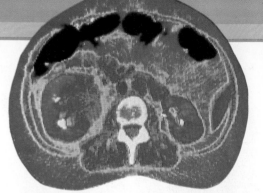

Chapter 14—Control Systems of the Body The nervous and endocrine systems play major roles in this athlete's performance. The spinal cord, seen here in cross section, is an important part of the nervous system.

Chapter 15 — Growth and Development A person begins life as a single cell. In some ways that cell is alike in all people. Yet in many ways, it also is quite different. In this chapter you will find out why people who are related to each other may look more alike than do people who are not related. Also, you will learn how a person changes at various stages in life, from birth to adulthood.

335

CHAPTER 14
Control Systems of the Body

Little 6-year-old Brittney Blye dove into the icy water to save her friend Tara Turchetti. Tara had fallen through the ice of a partly frozen pond. Both girls quickly slipped down into the cold depths. When the rescue workers came to pull the girls out of the water, Brittney and Tara were not breathing. They showed no heartbeat. Their skin was blue. Were these two girls drowning victims? No. Brittney, shown in the inset on the next page, soon recovered. After a slightly longer time, Tara also recovered.

What accounts for the happy ending of this near tragedy? The girls were in danger of drowning. To keep them alive, their bodies' control systems took over. Both girls underwent something called the diving reflex. The diving reflex is a response to very cold water. The reflex begins when the face, especially the forehead and nose, is hit by very cold water. The reflex will not continue unless the person is also under the pressure of water. The cold water and high pressure of the water cause many things to happen. The lungs shut down and the heart is slowed. Blood is sent only to the vital organs—the brain and heart.

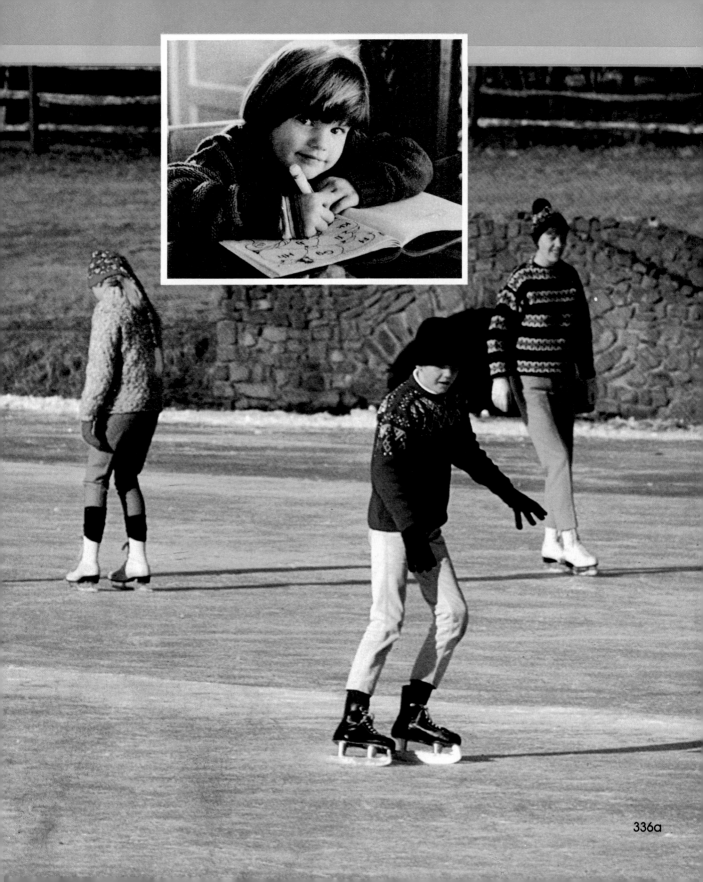

Right now you may be struggling with two questions: Isn't it true that a person cannot survive more than a few minutes without oxygen? Won't a person suffer brain damage without oxygen? Often the answer to these questions is yes. But with the diving reflex, precious oxygen goes only to the body parts where it is most needed. The heart and brain receive blood and oxygen. This reflex can save a person's life.

The diving reflex is more likely to occur in some people than in others. It occurs most often in young people. The reflex is strongest in infants and weakest in old people. Yet there are adults who have survived because of the reflex. These people have lived even though they have not breathed for many minutes underwater.

The diving reflex is more likely to occur in cold weather than in warm. In warm weather the water

1. *Cold water strikes the forehead and nose. Nerve signals are sent to the brain.*

2. *The brain sends information to the base of the brain, known as the brain stem.*

3. *The brain stem sends signals along a nerve to the chest. The breathing rate is then slowed down.*

4. *Signals are sent along this same nerve. The heartbeat is then slowed down a great deal.*

5. *Signals are sent to nerves in the arms, legs, and skin. Signals are also sent to digestive organs. Blood is sent mainly to the brain, heart, and lungs.*

Work with a partner. You will need a house key. Have your partner remove one shoe. Students wearing a heavy sock should remove the sock. Have your partner lie down on the floor or on a table. Stroke the key across the bottom of your partner's foot. (See the drawing.) How does your partner respond? Change places. Have your partner stroke the key across the bottom of your foot. How do you respond? How do you think the other foot would respond?

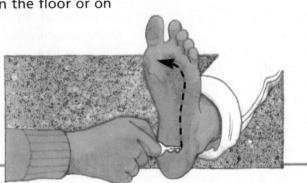

temperature is likely to be high. In general the diving reflex is triggered by a fall into cold water. But the reflex can occur when a person begins to drown in warm water. What matters most is the temperature of the water into which a person *sinks*. Even in warm weather the person may sink into a pocket of cold water. This cold water may set off the diving reflex.

Suppose the diving reflex has been triggered. People are more likely to survive if they are not underwater long. The shorter the time underwater, the greater the chance a person will survive. However, there are people who have survived after being underwater for up to 40 minutes.

Dr. Martin Nemiroff is an expert on the diving reflex. He believes that many people die without cause each year. There are about 1,000 cold-water drownings each year in the United States. In many cases the victim is declared dead at the scene. But knowledge of the diving reflex might save many of these lives. Rescuers must learn about the diving reflex. They might save many people by doing cardiopulmonary resuscitation (CPR). This is a technique for restoring heart and lung function. CPR can often save the life of a "dead" drowning victim.

You will probably never undergo the diving reflex described in the story. But when you were a baby, a doctor probably tested your foot responses. This test is often done on young children. The ways in which you respond are controlled by the nervous system. In this chapter you will learn about the nervous system and another control system of the body.

The Nervous System

What are the parts of the nervous system?

Why are these champion volleyball players winners? It is because while they are playing, they think and act almost as if they were one person. The eyes of each player follow the ball. Information about the ball is carried from the eyes to the brain. A decision about whether the ball can be reached and how to hit it is quickly made. The brain sends that message to the muscles, and the muscles respond accordingly. All of these actions are voluntary. At the same time that they are taking place, each player's heart is beating. The players are also breathing. These actions are involuntary—they happen automatically.

Both the voluntary and the involuntary actions of your body are controlled by the nervous system. The **nervous system** is made up of the brain, the spinal cord, and all the nerves of the body. It can be divided into two main parts. You can see from the drawing that the **central nervous system** is in the middle of the body. It is made up of the brain and the spinal cord.

The other part is the **peripheral** (pə rif′ər əl) **nervous system.** The word *peripheral* means "outside" or "edge." This system includes all the nerves that extend from the central nervous system to the edges of the body. It also includes all the nerves that lead from the outer parts of the body to the brain or spinal cord.

Just as with the volleyball players, some of your nerves control the actions that you must think about to do. Walking, talking, eating, and drinking are examples of such actions. They are voluntary responses controlled by messages sent from your brain to certain muscles.

Other nerves control the body activities that you do not have to think about. Breathing and heartbeat are examples of such activities. They are involuntary responses. Nerves carry messages to the heart and to muscles near the lungs. The messages are sent without your having to think about them.

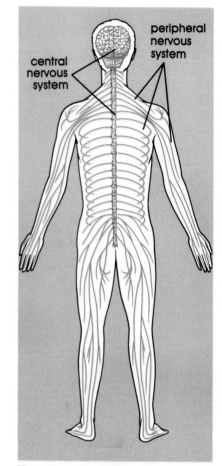

The nervous system

Voluntary muscles in action

For Lesson Questions, turn to page 410.

Nerve Cells and Nerves

What are the jobs of the three kinds of nerve cells?

How do messages travel through the nervous system? Messages move along a series of **nerve cells.** Each nerve cell has three main parts. These are shown in the drawing. One part is called the cell body. Many short fibers can be seen extending from the sides of the cell body. These fibers pick up messages and carry them to the cell body. Also extending from one side of the cell body is a single long fiber. This long fiber carries messages from the cell body to another nerve cell. Compare the drawing of a nerve cell with the nerve cells in the picture. What parts of a nerve cell can you identify in the picture?

Nerve cells are grouped in "bundles" that form nerves. This is something like the bundles of wires in a telephone cable. Nerves carry messages from parts of the body to the brain. They also carry messages from the brain to parts of the body. Nerves are various sizes. Some nerves in the fingers and toes are almost invisible. Others, like those that enter the spinal cord, are almost as thick as a pencil.

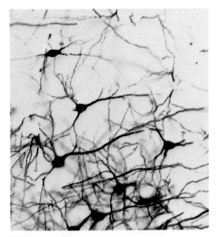

Nerve cells

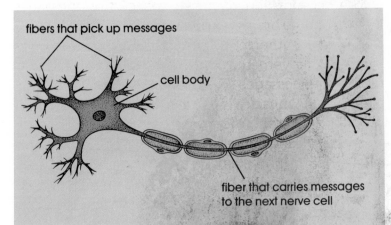

fibers that pick up messages

cell body

fiber that carries messages
to the next nerve cell

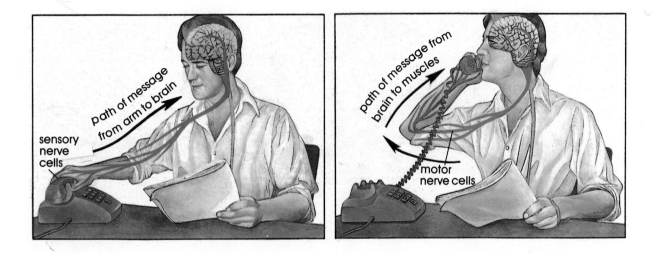

There are three main kinds of nerve cells. Each kind performs a different function. The first kind of nerve cell can respond to a stimulus from outside the body or from internal parts of the body. For example, nerve cells in the skin respond to an external stimulus such as pressure, pain, heat, and cold. When you have a stomachache, nerve cells are responding to an internal stimulus. Nerve cells that respond to an internal or external stimulus are called **sensory nerve cells.** They send messages to the brain. In the drawing the brain is receiving a message that the hand has gripped the telephone receiver.

The second kind of nerve cell carries messages away from the brain and spinal cord. These cells carry messages to other parts of the body. The messages can cause movement of the muscles. Nerve cells that carry such messages are called **motor nerve cells.** In the drawing, muscles in the arm have received a message to pick up the receiver.

The third kind of nerve cell connects sensory nerve cells to motor nerve cells. These cells are called **connecting nerve cells.** They are part of the central nervous system. That is, they are located in either the brain or the spinal cord.

Messages sometimes take shortcuts. They can by-pass the brain. For instance, you will quickly pull your hand away if you touch a hot pan. Such a reaction is called a **reflex.** A reflex is a rapid, unlearned response. You do not think about reflexes. They are automatic responses. The message travels over sensory nerve cells to your spinal cord. In the spinal cord the message passes over connecting nerve cells to motor nerve cells. You instantly remove your hand when the muscles receive messages from the motor nerve cells. A reflex can prevent serious injury. Follow the path of the message in the drawing.

(3) motor nerve cells send message to **muscles**—person pulls hand away

(1) person touches hot pan—message travels along sensory nerve cells

(2) in spinal cord, message passes over connecting nerve cell to motor nerve cells

Reflex messages allow you to respond quickly. Messages that must travel to and from the brain result in delayed reaction. The time that it takes for you to react is called **reaction time.** These basketball players must react quickly to actions around them. They need to have short reaction times.

342

For Lesson Questions, turn to page 410.

How fast is your reaction time?

Materials meterstick

Procedure

A. Do this activity with a partner. Stand facing each other. Have your partner hold the meterstick from the top end (the 100-cm mark). The meterstick should be held high.

B. Place your thumb and forefinger around the meterstick, but do not touch it. Have your fingers at the 50-cm mark.

C. Your partner will drop the meterstick without warning. Try to catch it with your thumb and forefinger.
   1. At what mark did you catch it?

D. Find the distance the meterstick fell by subtracting 50 cm from the mark at which you caught it. This is a measurement of your reaction time.
   2. Record this measurement.

E. Repeat the activity four more times.
   3. Record each measurement.

Results

Graph your reaction time (the distance the meterstick fell) versus the number of times you tried the activity.

Conclusion

How did your reaction time change with practice?

Using science ideas

1. How does a fast reaction time help a person when playing games or riding a bicycle?
2. What other reaction times do you think can be improved by practice? Give examples.
3. Name some animals that depend on fast reaction times for survival.

343

The Brain and Spinal Cord

What are the functions of the three main parts of the brain?

There are two parts to the central nervous system. They are the brain and the spinal cord. The central nervous system receives as well as sends messages to all parts of the body.

The brain is the most important part of the nervous system. It is made up of delicate nerve tissue. The brain of an adult weighs about 1.5 kg. The brain is enclosed in the skull which helps to protect it from damage. Between the brain and the skull, there is a thin layer of liquid. This liquid, which covers the brain, acts like a shock absorber. It further protects the brain from damage that might result from a hard blow to the head.

The brain has three main parts. As you can see in the drawing, they are the brain stem, the cerebellum (ser ə bel'əm), and the cerebrum (ser'ə brəm). The **brain stem** is the part of the brain that connects with the spinal cord. It controls many involuntary actions,

cerebrum
- controls thinking, reasoning, problem-solving, and memory
- each half controls the opposite half of the body

cerebellum
- controls body balance
- coordinates muscle movement

brain stem
- controls involuntary actions

such as breathing and heartbeat. It is also the control center for actions such as sneezing, coughing, and blinking.

The **cerebellum** is found above and behind the brain stem. The main function of the cerebellum is to control body balance and the movements of muscles.

The cerebellum sends messages to the correct sets of muscles so that they work together. When you catch a ball, the muscles of your eyes, arms, and hands must work together. Your cerebellum coordinates the movements of these muscles.

The largest and most important part of the brain is the **cerebrum.** In fact it makes up about 80 percent of the brain. It is divided into a right half and a left half. The right half controls the left side of the body. The left half controls the right side.

Look at the pictures. What parts of the brain are being used by the person in each picture?

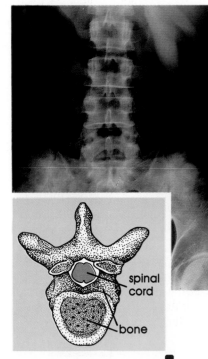

spinal cord

bone

The outer layer of the cerebrum has many deep folds and ridges. It looks something like a large walnut. This arrangement allows a great amount of nerve tissue to fit in the skull. In fact, half of the nerves in the body are located in the cerebrum. Thinking, reasoning, problem solving, and memory are controlled by the cerebrum. As mentioned earlier, the cerebrum is the largest part of your brain. In some wild animals, however, the cerebellum is large and the cerebrum is small. Why is it important that your cerebrum is large?

Messages travel to and from the brain along the spinal cord. The spinal cord is made up of bundles of nerve cells. The tissue of the spinal cord is soft and delicate. The drawing shows how the backbone completely surrounds and protects the spinal cord. Why is this protection necessary? Nerves from all parts of the body are connected to the spinal cord.

SKILLS: Making a model, Interpreting data

Finding Out

How do folds and ridges increase the brain's surface area?

Get a sheet of aluminum foil that is 50 cm square. If you do not have an extra-wide roll of foil, you can tape two pieces together. Be sure to cut them to the right size. This sheet is about the size of the outer layer of your brain if it were smoothed out. It is 2,500 square centimeters (cm^2).

Now find a medium-size plastic bowl. It should be a little smaller than your head. A whipped-topping container — the 340-g size — is just right. It will be about the size of your brain.

Fit the sheet of foil around the bowl. Fold and pinch the foil so that it covers the outside surface of the bowl. How does this show how a large amount of brain tissue can fit inside your skull?

For Lesson Questions, turn to page 410.

How good is your memory?

Materials   watch or clock with a second hand

Procedure

A. Do this activity with a partner. Have your partner hold up your book so that you can see Chart 1. Try to memorize the list of nonsense words. Your partner will give you 30 seconds to do this.

B. Try to write down the nonsense words in the correct order from memory.
  1. How many nonsense words did you remember?

C. Repeat the procedure, using Chart 2.
  2. How many words did you remember?

D. Repeat the procedure, using Chart 3.
  3. How many words did you remember?

Conclusion

1. Which chart was the easiest to memorize? Why do you think it was easiest?
2. Which chart was the hardest to memorize? Why do you think it was hardest?

Using science ideas

1. Make a chart containing 10 three-digit numbers. Repeat the activity with this chart. Is it easier to remember numbers or words?
2. People sometimes use a "memory aid" to help them remember certain facts. For example, the name ROY G BIV may be used to remember the order of the colors in the light spectrum. The letters that spell ROY G BIV are the first letter of each color in the spectrum in the correct order. Why would this memory aid be a help in remembering the colors and their order?

Chart 1
wot
lom
eam
zel
kac
nik
bem
gur
fam
pon

Chart 2
milk
kitten
house
jump
school
many
star
work
sail
pen

Chart 3
only
a
scientific
people
can
survive
in
a
scientific
future

347

Disorders of the Nervous System

What are three problems of the nervous system?

You know by now how important your nervous system is. Problems with parts of the nervous system can be very serious. A cut finger will heal, but an injury to the spinal cord may never heal. Since the nervous system is the body's control center, damage to it can affect other parts of the body.

The brain may become diseased. Fortunately, however, brain tissue itself does not have nerves that receive pain messages. Therefore, most diseases of the brain do not cause pain. The spinal cord can be damaged by an accident or an infection. Either trouble may cause paralysis. *Paralysis* means that one or more parts of the body cannot move.

Cerebral palsy (ser′ə brəl pôl′ze) is a disorder of the brain. It may result from infection or injury to the part of the brain that controls the movement of muscles. A person with cerebral palsy has trouble moving. He or she may also have trouble speaking. This is

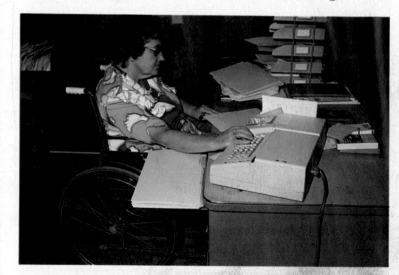

Therapy for cerebral palsy

because the muscles do not work together. There is no cure for this disorder. But training can help a person with cerebral palsy lead a nearly normal life.

Drugs that are misused affect the nervous system, too. They may destroy the natural way the brain handles the messages it receives. A person who misuses drugs may not be able to think normally. He or she may see things that are not there and hear sounds when there are no sounds. The parts of the body may not work together as they should. Drugs should be used only according to directions on the label.

For Lesson Questions, turn to page 410.

Science & Technology

Computers are helping people to walk. This Ohio woman, paralyzed from the ribs down, is walking with the aid of a computer. Wires are used to connect the computer to muscles in her legs. The computer then triggers bursts of electricity that cause the muscles to work properly. The lower picture shows the woman with the computer-controlled walking system in 1982. Due to its size, the system could be used only in one location. Since then, many changes have been made in the system. It is now portable and more efficient. The upper picture shows the woman walking with the new system. Because it is portable, it can be worn as she moves around her kitchen, fixing lunch or washing dishes. She even wore it as she danced for the first time since becoming paralyzed.

The Endocrine System

What is the function of the endocrine system?

You have learned that much of what you do is controlled by your nervous system. But there is a second control system in your body. This system is the **endocrine** (en'dō krin) **system.** It controls the rate of many of your body's activities. For example, your endocrine system controls the rate at which you grow. It also controls how quickly energy is released from food in your body's cells. This system can both speed up and slow down activities in your body.

The endocrine system is made up of several glands. **Glands** are special organs or tissues in the body that make chemical substances. The chemical substances

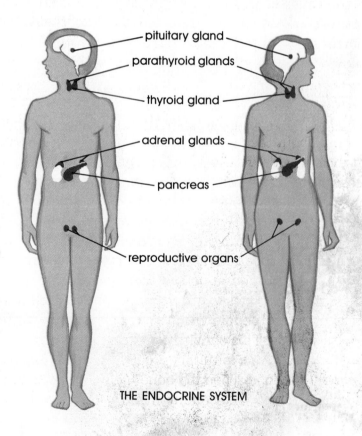

- pituitary gland
- parathyroid glands
- thyroid gland
- adrenal glands
- pancreas
- reproductive organs

THE ENDOCRINE SYSTEM

that the endocrine glands make are called **hormones** (hôr′mōnz). *Hormone* comes from a Greek word meaning ''to excite.'' Hormones ''excite'' your body to do certain activities. The drawing shows some of the glands of the endocrine system. As you can see the glands of the endocrine system are not directly connected to one another.

You know that nerves connect the central nervous system to all parts of your body. The glands of the endocrine system, however, are different. They are not connected to the body parts they control. How, then, do the glands ''excite,'' or stimulate, those body parts? Each gland makes one or more kinds of hormones. The hormones move from the glands into the blood. When the blood reaches a part of the body controlled by a particular gland, hormones from that gland cause changes to take place in that body part. Many of the changes occur slowly. Eventually the hormones are carried by the blood to the liver. There they are changed to inactive chemicals. Finally they are excreted by the kidneys.

The **pituitary** (pi tü′ə ter ē) **gland** may be the most important gland of the endocrine system. This gland is only about the size of a pea and is on the underside of the brain. Find the pituitary gland in the drawing. It produces several hormones. Some of these hormones control other endocrine glands in the body. For this reason the pituitary is called the master gland.

One of the pituitary hormones regulates the growth of bones. Too much or too little of this growth hormone can affect a person's body size. Too much can cause the bones to grow longer than their normal lengths. Some people with this condition grow to be as tall as 3 m. This condition is called giantism.

Sometimes the pituitary does not make enough growth hormone. Then the bones do not grow to their normal lengths. This condition is known as dwarfism.

Giantism

Dwarfism

351

The **thyroid** (thī′roid) **gland** is in the neck. Can you feel your Adam's apple, or voice box? The thyroid is just below and in front of the voice box. Find the thyroid gland in the drawing on page 350. It makes an important hormone called thyroxine (thī rok′sēn). This hormone controls how fast the cells in your body obtain energy from food.

Too little thyroxine slows down the release of energy from food. Some of the food is stored as fat. In this case a person would become overweight. He or she would also feel tired, since the body would not be getting enough energy from the food.

Too much thyroxine causes the body to use up food too quickly. In this case a person would lose weight and might have a lot of nervous energy. When the thyroid produces too much thyroxine, part or all of the gland may need to be removed. People whose thyroid has been removed or whose thyroid is underactive must take medicine containing thyroxine. Years ago this medicine was a purified form of thyroxine from an animal. Today most thyroxine medicine contains a manufactured duplicate of the real hormone.

The thyroid gland uses the chemical called iodine to make thyroxine. You usually get as much iodine as you need from the food you eat. But iodine is sometimes added to table salt. What does the label on this salt box tell you?

The four **parathyroid** (par ə thī′roid) **glands** are on the back of the thyroid. Find them in the drawing on page 350. They are the smallest endocrine glands. They make hormones that control the amount of calcium and other minerals contained in the blood. These minerals help to make strong bones and teeth. Calcium is needed for the blood to clot properly.

The **pancreas** (pan′krē əs) is a double-purpose organ. It is located behind the stomach. It makes substances that help to digest food.

The pancreas is also an endocrine gland. It makes a hormone that helps to control how the cells use sugar. This hormone is called insulin (in'sə lin). If the body does not have enough insulin, the cells cannot use the sugar in the blood. Too much sugar builds up in the blood. This condition is called diabetes (dī ə bē'tis). People with diabetes have to take medicine that contains insulin. A person with diabetes may wear a Medic Alert bracelet like the one shown. If a person with diabetes passes out, the bracelet can make others aware of the person's medical problem. The person may have too much sugar in the blood. But it may also be that the person temporarily has too much insulin. This is called insulin shock. Rapid medical treatment can solve the problem.

Do You Know?

By combining their knowledge of biology and electronics, scientists may soon be able to help people who have diabetes. This drawing shows a biosensor surrounded by blood cells in the bloodstream. This biosensor will be connected to a device that holds insulin. The tip of the sensor will contain a chemical that will react with sugar in the blood. The reaction will produce an electric signal. As the amount of sugar in the blood varies, so will the signal the sensor sends. As the signal varies, so will the amount of insulin that is released. By using a biosensor such as this, a person with diabetes might not have to worry about taking the correct amount of insulin.

There are two **adrenal** (ə drē′nəl) **glands,** one on top of each kidney. Can you find these glands in the drawing of the endocrine system on page 350? The adrenal glands have an inner part and an outer part. The outer part makes hormones that help to control how the body uses food. These hormones also help the body deal with stress. The inner part makes a special hormone called adrenalin.

Adrenalin (ə dren′ə lin) is released when you are frightened, hurt, or in danger. This hormone triggers many body actions. Your eyes open wider. Your heart beats faster. You breathe faster. If you are cut, your blood clots faster. Also, your muscles can work harder and longer than they normally do.

Perhaps you have heard stories of unusual strength or endurance. For example, people have been known to lift very heavy objects to free trapped victims. Normally they would not have been able to do so. But in an emergency, adrenalin causes many parts of the body to work harder.

Doctors sometimes inject adrenalin into someone whose heart has stopped working. The adrenalin can stimulate the heart and may start it beating again.

The reproductive organs are also parts of the endocrine system. These organs produce hormones that cause sex characteristics. These are traits that make males different from females. For example, males have beards, as well as deeper voices and broader shoulders than females. Females have higher voices, narrower shoulders, and wider hips than males.

The table on page 355 is a summary of what you have learned about the endocrine system. Look at the table. What are the names of six endocrine glands? Which endocrine gland produces thyroxine? What is the function of the parathyroid glands? Where is the pituitary gland located? Which gland produces a hormone that is used by the body in emergencies?

For Lesson Questions, turn to page 410.

THE ENDOCRINE SYSTEM

Gland	Function
pituitary gland	• produces hormones that control other glands • produces growth hormone
parathyroid glands	• produce a hormone that controls the amounts of calcium and other minerals contained in the blood
thyroid gland	• produces thyroxine, which controls how fast cells obtain energy from food
adrenal glands	• produce hormones that help control how the body uses food, help the body deal with stress, and help in emergencies
pancreas	• produces a hormone that helps to control how cells use sugar
reproductive organs	• produce hormones that cause sex characteristics.

Ideas to Remember

▶ Body activities are controlled by the nervous system and the endocrine system.
▶ The nervous system consists of two main parts—the central nervous system and the peripheral nervous system.
▶ The thinking and reasoning actions of the body are controlled by the cerebrum.
▶ Injury, disease, and the use of drugs can damage the nervous system.
▶ The endocrine system releases hormones that control some body functions.
▶ Some of the endocrine glands are the pituitary, thyroid, parathyroid, pancreas, and adrenal glands.

Reviewing the Chapter

SCIENCE WORDS

A. Use all the terms below to complete the sentences.

hormones
central nervous system
motor nerve cells
glands

peripheral nervous system
sensory nerve cells
reflex
connecting nerve cells

The __1__ is made up of the brain and spinal cord. The __2__ includes the nerves that extend to the edges of the body. Nerve cells that carry messages to the brain and spinal cord are called __3__. Nerve cells that carry messages from the brain and spinal cord to other body parts are called __4__. Messages passing between these two types of nerve cells travel over __5__. In a reaction called a/an __6__, messages bypass the brain. The rate of many body activities is controlled by chemical substances called __7__. These substances are produced by tissues and organs of the endocrine system that are called __8__.

B. Write the letter of the kind of endocrine gland that matches the function.

1. Controls the amount of calcium contained in the blood
2. Helps the body deal with stress
3. Controls how fast the cells obtain energy from food
4. Regulates the growth of bones
5. Regulates the use of sugar

a. thyroid gland
b. adrenal gland
c. pancreas
d. parathyroid gland
e. pituitary gland

UNDERSTANDING IDEAS

A. Write the correct term for each number in the diagram.

B. Suppose you watch a traffic light turn green. You then begin to cross the street. Describe the paths that the messages take over your nerve cells so that you can begin to cross the street.

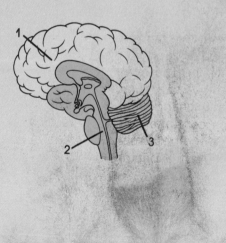

C. Explain the differences between the terms.

1. reaction time, reflex
2. cerebrum, cerebellum
3. hormone, gland
4. nerve cell, nerve

D. Both the nervous system and the endocrine system help to control body activities. How do they differ in the way that they control body activities?

USING IDEAS

1. Use your library to find out how biofeedback is used to help control activities that are normally involuntary, such as blood pressure.
2. The pituitary gland is sometimes called the master gland. Find out which endocrine glands are controlled by the pituitary gland.

3. Many educational toys are puzzles. Some are cubes, spheres, or other forms that have been divided into pieces. To solve the puzzles, the pieces must be put together in a certain way. How is the nervous system involved in solving such a puzzle? What part or parts of the brain are used?

THINKING LIKE A SCIENTIST

Answer the following questions. You may be able to answer some of the questions just by thinking about them. To answer other questions, you may have to do some research.

1. In science fiction movies wild-eyed doctors transplant brains from one person to another. If heart transplants are becoming more common, why do scientists believe that a successful brain transplant is unlikely in the near future? Use your understanding of how tissues, organs, and systems work to support your answer.
2. The nervous system of a sleeping person carries out certain body functions automatically. The heart continues to beat, the blood is circulated, and carbon dioxide is exchanged for oxygen. These functions continue in the same manner as when the person is awake. The nervous system of a person in a coma (kō'mə) carries out these same functions. How do you think the nervous system of a sleeping person differs from that of a person in a coma?

CHAPTER 15
Growth and Development

At the age of 2, Midori longed to play her mother's violin. On her third birthday, Midori's wish came true: Her parents gave her a wonderful gift—a violin just half normal size. She began studying the violin at 4. By 6 years of age, the little Japanese girl was thrilling audiences with her talents. She could play complex adult pieces on her violin.

When Midori was about 9 years old, an American heard her playing the violin. He was so astounded by Midori's talent, that he taped her playing. He sent the tape to a teacher at a famous music school in America. The teacher was also thrilled with her playing and invited her to perform in the United States. Playing in this country would be a fine chance for Midori. So mother and daughter left Japan for the United States.

Midori performing with a symphony orchestra

In just a few short years, Midori's career has rivaled that of people many times her age. She has recorded her own album. Midori has performed under great conductors, such as Leonard Bernstein. A world-famous violinist recently said, "A Midori comes along once in 50 or 75 years." When asked what she wants to do when she grows up, Midori has said, "I'm not sure yet what I want to do. I think I'll be a writer, or an archaeologist—or maybe a violinist."

Midori is a child prodigy (prod´ ə jē). Child prodigies show special talents in areas such as music, art, math, and sports. What causes these children to be so talented? Are they born talented? Or do their talents result from plain hard work?

Steveland Judkins Morris was born with two strikes against him. He was poor and blind. Yet he had a talent that could not be ignored. Like many small children, Stevie had a little toy harmonica. This toy had only four notes. But Stevie astounded family and friends with the music he produced on that toy.

By the age of 10, the "boy wonder" was entertaining people in his neighborhood in Detroit. Soon he was known as "Little Stevie Wonder." Today he plays and sings many kinds of music — rhythm and blues, rock, and ballads. He has appeared before millions of people and recorded dozens of songs. Stevie Wonder's music is known and loved throughout the world.

Nadia Comaneci (nod´ yə kō mə nēch´) is a gymnast who was born in 1961 in Romania. She began her training in gymnastics at the age of 6. At age 13 she was the European all-around gymnastics champion. At age 15 she did something never before done: She received 7 perfect (10.00) scores at the 1976 Summer Olympics. Was Nadia born with her talent? Or did she win her medals because of tough training?

Karl Gauss's grade-school teacher gave the class a tough math problem: Add up all the numbers from 1 to 100. Within a few seconds Karl wrote down his answer. The teacher assumed Karl had written down any old number. The rest of the students worked a long time at the problem.

Nadia Comaneci, world-famous gymnast

Nearly everyone can be creative in some way. You need not be a math wizard or a musical genius. You can show creativity just by thinking of new ways to use common objects. Try to invent new ways to use an object you might see every day—a milk carton.

List at least 10 different uses, other than holding milk, for a milk carton. For example, you might want to use the milk carton to build a toy. There is no limit to the number of cartons you can use. You can also use other materials. For example, you can use such things as scissors, glue, string, and thumbtacks.

Choose one of your ideas. From your teacher, obtain the materials you need. Construct the object. Test it out to see that it does what you want it to do. Change the design if needed. Give your invention a name. Show someone how to use your invention.

At the end of the period, the teacher checked Karl's answer. It was correct! In his head Karl had arranged the numbers in pairs:

$$100 + 1 = 101$$
$$99 + 2 = 101$$
$$98 + 3 = 101 \text{ and so on}$$

He realized that there would be 50 such pairs. So he multiplied 101 by 50 to get the answer 5050. Ten-year-old Karl had figured out a quick method for solving this tough problem.

Karl Friedrich Gauss, born in Germany in 1777, showed many other signs of math genius. Before he could even speak, Karl had figured out the basic elements of mathematics. At 3 years of age he caught an error in his father's tally of the payroll for the men he employed. During his life he made many discoveries in math and astronomy. He also built a working telegraph two years before Morse invented his telegraph.

Did Gauss inherit his talents from his mother and father? In this chapter you will learn how living things inherit traits from their parents.

Karl Friedrich Gauss, math genius

Reproduction

Why is reproduction important?

Everything on the earth can be classified as either living or nonliving. There are many ways in which living things differ from nonliving things. But one of the most important differences is the ability of living things to reproduce.

Reproduction is the process by which living things produce other living things of the same kind. If a certain kind of living thing stopped reproducing, it would die out. For example, if pandas stopped reproducing, they would die out, or become extinct. The California Condor is an animal now in danger of becoming extinct. One reason is because the condor's breeding grounds are disappearing. Breeding grounds are the places where some animals reproduce and raise their young.

Living things reproduce in different ways. In some kinds of living things, reproduction requires only one parent. In some cases a new living thing can grow from a part of the parent organism. For example, a new plant can often be grown from a leaf taken from the parent. If certain kinds of worms are cut in pieces, the pieces will grow into new worms. How many new worms have formed in the drawing?

Pandas

California Condor

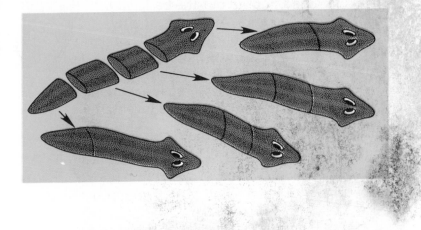

Some single-celled organisms reproduce by dividing. The parent cell simply divides into two new cells, each having the same parts as the parent cell. This type of reproduction, where one cell splits into two, is called **fission** (fish′ən). The amoeba in the pictures is reproducing by fission. If the two new amoebas divide again, how many amoebas will there be?

Some living things reproduce by growing small parts called buds. The buds grow out from the parent organism. The buds grow larger and then break off from the parent. Yeasts, shown in the picture, reproduce by budding. The hydra shown in the picture has a bud growing from it. The bud will break off and a new hydra will have formed. What kinds of living things are yeasts and hydras?

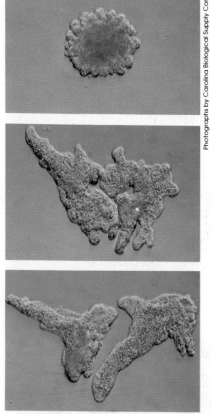

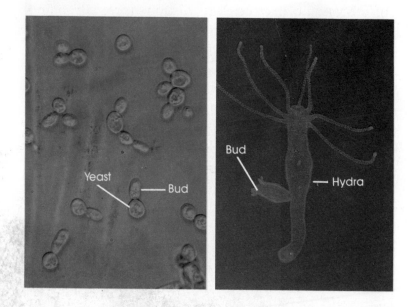

Amoeba reproducing

In many other kinds of living things, reproduction requires two parents. In this kind of reproduction, cells from a male and a female must join. When they join, a new living thing — an offspring — begins. To understand how an offspring forms, you must know something about male and female reproductive cells.

For Lesson Questions, turn to page 412.

Reproduction and Cells

How are reproductive cells different from other kinds of cells?

You know that all living things are made up of cells. Some living things are made up of only one cell. Others, like people, are made up of trillions of cells. A person may have as many as 50 trillion cells. Most are so small that 100,000 would fit on the head of a pin! Even though cells are very small, they are complex. Each cell has many different parts, and each part performs its own specific function.

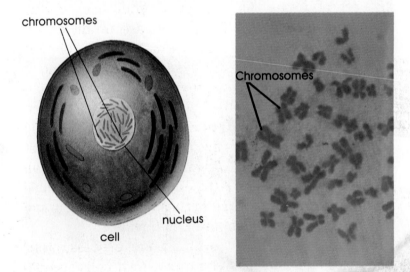

chromosomes

Chromosomes

nucleus

cell

The control center for a cell is the nucleus. It is also the information center for a cell. It stores all the information the cell needs to grow, reproduce, and do its job. This information is found inside the nucleus, on the threadlike structures called chromosomes.

Each cell in a living thing has a certain number of chromosomes. The chromosomes are usually arranged in pairs. Different organisms have different numbers of chromosome pairs. In a person there are

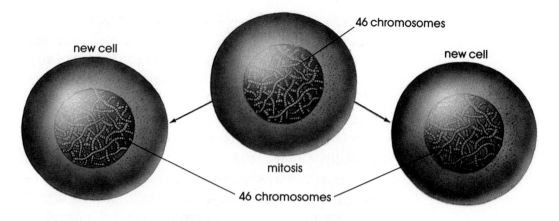

new cell

46 chromosomes

new cell

mitosis

46 chromosomes

23 pairs of chromosomes in the nucleus of every body cell. This means that each of your body cells contains 46 chromosomes. As you grow, your body forms more and more cells. These cells are produced by mitosis. Mitosis is a process in which one cell divides to form two cells. Mitosis is shown in the drawing.

Before a cell undergoes mitosis, it makes a duplicate set of chromosomes. So the cell at that time contains two complete sets of chromosomes. The cell then divides into two new cells. Each new cell receives a complete set of chromosomes. In this way, all the body cells have the same information. When a cell with 16 chromosomes undergoes mitosis, how many chromosomes will each new cell have?

Mitosis is a very important body process. Your body adds new cells as you grow. New cells also replace worn out cells and cells that have been damaged by an injury. Mitosis supplies these new cells.

In many living things, reproduction requires two parents. Each parent produces a special kind of cell called a reproductive cell. The male parent produces a **sperm cell.** The female parent produces an **egg cell.** Sperm cells are produced in the male's testes. Sperm cells are among the smallest cells in the body. Egg cells are produced in the female's ovaries. Egg cells are larger than most other cells in the body.

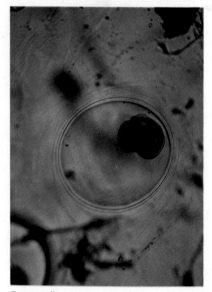

Egg cell

363

Reproductive cells differ from other body cells. They are not formed by mitosis. Instead they are formed by a special kind of cell division called reduction division. It has this name because the number of chromosomes is reduced by one half. So sperm cells and egg cells have only half the number of chromosomes that other cells have. Human body cells have 46 chromosomes. How many chromosomes would each egg cell or sperm cell have in a person?

When an egg cell and a sperm cell join, or unite, they form a cell called a **zygote** (zī′gōt). The zygote has as many chromosomes as were in both the sperm cell and the egg cell. Half of the zygote's chromosomes come from the egg cell, and half come from the sperm cell. Look at the drawing below. The egg cell and the sperm cell each have 20 chromosomes. How many chromosomes would the zygote have?

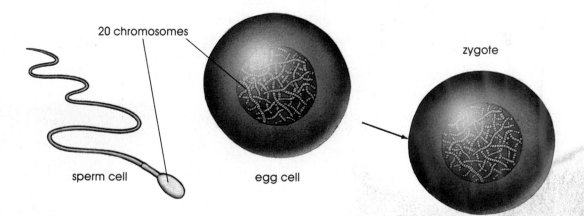

20 chromosomes

zygote

sperm cell   egg cell

A new organism begins when a sperm cell joins with an egg cell to form a zygote. This process is called **fertilization** (fėr tə lə zā′shən). After an egg has been fertilized, other sperm cells cannot join with it. The zygote that is formed has a complete set of chromosomes and is able to divide by mitosis. How does mitosis differ from reduction division?

For Lesson Questions, turn to page 412.

A New Organism Develops

How does a new organism develop from a single cell?

After fertilization the zygote develops into a new organism. It begins as a single cell with chromosomes from both parents. This cell then undergoes mitosis. In other words, it begins to divide and to form new cells. Each new cell then divides. As this process continues, many new cells are formed. The organism grows and develops as new cells are added.

As new cells form, they begin to carry out different functions. Many different kinds of cells form. For example, in humans some of the new cells become skin cells. Others become muscle cells and bone cells. What other kinds of cells can you name?

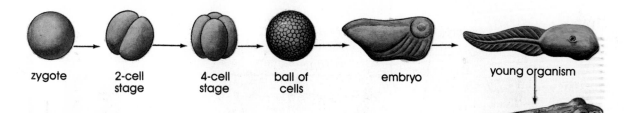

| zygote | 2-cell stage | 4-cell stage | ball of cells | embryo | young organism |

adult

The drawing shows some of the stages in the development of a frog. Humans develop in somewhat the same way. In humans the zygote divides into two cells about a day after fertilization. Less than a day later, the two cells become four. After a few hours the four cells become eight. By the third day a tiny ball of cells has formed. Mitosis continues and the new cells become specialized as the organism develops.

In time the growing organism develops organs and systems. In the early stages of development, an organism is called an **embryo** (em′brē ō). By the time of birth or hatching, the embryo has developed into a young organism that resembles its parent. The pic-

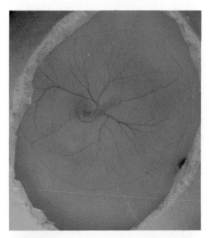

3 days

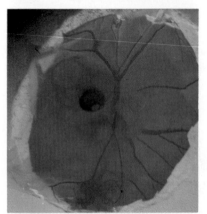

7 days

14 days

tures show several stages in the development of a chicken. By studying the stages of development in chickens and other animals, scientists have been able to learn about human development.

The amount of time the embryo needs before birth or hatching varies from one kind of organism to another. In humans the embryo usually needs 280 days. Look at this table. How much time does a cat embryo need to develop?

DEVELOPMENT TIME BEFORE BIRTH

Animal	Approximate time (days)
Mouse	21
Rabbit	30–43
Kangaroo	40–45*
Dog	58–65
Cat	60
Lion	106
Armadillo	150
Horse	330–380
Whale	334–365
African elephant	641

* Young are born undeveloped; growth continues in a pouch.

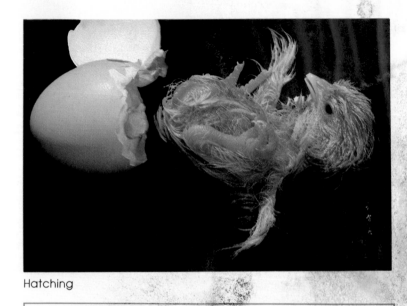

Hatching

366

For Lesson Questions, turn to page 412.

Passing on Information

How are features of parents passed on to their offspring?

Perhaps someone has said to you, "You look just like your mother." Or "You look like your uncle when he was a boy." Most of us have heard statements like these. We all have features of our parents and other relatives. You may be tall like your father, or you may have blue eyes like your mother. Such features are called traits.

As you have learned, half of your chromosomes came from your mother. Half came from your father. So your chromosomes carry information from both parents. This information determines many of your traits. The information helps to determine your height. It also determines traits such as your hair color and eye color. What other traits are passed along on chromosomes? What traits do the mother and child in the picture have in common?

Scientists estimate that each cell carries between 10,000 and 100,000 different instructions. Besides

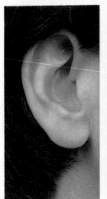
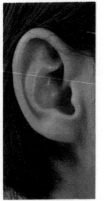

Free earlobes   Attached earlobes

body features, traits such as ability in art, music, or sports may be partially determined by information on chromosomes. Of course, the environment in which you grow up also determines many of your traits. Traits or features that are passed on from parents to offspring are often called **inherited traits.**

Some traits that you inherit may not seem important. For example, look at the ears of the people in your class. In some people the earlobes are attached to their head. In others the earlobes may hang free. The pictures show free and attached earlobes.

SKILLS: Observing, Communicating, Inferring

Finding Out

Can you roll your tongue?

The picture shows a person who can roll up the sides of her tongue. Most people can do it. But if you cannot, it is because of chromosomes in your cells. Check your classmates. Also check members of your family. Check friends in your neighborhood. Keep a record of the number of tongue rollers and nonrollers you find. No amount of practice can make a roller out of a nonroller. How important do you think this inherited trait is?

Activity

What traits do your classmates have?

Procedure

A. Copy the table on a sheet of paper.

B. Look at your classmates to find out what color eyes each one has. Record the numbers in the table. Be sure to include yourself in the tally.

C. Fill in the rest of the table after observing the remaining traits in each of your classmates.

Results

1. What is the most common eye color among your classmates?

2. What is the most common hair color among your classmates?

3. Make bar graphs showing your data for eye color and hair color.

4. Do more of your classmates have straight hair or curly hair?

5. Do more of your classmates have earlobes that are attached or not attached?

Conclusion

1. For each trait that you studied, identify the variation that is the most common.

2. Based on your data, identify the trait expressions that you think are dominant.

Trait	Number

Eye color:
  Brown
  Blue
  Green
  Gray
  Other	

Hair color:
  Black
  Brown
  Blond
  Red	

Hair:
  Straight
  Curly	

Earlobes:
  Attached
  Not attached	

What inherited traits can you observe in the family shown in the picture? Often the chromosomes from both parents contain the same information for a trait. For instance, both parents may have brown hair. In such a case there is a strong likelihood that their offspring will have brown hair. But in some cases the information coming from the parents is not the same for a trait. One parent may have black hair, and the other may have red hair. What happens in such a case?

To understand how the traits of an offspring are determined, let's look more closely at chromosomes. On the chromosomes are special units called genes. The genes are the units that carry information about an organism's traits. When a sperm cell and an egg cell join, genes from both parents are brought together. The genes for hair color that are received from both parents may be the same or different.

When two genes carrying different information for a trait join, one gene may determine that trait in the offspring. Such a gene is said to be dominant. A **dominant gene** is one that when present always determines a trait. A gene that does not determine a trait when paired with a dominant gene is a **recessive gene.** A recessive gene can only determine a trait when paired with the same kind of recessive gene. When a recessive gene is paired with a dominant gene, the dominant gene masks, or hides, the recessive trait.

Eye color is a trait for which there are dominant and recessive genes. The gene for brown eyes can mask the gene for blue eyes. So we say brown eye color is dominant. Blue eye color is recessive.

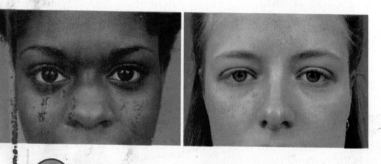

Do You Know?

Certain kinds of diseases can be inherited. For example, sickle-cell anemia, a blood disease, can be inherited. In this disease some of the red blood cells are shaped like sickles, or crescents, so they cannot carry oxygen. The disease is caused by a recessive gene that controls the formation of the sickle-shaped cells. Sickle-cell anemia occurs mostly among black people. Scientists are searching for ways to prevent this and other inherited diseases.

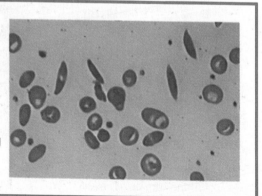

You can trace how eye color is inherited by looking at the drawings. Because the gene for brown eyes is dominant, we use the symbol **B** for it. Because the gene for blue eye color is recessive, we use the symbol **b** for it. Remember that you get a gene for eye color from each parent.

If you get a **B** from each parent, you will have brown eyes (**BB**). If you get a **B** from one parent and a **b** from the other, you will also have brown eyes (**Bb**). The gene for brown eyes (**B**) masks the gene for blue eyes (**b**). The only way you can have blue eyes is if you get a **b** gene from each parent. Then the message that your cells carry for eye color will be **bb.**

The study of inherited traits is an interesting branch of science. It is the science of **genetics** (jə net'iks). Scientists use what they have learned to develop special kinds of plants and animals. For example, someone who breeds show dogs can determine the traits of the offspring by selecting parents with certain traits. Plants that are disease-resistant or that grow in certain soils can also be developed.

For Lesson Questions, turn to page 412.

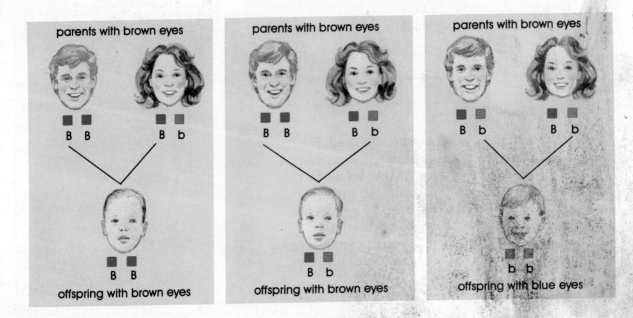

parents with brown eyes

B B   B b

B B

offspring with brown eyes

parents with brown eyes

B B   B b

B b

offspring with brown eyes

parents with brown eyes

B b   B b

b b

offspring with blue eyes

How is color inherited in bean seeds?

Materials 2 brown paper bags / 10 brown bean seeds / 10 white bean seeds

Procedure

A. The brown beans and white beans will be used to represent genes for seed color. Each brown seed represents a gene for the dominant color brown (B). Each white bean represents a gene for the recessive color white (b).

B. Label one paper bag *Parent A.* Label the other one *Parent B.*

C. Put 10 brown beans in bag *A.* Put 10 white beans in bag *B.*

D. Take 1 bean from each bag. Make a table in which to record the combination you drew and the seed color that would result from this combination. Replace the beans in their proper bags. Repeat the procedure nine times.

E. Empty the bags. Place 5 brown beans and 5 white beans in bag *A.* Do the same with bag *B.*

F. Repeat step **D**. Record your results.
  1. Compare your two trials. How do they differ?

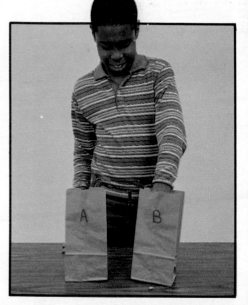

Conclusion

1. What would the seed color be if both parents are brown?

2. What would the seed color be if both parents are white?

3. What would the seed color be if one parent is brown and the other parent is white?

Using science ideas

Flower color in plants is an inherited trait. In some flowers, red color may be dominant over white. But sometimes when a red (R) combines with a white (r), a pink flower is produced. This is called incomplete dominance. Explain why this term is used.

The Life Cycle

What are the stages of the human life cycle?

All living things reproduce. Living things also grow and change. The stages that a living thing goes through make up the organism's **life cycle.**

A person goes through a life cycle too. A person begins as a single cell. The cell divides again and again as an embryo. After about 280 days a new baby is born. Look back to the table on page 366 to compare the time for human development with that of other living things. For several months after birth, a baby is in the stage called **infancy.** An infant depends on its parents for food and protection.

In about a year an infant enters the stage called **childhood.** A child depends less on its parents than does an infant. A child continues to grow and develop. During this stage a child learns many skills. For example, a child learns to walk and talk. A child also learns many of the social skills needed to get along with others.

Infancy

Childhood

Adolescence

After childhood a person enters a stage of rapid growth and change. This stage is called **adolescence** (ad ə les′əns). Adolescence occurs when a person is in his or her teens. The beginning of adolescence is called **puberty** (pyü′bər tē). Many important body changes take place during puberty. Also, during this stage young people take on new responsibilities. An adolescent also begins to learn to make his or her own decisions.

The stage that follows adolescence is **adulthood.** This is the longest stage in the life cycle. As an adult a person is fully grown. While in this stage, some adults have offspring. The cycle then begins for the off-spring. Like all other organisms, people grow old. They also die. When this happens, the life cycle for an individual ends.

Adulthood

Ideas to Remember

► The nucleus of a cell stores the information for the growth and development of the cell. This information is carried on the chromosomes.
► Sperm cells and egg cells have half the number of chromosomes that regular body cells have.
► A new living thing begins when a sperm cell joins with an egg cell.
► Many traits are passed on from parents to off-spring. These are called inherited traits.
► Traits are carried on the chromosomes, on units called genes.
► Each living thing goes through a life cycle.
► The human life cycle includes infancy, child-hood, adolescence, and adulthood.

For Lesson Questions, turn to page 412.

Reviewing the Chapter

A. Use all the terms below to complete the sentences.

adulthood   reproduction   fertilization   infancy
life cycle   adolescence   childhood   zygote

The process by which living things produce other living things of the same kind is called __1__. In humans a new organism begins when a sperm cell joins with an egg cell, a process called __2__. The cell that is formed is called a/an __3__. All living things go through changes that make up the __4__ of the organism. In humans the stage that occurs immediately after birth is called __5__. During __6__ an individual learns many skills, such as the ability to walk and talk. During __7__, rapid growth and change occur. During the stage called __8__, physical growth stops.

B. Copy the sentences below. Use science words from the chapter to complete the sentences.

1. The female reproductive cell is the _____.
2. During the early stages of its development, an organism is called a/an _____.
3. Features or traits that are passed on from parents to offspring are called _____.
4. The male reproductive cell is the _____.
5. A gene that when present always determines a trait of an offspring is called a/an _____.
6. The beginning of adolescence is called _____.
7. _____ is the branch of science that deals with the study of inherited traits.

A. In what ways do egg cells and sperm cells differ from the other cells of the body?

B. Explain how the cells formed by reduction division differ from those that are formed by mitosis.

C. What changes occur in an organism during the time that it is an embryo?

D. Explain why offspring have traits of both parents.

E. Study the drawing. The gene for brown hair (**B**) is dominant. The gene for red hair (**b**) is recessive. Determine the hair color of the offspring in each case.

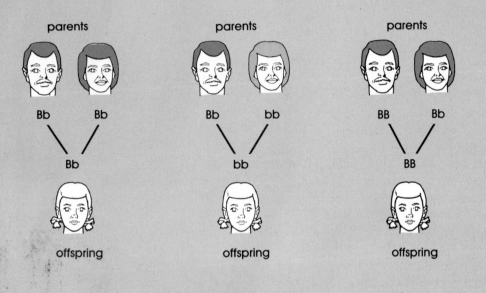

USING IDEAS

1. Find out about some genetic diseases, such as Tay-Sachs and phenylketonuria. For each disease, state whether the gene that causes it is dominant or recessive.

2. How can keeping records on milk production help a farmer develop the best possible herd of cows?

THINKING LIKE A SCIENTIST

Answer the following question. You may be able to answer the question just by thinking about it, or you may have to do some research.

Nurses who work in hospital nurseries have always noticed differences in newborn babies. They report that some babies seem irritable from the moment they are born. These babies have trouble sleeping, and they cry frequently. Other babies sleep peacefully and rarely cry. After careful research, many scientists now hypothesize that "reactivity"—what the nurses call irritability—is inherited. What evidence would support such a conclusion?

377

Science in Careers

Did you visit a doctor the last time you were sick? A **doctor** is well trained in how the organs and systems of the human body work. A doctor can usually recognize problems in the body and frequently can help to heal the body. But a doctor is just one member of the team of workers who provide health care.

A **nurse** is another member of the health-care team. A nurse may assist a doctor in treating patients. Some nurses take special training to care for special cases, such as heart patients or burn victims.

A **medical technologist** performs laboratory tests on blood and other body tissues. These tests help to determine which disease a person may have. A **laboratory assistant** is a laboratory worker who helps to perform the tests.

Inhalation therapist

A **pharmacist** is trained in the science of drugs. A pharmacist prepares drug prescriptions that are ordered by a doctor.

A **physical therapist** works with people who must rebuild their muscles or relearn to walk. A physical therapist teaches exercises and may use special equipment to help to strengthen a person's muscles.

People who have become addicted to drugs often need counseling to help them with problems. A **drug counselor** can help a person understand why he or she was using drugs.

If the functioning of the human body interests you, perhaps a career in health care is for you.

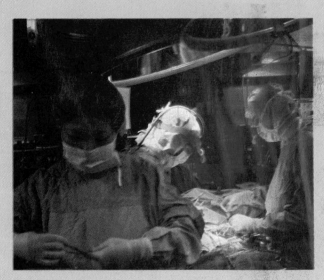
Doctors and nurses

People in Science

KO KUEI CHEN
(1898–   )

Dr. Chen has been involved in research in pharmacy, the science of drugs. His studies have led to the development of a medicine that helps to relieve the symptoms of asthma and bronchitis. He has also developed drugs for treating cyanide poisoning. In addition to doing research, Dr. Chen has also taught at several universities.

Drugs being manufactured at a pharmaceutical company

Developing Skills

WORD SKILLS

Many English words come from Latin, Greek, and other languages. If you know the meanings of words in other languages, you can often understand the meanings of English words. The tables below list word parts that come from other languages and give their meanings.

Use the tables for help in writing a definition for each of the following words. You can do this by breaking each word into parts.

For example, the word histology is made of these parts: histo- + -logy. Check your definitions by finding the meanings of the words in a dictionary.

1. histology
2. spermatocyte
3. neural
4. ambidextrous
5. epidermis
6. psychology
7. somatic
8. osteocyte

Word part	Meaning
ambi-	both
epi-	on the outside
histo-	tissue
neur-	nerve
osteo-	bone
psycho-	mind
somat-	body
spermato-	sperm, seed

Word part	Meaning
dextr-	toward the right
-al	of, like
-cyte	cell
-dermis	skin
-ic	having to do with
-logy	science of
-ous	full of

READING A TABLE

A table can contain many types of information. The table shown here gives information about the effects that various drugs have on the body. Use the table to answer the following questions.

1. What are the four types of drugs shown in the table?
2. Which drugs are examples of stimulants?
3. In which group of drugs does morphine belong?
4. Which of the groups of drugs shown can cause the body to depend on them?
5. Which of the drugs can cause long-lasting damage to the mind?
6. Give three examples of narcotics.
7. Name three drugs that speed up body functions.
8. Name three drugs that slow down the nervous system.
9. Nicotine is found in cigarettes. How do cigarettes effect the body?

380

HOW DRUGS AFFECT THE BODY

Type of Drug	Examples	Effect on the Body
depressants	• alcohol • barbiturates • tranquilizers	• slow down nervous system • cause the body to depend on the drug • can affect judgement
hallucinogens	• hashish • LSD • marijuana	• can have strange and frightening effects on the mind • LSD can cause long-lasting damage to the mind
narcotics	• heroin • morphine • opium	• often used to stop pain • often cause the body to strongly depend on the drug
stimulants	• amphetamines • cocaine • nicotine	• speed up body functions • cause the body to depend on the drug

USING THINKING SKILLS

Drugs can affect you in many ways. First, drugs affect your mind and body, as shown in the table. Drugs can also affect your life in other ways. Think about this as you answer the following questions.

1. In what ways can drugs affect your life?

2. Look up the word *drug* in an unabridged dictionary (you should be able to find one in a library). What is a drug?
3. Why are cigarettes and alcohol drugs?
4. Is it all right to use drugs? Explain your answer. If you say it is not all right, what can you do to avoid taking drugs?

Study Guide

Reading your book will help you learn more about the world around you. Your book will provide answers to many questions you may have about living things, the earth, space, matter, and energy.

On the following pages you will find questions from each lesson in your book. These questions will help test your understanding of the terms and ideas you read about.

There are three sections for each chapter. You can answer questions in the first section, "Lesson Questions," by using the information you read in each chapter. Careful reading will help answer these questions.

The second section is called "Problem Solving." These questions are more challenging. The answer may not be found just by reading the lesson. You may have to think harder.

The third section is called "Skills." In this section you will be asked to read tables and graphs.

Chapter 1

Living Things

LESSON QUESTIONS

Living and Nonliving (pp. 4–6)
1. Describe four life processes.
2. Why do living things need energy?
3. What is an organism? How are all organisms alike?
4. What is a virus? Is a virus living or is it nonliving?

Animal Cells (pp. 7–9)
1. What is the nucleus of a cell? What structures are found within the nucleus?
2. Why is the nucleus referred to as the cell's control center?
3. What is the function of a vacuole?
4. What structure surrounds animal cells? What is the function of this structure?

Plant Cells (pp. 10–13)
1. How are the cell membrane of an animal cell and the cell wall of a plant cell alike? How are they different?
2. What are chloroplasts? What is the function of chloroplasts?
3. How do plant vacuoles differ from animal vacuoles?

How Cells Reproduce (pp. 14–16)
1. What is the purpose of mitosis?

2. Describe what happens as mitosis begins.
3. Describe what happens during mitosis.
4. Why is it important that chromosomes make copies of themselves during mitosis?

Single Cells (pp. 17–20)
1. What is a protist?
2. What are animallike protists called? Describe the characteristics of these protists.
3. Compare the ways an amoeba, a paramecium, and a euglena move.
4. How are plantlike protists different from animallike protists? Give an example of a plantlike protist.
5. How do bacteria differ from both plantlike and animallike protists?
6. How are bacteria classified? What are three groups of bacteria?
7. Describe how bacteria are important.

Tissues, Organs, and Systems (pp. 21–23)
1. What is a tissue? Give two examples of tissues.
2. What is an organ? Give an example of an organ.
3. What is a system? Describe two systems.

PROBLEM SOLVING

Use after page 13. Not all plants are able to make their own food. If you were given 12 plants, how could you determine which plants could make their own food?

Use after page 20. Why is it an advantage for a large animal to be made of billions of cells rather than just one cell?

Reading a Line Graph

Suppose you were a scientist studying a new type of bacteria. You let the bacteria grow in one place. Every hour you count the number of bacteria cells. You use this data to make a line graph like the one shown here. Use the line graph to answer the following questions.

1. Over how many hours did you observe the bacteria, according to the line graph?

2. What was the greatest number of bacteria observed?

3. At what hour were the greatest number of bacteria observed?

4. What happened to the number of bacteria from the fourth hour to the fifth hour?

5. How many bacteria were observed at the sixth hour?

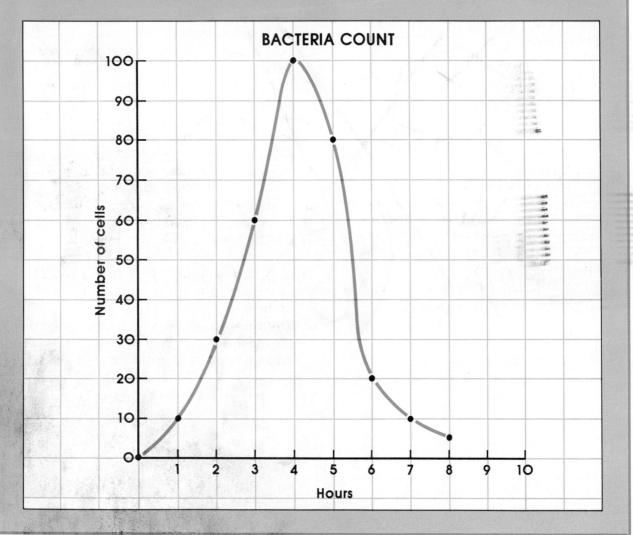

BACTERIA COUNT

Chapter 2 Plant Growth and Responses

LESSON QUESTIONS

How Plants Grow (pp. 28–31)
1. What is a growth region? Describe two kinds of growth regions.
2. What kind of tissue is found in all growth regions?
3. Describe two ways in which stems, branches, and roots grow.
4. What is an annual ring? How is it formed? What can it tell you?

Growth and Survival (pp. 32–35)
1. What is an environment? Name three things that must be found in a plant's environment for the plant to survive.
2. Distinguish between a response and a stimulus.
3. What is phototropism? How can phototropism help a plant survive?
4. What causes a plant to bend toward the light?

5. In addition to light, name two other things that plants respond to.

Other Adaptations of Plants (pp. 36–41)
1. Describe how seeds are adapted to be spread around.
2. How do poisons help plants survive?
3. How are needles of evergreen trees a kind of adaptation?
4. Describe how certain plants are adapted to live in hot, dry places.
5. How are the seeds of some kinds of shrubs adapted to forest fires?

Biological Clocks (pp. 42–45)
1. What is a biological clock?
2. How can plants be used to tell time?
3. How can a plant's biological clock be fooled?
4. How does a plant's biological clock help it to survive?

PROBLEM SOLVING

Use after page 31. Suppose a beaver gnawing on the trunk of a tree was suddenly frightened away and didn't return. If the tree grew 30 cm taller in the next two years, where would the scar from the beaver's teeth be? Why?

Use after page 35. The trunks of young trees bend easier than the trunks of older trees. Why might this be an advantage? Explain your answer.

Use after page 41. What adaptations would a maple tree need to grow in a desert? Make a drawing of a maple tree that has these adaptations.

Use after page 45. Design an experiment that could be done to prove that plants have biological clocks.

SKILLS

Reading a Bar Graph

A scientist wanted to see how one type of plant grew under different conditions. To do this, she used six groups of plants of one type. She varied the number of hours of light each plant received each day. After four weeks, she measured the plants. Her results are shown here. Use the bar graph to answer the following questions.

1. Which group of plants grew the most?
2. Which group of plants grew the least?
3. How much more did the plants receiving 10 hours of light each day grow than the plants receiving 8 hours of light?
4. Which group of plants grew more — the plants grown with 14 hours of light or the plants grown with 8 hours of light?
5. When would plants of this type grow best — during the early summer when the days are long or during the late summer when the days are shorter? Explain your answer.

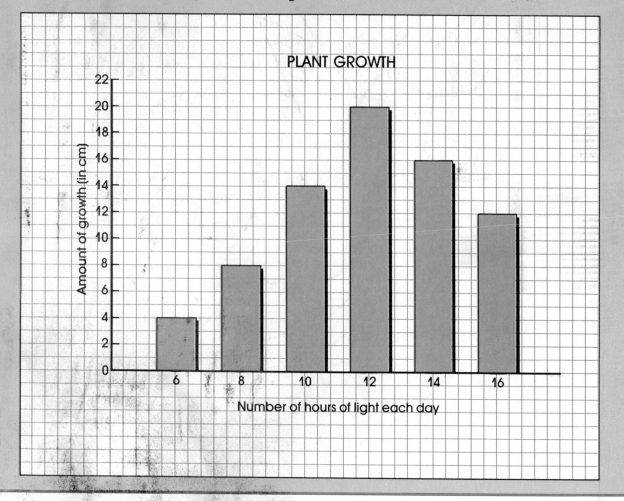

PLANT GROWTH

Amount of growth (in cm)

Number of hours of light each day

Chapter 3 Animal Adaptations

LESSON QUESTIONS

Structural Adaptations (pp. 50–58)

1. What is a structural adaptation?
2. How do the teeth of rodents, grazing animals, and meat-eating animals differ?
3. What structural adaptations relating to feeding do birds have?
4. Describe some specialized mouth parts for feeding that are found on insects.
5. Describe the structural adaptation for moving that is found on animals that hop.
6. What structural adaptations for moving does a cheetah have?
7. What structural adaptations for flying does a frigate bird have?
8. Describe how body coverings can be structural adaptations.

Looks That Protect (pp. 59–61)

1. What is protective coloration? How does protective coloration help an animal survive? Give two examples of protective coloration.
2. How does protective resemblence differ from protective coloration? Give an example of protective resemblance.
3. What is mimicry? How does mimicry help an animal survive?

Behavior and Instinct (pp. 62–66)

1. What is behavior? Give an example of a learned behavior.
2. What is instinct? Give two examples of this type of behavior.
3. What is migration? Describe the migratory behavior of two animals.

Hibernation (pp. 67–70)

1. What is hibernation? What happens to an animal's body during hibernation?
2. Describe how different cold-blooded animals hibernate.
3. Describe how different warm-blooded animals hibernate.
4. How is hibernation an adaptation?

Learned Behavior (pp. 71–73)

1. What is learning?
2. Why is it important that animals be able to learn?
3. Describe two steps that must take place for most kinds of learning.
4. What is imprinting? Give an example of imprinting.

PROBLEM SOLVING

Use after page 58. An animal's eyes, ears, and nose are adaptations that help the animal find and identify its predators and prey. Look at the pictures in Chapter 3. Choose three animals. Describe how each animal's eyes, ears, or nose help the animal survive.

Use after page 66. People called nomads live in the desert. They travel from place to place to follow animals, to look for sources of water, and to avoid harsh weather. Would you classify this behavior as migration? Explain your answer.

Reading a Map

A map is a representation of all or part of a region. This map shows where the mallard duck lives in eastern North America. This duck migrates from north to south in the fall. It migrates from south to north in the spring. It breeds during the summer months. Use the map to answer the questions.

1. If you live in Georgia, during what season will you most likely see a mallard duck?

2. While in Canada in October, you spot some migrating mallards. In which direction will the mallards probably be flying?

3. In which of the following places does the mallard **not** breed—Iowa, New Jersey, Tennessee, Canada?

4. A friend in northern Minnesota tells you that some mallards are living in a marsh near her home. What time of year is it?

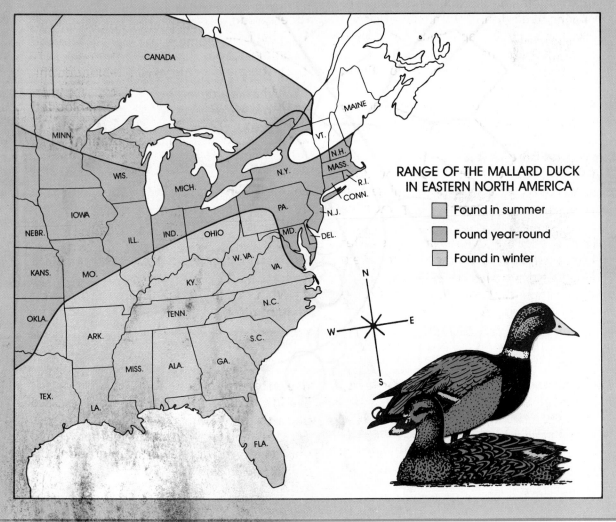

RANGE OF THE MALLARD DUCK
IN EASTERN NORTH AMERICA

Found in summer

Found year-round

Found in winter

Chapter 4

Climate and Life

LESSON QUESTIONS

Life Zones (pp. 78–80)
1. What is the biosphere? Where is the bio-sphere found?
2. What is a biome? Name six major biomes.
3. What is climate?

The Tundra (pp. 81–83)
1. What is the tundra?
2. How are animals adapted to survive winter in the tundra?
3. Describe summer in the tundra.

The Taiga (pp. 84–85)
1. What is the taiga?
2. Describe the type of trees found in the taiga. How are these trees important to animals in the taiga?
3. Describe winter in the taiga.

The Deciduous Forest (pp. 86–88)
1. Describe the deciduous forest biome.
2. Describe the layers found in a deciduous forest.
3. What animals and plants are found in a deciduous forest biome?

The Tropical Forest (pp. 89–91)
1. What is a tropical forest?

2. How is a tropical forest like a deciduous forest?
3. Describe the adaptations of plants and animals in a tropical forest biome.

The Grassland (pp. 92–94)
1. What is a grassland?
2. How has the grassland biome changed?
3. Describe the adaptations of animals in a grassland biome.

The Desert (pp. 95–97)
1. What is a desert?
2. How are deserts different? How are they alike?
3. Describe the adaptations of plants and animals in a desert.

Aquatic Habitats (pp. 98–101)
1. What is an aquatic habitat?
2. Distinguish between a freshwater habi-tat and a marine habitat.
3. What is plankton? Why is plankton im-portant?
4. What is upwelling? Why is upwelling im-portant?
5. Describe an estuary.

PROBLEM SOLVING

Use after page 80. The map on page 78 shows the locations of six major biomes. Do you think it is possible to find a biome out-side the area described in this map? Explain your answer.

Use after page 91. If you have ever seen a movie that was filmed in a jungle, you know how noisy a jungle can be. Why are jungle animals so noisy? Why aren't animals in a grassland or desert so noisy?

Reading a Line Graph

A line graph can be used to show many things. This line graph shows the temperature of the water in a particular pond at various depths. Use the graph to answer the following questions.

1. How deep is the pond?
2. What is the coldest temperature in the pond? At what depth is this temperature?

3. What is the temperature of the pond at the surface?
4. How much colder is the water at the depth of 7 m than at the depth of 2 m?
5. Suppose you read that a particular type of fish could be found where the water temperature ranges between 8°C and 14°C. Between what depths would you look for this fish in the pond?

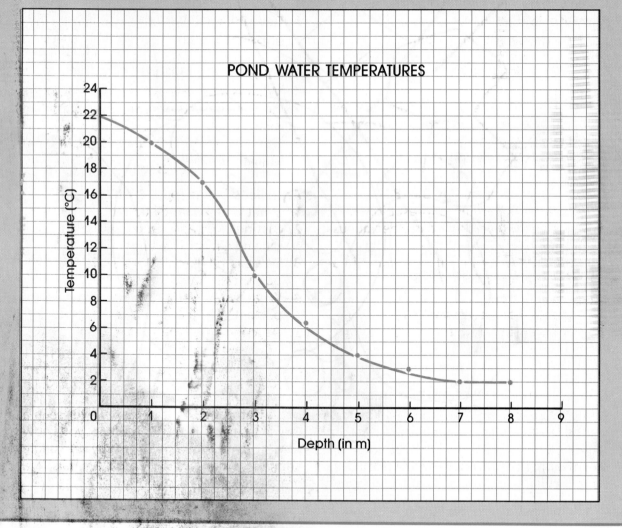

POND WATER TEMPERATURES

Chapter 5 — Matter and Atoms

LESSON QUESTIONS

Matter and Mass (pp. 112–114)
1. Describe two characteristics of matter.
2. What is mass? Compare your mass on the earth with your mass on the moon.
3. Compare the terms *mass* and *weight*.
4. How would your weight at sea level compare with your weight on the top of a high mountain?

Atoms (pp. 115–116)
1. What is an atom?
2. How do scientists know about atoms?
3. Describe the particles that make up an atom.

Grouping the Elements (pp. 117–121)
1. What is an element?
2. How do atoms differ?
3. What does the term *atomic number* refer to?
4. Define the term *mass number?* How can you use the atomic number and the mass number of an atom to find the number of neutrons in the atom?

5. What is an isotope?
6. What information does the periodic table give you?

Compounds and Molecules (pp. 122–123)
1. What is a compound?
2. Compare a compound and a molecule.
3. What does the formula $C_6H_{12}O_6$ tell you?

Kinds of Compounds (pp. 124–129)
1. What is an acid? Describe some characteristics of acids.
2. Describe the uses of two acids.
3. Describe the characteristics of bases.
4. Describe the uses of two bases.
5. What is an indicator? Give an example of one indicator and tell how it is used.
6. What is a salt? How is a salt formed?
7. Describe two ways salts are used.
8. What is an oxide? Give an example of an oxide.

PROBLEM SOLVING

Use after page 114. Suppose you have two 1-L containers filled with water. You freeze one container. Which weighs more—the container of ice or the container of water? Explain your answer. Which has more mass? Explain your answer.

Use after page 121. Nearly 2000 electrons equal the mass of 1 proton. About how many electrons would it take to equal the mass of the protons in one atom of the element neon?

Use after page 129. About 100 years ago, coin collectors shined copper coins by using a mixture that included lemon juice. Why, do you suppose, was lemon juice used?

Using a Diagram

This diagram shows the masses of different types of balls. Use the diagram to answer the following questions.

1. Which of the balls shown has the greatest mass?
2. Which has the least mass?
3. How much greater is the mass of a baseball than the mass of a tennis ball?
4. Which is greater — the total mass of a soccer ball and a softball or the mass of a basketball?
5. Which of the balls shown has a mass that is greater than the mass of a volleyball?

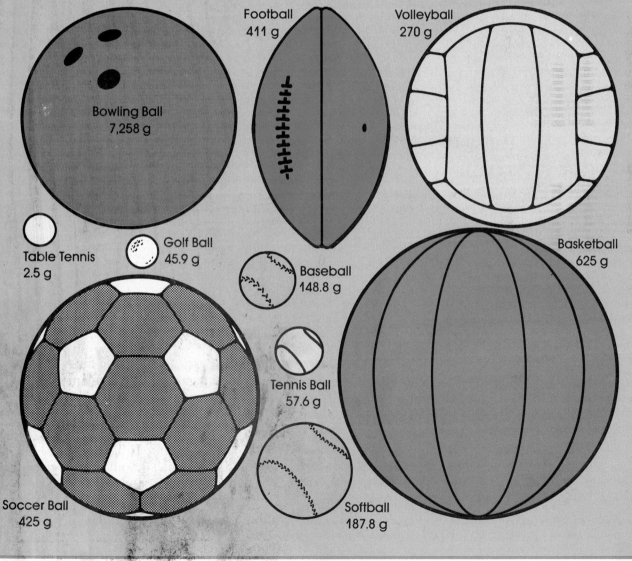

Football
411 g

Volleyball
270 g

Bowling Ball
7,258 g

Table Tennis
2.5 g

Golf Ball
45.9 g

Baseball
148.8 g

Basketball
625 g

Tennis Ball
57.6 g

Soccer Ball
425 g

Softball
187.8 g

Chapter 6

Chemical Changes in Matter

LESSON QUESTIONS

Properties and Changes (pp. 134–137)

1. What is a physical change? What happens during a physical change?
2. What is a physical property? Give three examples of physical properties.
3. What is a chemical change? What happens during a chemical change?
4. What is a chemical property?
5. What is density? How is the density of a substance stated?
6. What would it mean to say that a particular substance has a specific gravity of 0.94?

4. Explain the law of conservation of energy.

Chemical Bonds (pp. 143–144)

1. What are chemical bonds?
2. How are chemical bonds formed?
3. What is chemical energy? Why do some chemical reactions release chemical energy?

Chemical Reactions (pp. 138–142)

1. What is a chemical reaction? Give an example of a rapid chemical reaction. Give an example of a slow chemical reaction.
2. Describe and compare four types of chemical reactions.
3. Explain the law of conservation of matter.

Other Changes in Matter (pp. 145–149)

1. What is a nuclear reaction?
2. What is nuclear energy?
3. Compare nuclear fission with nuclear fusion.
4. Describe the law of conservation of mass and energy.
5. What is a radioactive element?

PROBLEM SOLVING

Use after page 137. Every chemical change is accompanied by a physical change. Describe three chemical changes that involve a change in one physical property — color.

Use after page 142. Explain how people in the following professions are involved with chemical reactions: auto-body mechanic, grocer, photographer, steelworker.

Use after page 144. Why is it easier to separate a mixture into its various elements than it is to separate a compound into its various elements?

Use after page 149. Suppose the underground water supply in your area was found to be slightly radioactive. What could have caused this?

SKILLS

Reading a Table

A large amount of information can be organized in a table. Then by using the table, you can easily compare the information. This table provides information about common chemicals. Use the table to answer the following questions.

1. What is the chemical name for baking soda?

2. What elements are found in methane?
3. What is the common name for acetylsalicylic acid? What is this compound used for?
4. Which of the compounds shown here contain sodium?
5. What are two uses for potash?
6. What is the formula for bleach?

Common Name	Chemical Name	Formula	Uses
alcohol	ethyl alcohol	C_2H_5OH	antifreeze, fuel
aspirin	acetysalicylic acid	$CH_3COOC_6H_4COOH$	medicine
baking soda	sodium bicarbonate	$NaHCO_3$	antacid, mouthwash
bleach	sodium perborate	$NaBO_2$	whitener
lime	calcium oxide	CaO	sewage treatment
marsh gas	methane	CH_4	fuel
potash	potassium carbonate	K_2CO_3	color TV tubes, soap
salt	sodium chloride	$NaCl$	seasoning
sugar	sucrose	$C_{12}H_{22}O_{11}$	sweetener

Chapter 7

Light Energy

LESSON QUESTIONS

Radiant Energy (pp. 154–159)

1. What is the electromagnetic spectrum?
2. How are all forms of radiant energy alike?
3. Describe three characteristics that describe the wave motion of radiant energy. How are the three characteristics related?
4. Describe infrared waves.
5. What are ultraviolet waves? How do they affect living things?
6. Describe the forms of radiant energy beyond ultraviolet in the electromagnetic spectrum.

The Behavior of Light (pp. 160–163)

1. Describe some characteristics of visible light.
2. What three things can happen to light that strikes matter?
3. Distinguish between the terms *transparent, translucent,* and *opaque.*

Seeing Colors (pp. 164–167)

1. What colors of light make up white light? How can white light be separated into these colors?
2. Explain why an apple looks red.
3. What happens when white light passes through matter?

Reflection and Mirrors (pp. 168–169)

1. How is the way light is reflected from a shiny frying pan different from how it is reflected from dirt?
2. Distinguish between a virtual image and a real image.
3. What is a convex mirror? Describe the image seen in a convex mirror.
4. How is a concave mirror different from a convex mirror? Describe the image seen in a concave mirror.

Bending Light Waves (pp. 170–172)

1. What happens to light as its speed changes?
2. Describe what causes a pencil in a glass of water to look bent.
3. What is refraction?
4. What is a convex lens? What happens to light that passes through a convex lens?
5. What is a concave lens? What happens to light that passes through a concave lens?

Modern Uses of Light (pp. 173–175)

1. What is a laser?
2. How can a laser be used in medicine?
3. How can laser light be used to carry voice signals?
4. Describe a new use for sunlight.

PROBLEM SOLVING

Use after page 159. What would happen if the sun suddenly disappeared? How long would it take for people on the earth to know that it disappeared? How would life on the earth be different?

Use after page 167. In 1819, Dr. Jan Purkinje observed that at twilight, red objects appear to fade faster than blue objects of the same brightness. Describe a simple experiment you could do to test this observation.

Reading a Diagram

This diagram compares the speed of light with the speed of other things on the earth. Use the diagram to answer the following questions.

1. What is the speed of light?
2. What is the slowest thing shown here?

3. In 1 hour, how much farther does light travel than a jet can travel?
4. How fast can a cheetah run?
5. How many times faster does light travel than the vehicle that holds the land speed record?

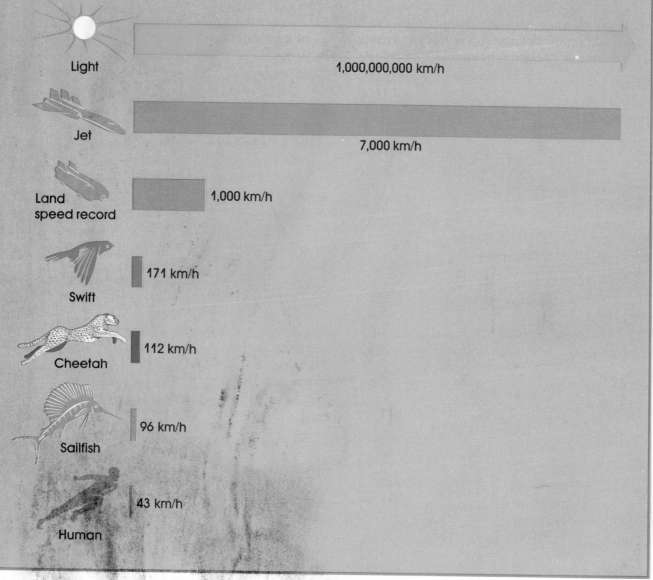

Light — 1,000,000,000 km/h

Jet — 7,000 km/h

Land speed record — 1,000 km/h

Swift — 171 km/h

Cheetah — 112 km/h

Sailfish — 96 km/h

Human — 43 km/h

Chapter 8 Sound Energy

LESSON QUESTIONS

Energy You Can Hear (pp. 180–182)
1. How does sound travel?
2. Describe how sound energy is transferred.
3. Describe a longitudinal wave.
4. Distinguish between a compression and a rarefaction. How are compressions and rarefactions related to the wavy line used to show a sound wave?

The Behavior of Sound (pp. 183–186)
1. Describe three things that can happen to sound energy that strikes matter.
2. On what does the amount of sound energy that is absorbed by matter depend?
3. Explain what happens to absorbed sound.
4. How does the matter that sound waves strike affect the loudness or softness of the reflected sound?

Describing Sound Waves (pp. 187–189)
1. What is wavelength?
2. Describe the characteristic of frequency. How are frequency and wavelength related?
3. What is pitch? How does pitch depend on frequency?

4. Describe the Doppler effect.

Pleasant and Unpleasant Sounds (pp. 191–192)
1. What is amplitude?
2. How is amplitude related to the loudness of a sound?
3. What is unpleasant sound called? Compare the wave patterns of pleasant and unpleasant sounds.

How Sounds Travel (pp. 193–194)
1. Why can't sound travel in a vacuum?
2. How is the speed of sound related to the type of matter it is traveling through?
3. How is the speed of sound affected by temperature?
4. What does the term *supersonic* mean? Explain what causes a sonic boom.
5. What is a Mach number? What does it mean to say that an object is traveling at a Mach number of 5?

Using Sound (pp. 195–197)
1. What is ultrasonic sound? Describe two uses for ultrasonic sound.
2. What is sonar? How can sonar be used?
3. How is the loudness of sound measured?

PROBLEM SOLVING

Use after page 186. It is usually very quiet after a snowstorm. Even passing trucks do not seem to make as much noise after a snowstorm as they do at other times. What can explain this observation? Why do you only observe this with fresh snow and not with snow that has been on the ground for several days?

Reading a Diagram

This diagram shows the range of sound frequencies heard by several animals. These frequencies are given in units called Hertz (Hz). Use the diagram to answer the following questions.

1. Which animal hears the greatest range of frequencies?

2. Which animal hears the smallest range of frequencies?

3. What is the range of frequencies heard by a frog?

4. Which has the greater range — a cat or a dog?

5. Which of the animals hears sounds at 20,000 Hz?

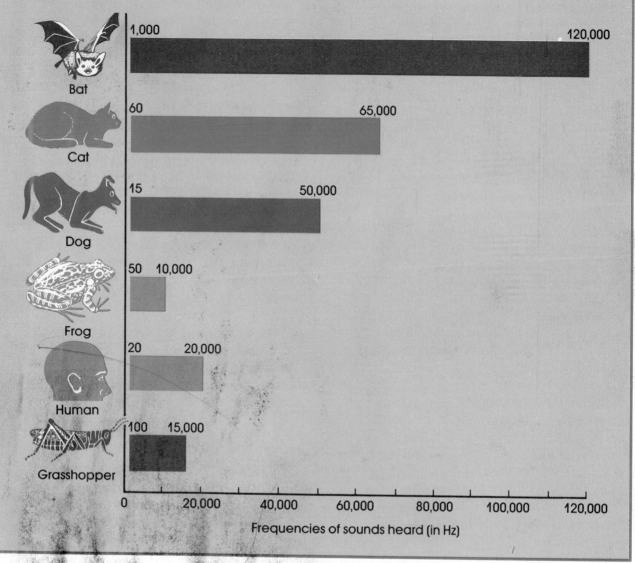

Bat — 1,000 to 120,000
Cat — 60 to 65,000
Dog — 15 to 50,000
Frog — 50 to 10,000
Human — 20 to 20,000
Grasshopper — 100 to 15,000

Frequencies of sounds heard (in Hz)

Chapter 9

Using Electricity

LESSON QUESTIONS

Electricity and Electrons (pp. 202–206)

1. What is energy? What is kinetic energy?
2. How is static electricity related to the movement of electrons?
3. Describe the two kinds of current electricity.
4. How are electricity and magnetism related?

Measuring and Controlling Electricity (pp. 207–210)

1. Describe four things that must be present to have an electric current.
2. What is a conductor? Describe what a good conductor is.
3. What is an insulator? How is a good insulator different from a good conductor?
4. What is electric resistance? How is electric resistance measured?
5. How does the thickness of a wire affect resistance? How does the length of a wire affect resistance?
6. How is the force needed to move elec-

trons measured? How is this force related to resistance?
7. What is an ampere?

Using Electricity (pp. 211–214)

1. Explain why electricity is our most useful form of energy.
2. Explain how an incandescent lamp works.
3. Explain how a fluorescent lamp works.

Circuits (pp. 215–223)

1. What is a circuit?
2. Distinguish between a series circuit and a parallel circuit.
3. Distinguish between a printed circuit and an integrated circuit.
4. What is a memory circuit? How is a memory circuit used?
5. What is a microprocessor? Describe three uses for microprocessors.
6. How does a computer work?

PROBLEM SOLVING

Use after page 210. A galvanometer is an instrument that detects electric current. How do you think this instrument works?

Use after page 223. Which do you think produces more electricity — two batteries connected in a series circuit or two batteries connected in a parallel circuit? Explain your answer.

Use after page 223. How do you suppose cordless telephones work?

Use after page 223. In what way is a computer like a human brain? How is it different?

Reading a Bar Graph

A bar graph can be used to compare information. This bar graph compares the amount of electrical energy used by various electrical appliances in 10 hours. This electrical energy is measured in units called kilowatt-hours. Use the bar graph to answer the questions.

1. Which uses more energy in 10 hours — a toaster or an iron?
2. How much energy does a radio use in 10 hours?
3. How much energy does a refrigerator use in 10 hours?
4. In 10 hours, how much more energy does an iron use than a television?
5. In 10 hours, how much more energy does a clothes washer use than a lamp?
6. Do you think a freezer uses more or less than 3 kilowatt-hours of electricity in 10 hours?

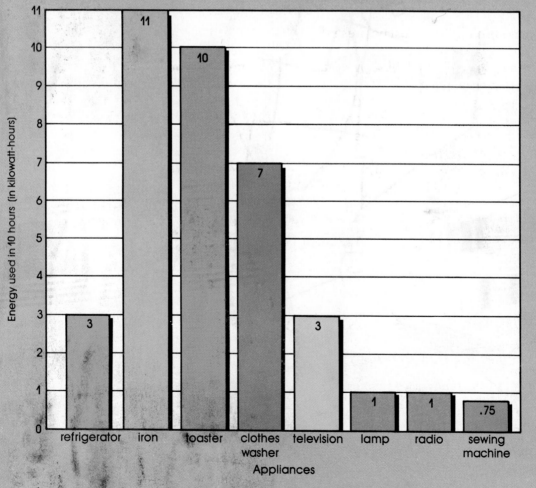

Chapter 10

The Earth's Resources

LESSON QUESTIONS

Living Renewable Resources (pp. 234–235)
1. What is a natural resource? Give three examples of natural resources.
2. Why are trees said to be renewable resources?
3. Give another example of a renewable resource.

Nonliving Renewable Resources (pp. 236–237)
1. Describe how water is renewed in the water cycle.
2. How is air renewed?
3. How can soil be renewed?

Nonrenewable Resources (pp. 238–241)
1. What is a nonrenewable resource?
2. What is a mineral? Give three examples of minerals.
3. What is an ore? How are ores obtained?
4. Give three examples of minerals that are often found as native metals.

Recycling (pp. 242–244)
1. What is recycling?
2. How is glass recycled? How can recycled glass be used?
3. How can recycled paper be used?

Fossil Fuel Resources (pp. 245–248)
1. What is a fossil fuel?
2. What are two main ways fossil fuels are used?
3. Describe how coal can be obtained.
4. How are oil and gas removed from the earth?
5. Describe fossil fuels that are found beneath the ocean floor.

Resources from the Oceans (pp. 249–255)
1. What resources can be found in seawater?
2. How can salt be removed from seawater? Why is it important that this is done?
3. What is a nodule? What minerals are found in nodules?
4. Explain how the oceans can be farmed.

PROBLEM SOLVING

Use after page 235. New inventions can affect renewable resources. Name an invention that has had a good effect on a renewable resource. Name an invention that has had a bad effect on a renewable resource.

Use after page 237. Farmers often vary the crops they plant in a field from year to year. Sometimes they plant crops and plow them under the ground without harvesting them. They might also plow their fields in curved rather than straight lines, and plant rows of trees between fields. How does each of these practices protect or renew resources?

Use after page 248. Oil companies employ many scientists. What skills would scientists be able to offer the oil companies?

SKILLS

Reading a Pictograph

A pictograph is a graph that uses pictures to represent data. Look at the pictograph on the opposite page. It shows how much crude oil was produced in the United States between 1945 and 1980. Use this pictograph to answer the questions.

1. How many barrels of crude oil were produced in the United States during 1945?

2. In which year was the most oil produced in the United States?

3. How many more barrels of oil were produced in 1960 than in 1955?

4. During which 5-year period did oil production decrease?

5. During which 5-year period did oil production increase most?

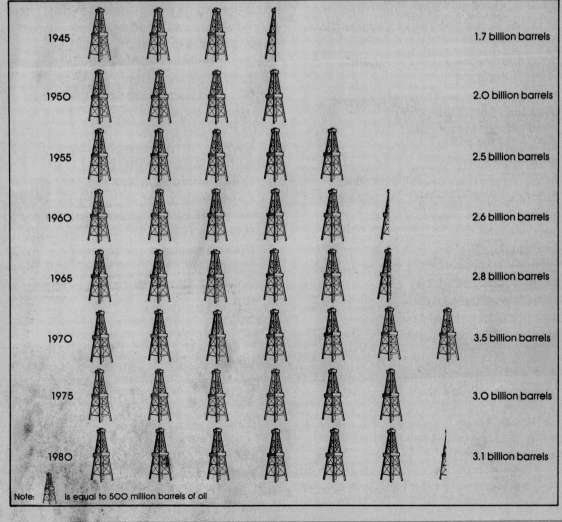

APPROXIMATE AMOUNT OF CRUDE OIL PRODUCED IN THE UNITED STATES (1945-1980)

1945	1.7 billion barrels
1950	2.0 billion barrels
1955	2.5 billion barrels
1960	2.6 billion barrels
1965	2.8 billion barrels
1970	3.5 billion barrels
1975	3.0 billion barrels
1980	3.1 billion barrels

Note: is equal to 500 million barrels of oil

403

Chapter 11

Changes in the Earth's Crust

LESSON QUESTIONS

The Floating Crust (pp. 260–265)
1. What is a theory?
2. What was Taylor's theory about the earth's crust?
3. Describe Wegener's theory of continental drift.
4. Describe two pieces of evidence that support Wegener's theory.
5. What is sea-floor spreading? How does sea-floor spreading help to support Wegener's theory?
6. Describe the plate tectonic theory.
7. What is Pangaea?

Earthquakes (pp. 266–269)
1. What is an earthquake? What causes earthquakes?
2. What is a fault?
3. What is the focus of an earthquake?
4. Describe how scientists measure earthquakes.
5. Describe the "gap theory" for predicting earthquakes.

Volcanoes (pp. 270–275)
1. What is a volcano?
2. Describe a benefit of volcanoes.
3. Describe the volcanic activity that occurs when two plates move away from each other. Name one place where this occurs.
4. Describe the volcanic activity that occurs when two plates collide. Name one place where this occurs.
5. Describe the volcanic activity that occurs when one plate sinks under another plate. Name one place where this occurs.
6. What is a hot-spot volcano? Give an example of a hot-spot volcano.
7. Describe what happens in the earth before a volcano erupts.
8. Describe two methods for predicting volcanic eruptions.

Mountain Building (pp. 276–279)
1. How are folded mountains formed? Give an example of a range of folded mountains.
2. How are fault-block mountains formed? Give an example of a range of fault-block mountains.
3. How is a dome mountain formed?
4. How does an old mountain range differ from a young mountain range? Explain what causes this difference.

PROBLEM SOLVING

Use after page 269. Why is fire often a problem after an earthquake? Do earthquakes start fires?

Use after page 275. Explain a way in which volcanoes might benefit people.

Use after page 279. What would the earth be like if all volcanoes, earthquakes, and mountain building stopped?

Reading a Diagram

This diagram shows the height of the highest mountain on each continent. Use the diagram to answer the following questions.

1. What is the highest mountain in Africa?
2. What is the height of the highest mountain in Europe?
3. What is the highest mountain shown?
4. How much higher is Mount Everest than Mount McKinley?
5. Which of the mountains shown are higher than 6,000 m?

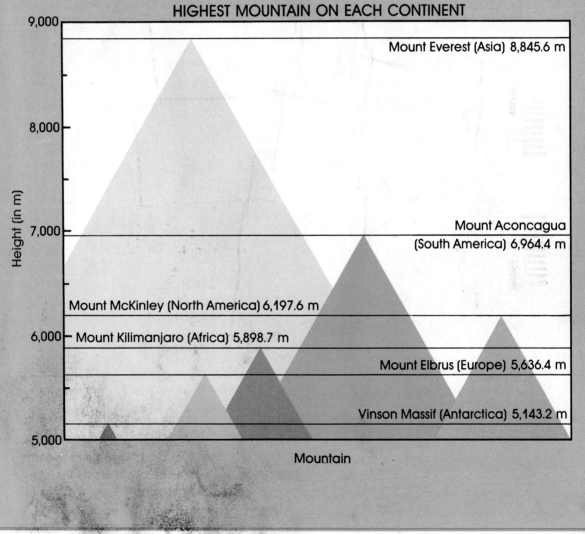

HIGHEST MOUNTAIN ON EACH CONTINENT

Mount Everest (Asia) 8,845.6 m

Mount Aconcagua (South America) 6,964.4 m

Mount McKinley (North America) 6,197.6 m

Mount Kilimanjaro (Africa) 5,898.7 m

Mount Elbrus (Europe) 5,636.4 m

Vinson Massif (Antarctica) 5,143.2 m

Height (in m)

Mountain

Chapter 12

Forecasting the Weather

LESSON QUESTIONS

Weather Instruments (pp. 284–288)
1. What is a forecast?
2. Describe three ways that wind speed and direction are measured.
3. What is relative humidity? How is relative humidity measured?
4. Explain what a relative humidity of 75 percent means.
5. What is air pressure? How is air pressure measured?

Collecting Weather Data (pp. 289–291)
1. Where is weather information for the National Meteorological Center gathered?
2. How are satellites used to gather weather data?

Weather Forecasts (pp. 292–295)
1. Distinguish between an air mass and a front.
2. How are air masses and fronts related to changes in weather?
3. What are the jet streams? How do jet streams influence weather?

4. Compare the accuracy of a short-range forecast with that of a long-range forecast.

Weather Maps (pp. 296–297)
1. What is a weather map?
2. Distinguish between isotherms and isobars.
3. What do the symbols H and L on a weather map indicate? What types of weather are usually associated with each of these symbols?

Storms (pp. 298–303)
1. Describe the formation of a thunderstorm.
2. How are hailstones formed?
3. What causes lightning?
4. What is a tornado?
5. What conditions are usually present when tornadoes form?
6. What is a hurricane?
7. Compare a hurricane and a tornado.

PROBLEM SOLVING

Use after page 288. Two people in different cities hang their clothes to dry on a clothesline. The temperature in city A is 25°C. The relative humidity is 50 percent. The temperature in city B is 25°C. The relative humidity is 90 percent. In which city will the clothes probably dry faster? Why?

Use after page 291. Many cities have weather records for every day of the past

100 years. Why are these old records important to meteorologists?

Use after page 297. On June 1 a computer is directed to make two forecasts. One is for the average temperature in the state of Texas for the entire month of June. The second is for the exact high temperature in Dallas on June 22. Which forecast is likely to be more accurate? Why?

Reading a Weather Map

There are many types of weather maps. One type is shown here. Use the map, including the map legend, to answer the following questions.

1. What is the high temperature for Washington, D.C.?
2. What is the weather like in Fargo?
3. In which city is the temperature expected to be higher—Denver or Chicago?
4. In which of these cities is it snowing—Santa Fe, Little Rock, Indianapolis, or Albany?
5. In which city is the temperature expected to be lower—El Paso or Nashville?
6. According to this map, what is the weather expected to be like in your town?

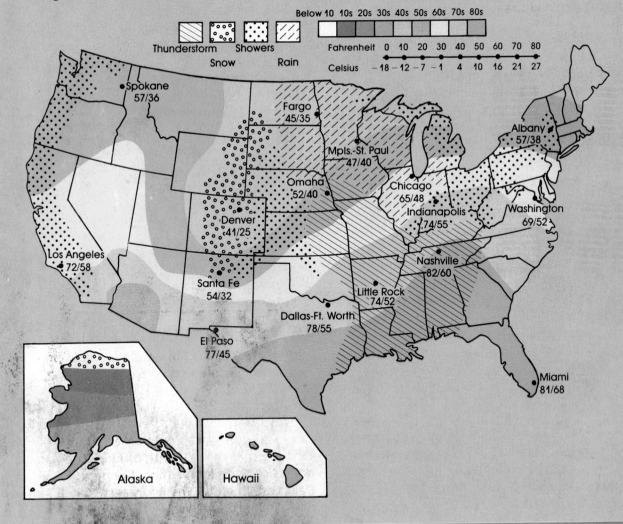

Thunderstorm   Showers   Snow   Rain

Below 10 10s 20s 30s 40s 50s 60s 70s 80s

Fahrenheit	0	10	20	30	40	50	60	70	80
Celsius	−18	−12	−7	−1	4	10	16	21	27

Spokane 57/36
Fargo 45/35
Mpls.-St. Paul 47/40
Omaha 52/40
Chicago 65/48
Albany 57/38
Indianapolis 74/55
Washington 69/52
Los Angeles 72/58
Denver 41/25
Santa Fe 54/32
Dallas-Ft. Worth 78/55
Little Rock 74/52
Nashville 82/60
El Paso 77/45
Miami 81/68

Alaska   Hawaii

Chapter 13

Exploring Space

LESSON QUESTIONS

Exploring from Earth (pp. 308–312)
1. What is astronomy?
2. Compare Ptolemy's model of the solar system with the model developed by Copernicus.
3. Distinguish between a refracting telescope and a reflecting telescope.
4. What is an observatory?
5. What is a radio telescope? Name two advantages of using a radio telescope over using an optical telescope.
6. Distinguish between a dish telescope and a linear array telescope.

Exploring from Space (pp. 313–319)
1. Explain how a rocket overcomes Earth's gravity.
2. What is a satellite? Describe some of the information obtained from satellites.
3. What is a Landsat satellite? What types of information are obtained from Landsat satellites?
4. How are satellites used to help forecast weather?
5. Describe how satellites are used to send radio and television signals.
6. Describe what was learned from IRAS.
7. What is a space probe?

8. Describe what was learned from the Voyager space probes.

People in Space (pp. 320–322)
1. Who were Yuri Gagarin and John Glenn?
2. Describe Project Apollo.
3. What was Skylab?
4. What is a space shuttle?
5. Describe some of the useful tasks a space shuttle can help to complete.

The Future of Space (pp. 323–324)
1. How would power plants in space work?
2. Name some advantages of having hospitals in space.

How Space Exploration Affects You (pp. 325–327)
1. Describe some spin-offs of the clothlike fabrics developed for the space program.
2. How have electronic games developed from the space program?
3. Describe methods that were developed for the space program and are now used by the food industry to keep food fresh.
4. What medical products are spin-offs from space?

PROBLEM SOLVING

Use after page 312. Many scientists are looking forward to the day when observatories will be located on orbiting space stations. What advantages would there be to having these observatories?

Use after page 319. Which satellite do you think is the most important? Why? Many uses for satellites were discussed in this lesson. Describe another way you would like satellites to be used in the future.

Reading a Line Graph

This line graph shows the total amount of time manned, American spacecraft have spent in space. The graph was made by taking the total amount of time spacecraft spent in space for a given year and adding it to the total from the previous years. Use the line graph to answer the following questions.

1. According to this graph, in what year was the first American manned spacecraft sent into space?

2. About how many days were spent in space by the end of 1968?

3. About how many days were spent in space by early 1984?

4. During which years was there the sharpest increase in days spent in space?

5. About how many days had been spent in space by 1986?

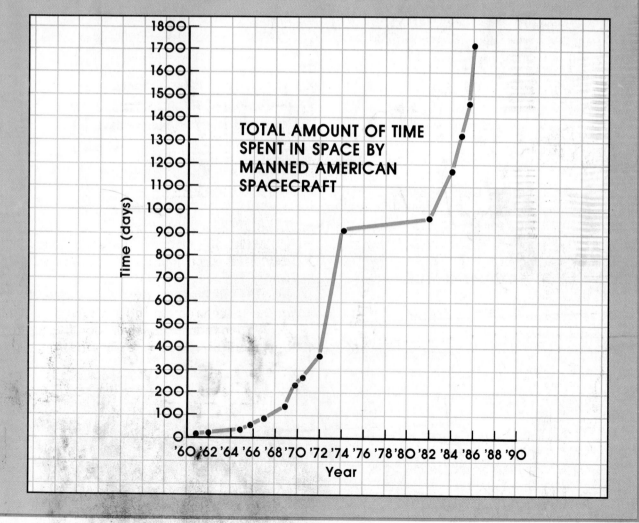

TOTAL AMOUNT OF TIME SPENT IN SPACE BY MANNED AMERICAN SPACECRAFT

Chapter 14

Control Systems of the Body

LESSON QUESTIONS

The Nervous System (pp. 338–339)
1. What is the nervous system?
2. Distinguish between the central nervous system and the peripheral nervous system.
3. Distinguish between voluntary and involuntary responses. Give two examples of each.

Nerve Cells and Nerves (pp. 340–343)
1. Describe three parts of a nerve cell.
2. Distinguish between a nerve cell and a nerve.
3. What is a sensory nerve cell?
4. What is a motor nerve cell?
5. What is a connecting nerve cell?
6. Explain what a reflex is.

The Brain and Spinal Cord (pp. 344–347)
1. Describe the brain.
2. Where is the brain stem located? What actions does the brain stem control?
3. Where is the cerebellum located? What is the main function of the cerebellum?
4. Where is the cerebrum located? Why is the cerebrum considered the most important part of the brain?
5. Describe the spinal cord.

Disorders of the Nervous System (pp. 348–349)
1. What is paralysis?
2. Describe cerebral palsy.
3. How do misused drugs affect the nervous system?

The Endocrine System (pp. 350–355)
1. What is the endocrine system?
2. What are glands?
3. What are hormones?
4. Describe the pituitary gland.
5. Describe the thyroid gland. What hormone does this gland produce? What does this hormone control?
6. Where are the parathyroid glands located? What do they control?
7. Where is insulin produced? What is the purpose of insulin?
8. Describe the adrenal glands. What does adrenalin do?

PROBLEM SOLVING

Use after page 339. What voluntary and involuntary actions take place to help your body produce and conserve heat when you are cold?

Use after page 347. Scientists do not do experiments on the brains of human beings. How do you think they learned what each part of the brain controls?

Use after page 349. When people suffer head injuries, a doctor will usually flash a bright light into the person's eyes. What do you think the doctor is observing?

Reading a Diagram

Diagrams can contain many types of information. This diagram shows the parts of the cerebrum. It indicates what functions are controlled by each part. Use the diagram to answer the following questions.

1. What is the front part of the cerebrum called?
2. What is the rear top part of the cerebrum called?
3. In which part of the cerebrum are body movement and coordination controlled?
4. In which part of the cerebrum is vision controlled?
5. In which part of the cerebrum is body position controlled?

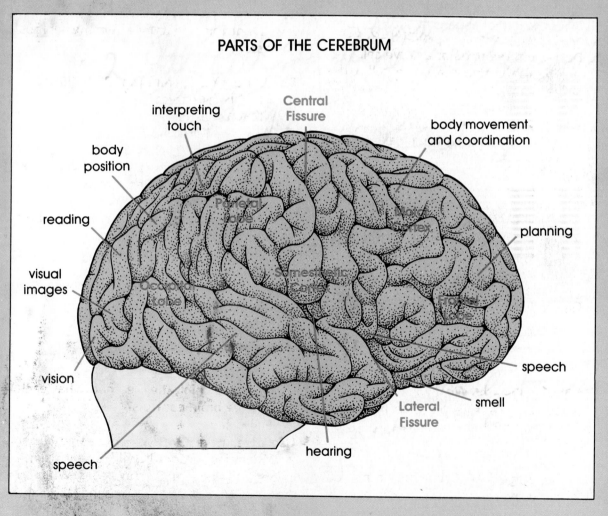

PARTS OF THE CEREBRUM

Chapter 15

Growth and Development

LESSON QUESTIONS

Reproduction (pp. 360–361)
1. What is reproduction?
2. Describe how single-celled organisms reproduce. What is this process called?
3. How do hydra and yeasts reproduce?

Reproduction and Cells (pp. 362–364)
1. Describe what happens to chromosomes before and after mitosis.
2. Distinguish between a sperm cell and an egg cell.
3. How do reproductive cells differ from other cells in the body?
4. What is a zygote?
5. What is fertilization?

A New Organism Develops (pp. 365–366)
1. What happens to a frog zygote during the first few days?
2. What is an embryo?

Passing on Information (pp. 367–373)
1. Explain why a child often has features of both parents.
2. What is an inherited trait? Give two examples of inherited traits.
3. What are genes?
4. Distinguish between a dominant gene and a recessive gene. For eye color, which gene is dominant, the gene for brown eyes or the gene for blue eyes?
5. Explain how two parents with brown eyes can have a child with blue eyes.
6. What is genetics?

The Life Cycle (pp. 374–375)
1. What is a life cycle?
2. Describe infancy.
3. What changes occur during childhood?
4. What is adolescence? What changes occur during adolescence?
5. What is the beginning of adolescence called?
6. Describe adulthood.

PROBLEM SOLVING

Use after page 361. Sometimes, pollution prevents living things from reproducing. For example, the eggshells of some pelicans were so thin that they often broke before the baby birds could hatch. A chemical called DDT is known to cause this problem. DDT is used to fight insects. But pelicans eat fish, not insects. How might the pelicans have taken in the DDT? Why is it important to protect living things from this type of pollution?

Use after page 364. Suppose a scientist observes three cells through a microscope. One cell contains 46 chromosomes, another contains 23 chromosomes, and the third contains 92 chromosomes. Explain what the scientist is observing.

Use after page 366. Study the table on page 366. What can you conclude about the relationship between an organism's development time and its size?

Reading a Line Graph

A line graph can be used to compare information. This line graph compares the average heights of boys and girls from birth to 18 months of age. Use the graph to answer the following questions.

1. On the average, who is taller at birth, boys or girls?
2. At what time during the first 18 months are the average heights of boys and girls the closest?
3. Would a 9-month-old boy who is 27 inches tall be above average or below average?
4. What is the average height of a 12-month-old girl?
5. On the average, who is taller at 18 months, boys or girls?

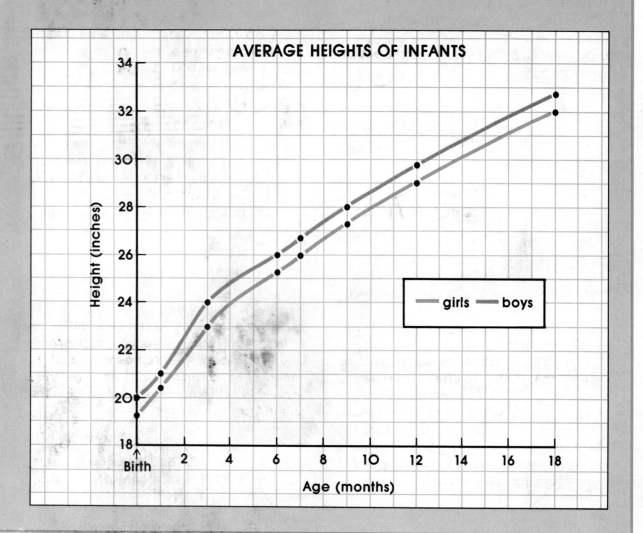

413

Glossary

Key to Pronunciation

a apple, bat	**i** if, pig	**sh** she, wish	**ə** stands for:
ā ate, page	**ī** idea, fine	**th** think, moth	a in asleep
â air, care	**ng** ring, sink	**ͲH** the, bathe	e in garden
ä father, star	**o** ox, top	**u** uncle, sun	i in pencil
ch chest, such	**ō** owe, no	**ù** pull, foot	o in button
e egg, bed	**ô** orbit, saw	**ü** glue, boot	u in circus
ē even, me	**oi** oil, joy	**zh** usual, vision	
ėr earn, bird	**ou** out, mouse		

This Key to Pronunciation is adapted from *Scott, Foresman Intermediate Dictionary*, by E. L. Thorndike and Clarence L. Barnhart. Copyright © 1983 by Scott, Foresman and Company. Reprinted by permission.

absorbed   Action in which light waves are trapped by matter. *pp. 161, 183*

acid   A compound that contains hydrogen and that has a sour taste. *p. 124*

adaptation   (ad ap tā′shən)   Any structure or response that helps an organism to survive. *p. 35*

adolescence (ad ə les′əns)   Stage of human life that follows childhood and that involves rapid growth and change. *p. 375*

adrenal (ə drē′nəl) **glands**   Two glands, one at the top of each kidney, that release hormones that help a person deal with stress and emergencies. *p. 354*

adulthood   The final stage of human life. *p. 375*

air mass   A large body of air with the same amount of moisture and humidity throughout. *p. 292*

air pressure   The push of air on all surfaces. *p. 288*

alternating (ôl′tər nā ting) **current (ac)**   Current electricity in which the electrons flow first in one direction and then in the opposite direction. *p. 204*

ampere (am′pir)   A unit of measurement used to indicate the number of electrons that move past a point in a conductor in one second. *p. 210*

amplitude   The amount of energy in a wave. *pp. 155, 191*

anemometer (an ə mom′ə tər)   An instrument that is used to measure wind speed. *p. 285*

annual rings   Rings of wood that are produced yearly by growth tissue in the stems of trees. *p. 30*

aquatic (ə kwat′ik) **habitat**   A body of water where organisms live. *p. 98*

astronomy (ə stron′ə mē)   The study of space and the many things it contains. *p. 308*

atom   The smallest particle of an element. *p. 117*

atomic number   The number of protons in the nucleus of an atom. *p. 118*

bacteria (bak tir′ē ə)   The simplest protists. *p. 19*

barometer (bə rom′ə tər)   An instrument that is used to measure air pressure. *p. 288*

base   A compound that contains oxygen and hydrogen and that has a bitter taste and feels slippery. *p. 125*

behavior   The activities and actions of an animal. *p. 62*

biological clock   A chemical clock by which an organism controls the timing of certain activities. *p. 43*

biome (bī′ōm)   A region of the earth that has the same climate throughout and where many of the same kinds of plants and animals live. *p. 79*

biosphere (bī′ə sfir)   The earth's life sphere. *p. 78*

brain stem   The part of the brain that controls such involuntary actions as breathing and heartbeat. *p. 344*

breeding grounds   Regions to which certain animals migrate to reproduce and to raise their young. *p. 64*

canines (kā′nīnz)   Sharp pointed teeth found near the front of the mouth. Such teeth are large in meat-eating animals. *p. 51*

cell   The smallest living part of an organism *p. 6*   A device in which chemical energy is changed to electrical energy. *p. 307*

cell membrane   The membrane that surrounds all animal cells. *p. 8*

cell wall   The thick wall that is found outside the cell membrane of a plant cell. *p. 10*

central nervous system   The brain and spinal cord. *p. 339*

cerebellum (ser ə bel′əm)   The part of the brain that controls body balance and helps the muscles work together. *p. 345*

cerebrum (ser′ə brəm)   The part of the brain that controls thinking and reasoning. *p. 345*

chemical bonds   The forces that hold together the atoms in a compound. *p. 143*

chemical change   A change in which one or more different kinds of matter are formed. *p. 135*

chemical energy   Energy stored in chemical bonds. *p. 144*

chemical property   A property that determines how an element or compound reacts with other elements or compounds. *p. 135*

chemical reaction (rē ak′shən)   A chemical change. *p. 138*

childhood   Stage of human life following infancy. *p. 374*

chlorophyll (klôr′ə fil)   The chemical in plant cells that traps energy from sunlight. *p. 11*

chloroplast (klôr′ə plast)   The structure in a plant cell that contains the green chemical called chlorophyll. Food is made in chloroplasts. *p. 10*

chromosomes (krō′mə sōmz)   Threadlike structures found in the nucleus that contain a cell's genes. *p. 7*

climate   The average weather for a large region over a long period of time. *p. 79*

climatologist (klī mə tol′ə jist)   A scientist who studies climate. *p. 294*

cold-blooded animal   An animal whose body temperature changes as the temperature of the environment changes. *p. 67*

combustion chamber   The chamber in a rocket in which fuel is burned. *p. 313*

compound (kom′pound)   A substance made up of two or more elements that are chemically joined. *p. 122*

compression   A region of crowded air particles. *p. 182*

concave lens   A lens that is thinner in the middle than at the edge. *p. 171*

concave (kon kāv') **mirror**   A mirror in which the reflecting surface curves inward. *p. 169*

conifers (kō'nə fərz)   Trees that produce seeds in cones. *p. 84*

connecting nerve cells   Nerve cells that connect sensory nerve cells with motor nerve cells. *p. 341*

continental (kon tə nen'təl) **drift theory**   The theory that the continents were once a single land mass that broke up, with the continents then drifting apart. *p. 261*

convex lens   A lens that is thicker in the middle than it is at the edge. *p. 171*

convex (kon veks') **mirror**   A mirror in which the reflecting surface curves outward. *p. 169*

cytoplasm (sī'tə plaz əm)   The jellylike material outside the nucleus of a cell. *p. 8*

decibels (des'ə bels)   Units used to measure the loudness of sounds. *p. 196*

deciduous (di sij'ü əs) **forest**   A biome in which broad-leaved trees are prominent. *p. 86*

density   The mass of a certain volume of a substance. *p. 135*

desalination (dē sal ə nā'shən)   The process by which salt is separated from seawater. *p. 249*

desert   A biome that receives little or no rain. *p. 95*

direct current (dc)   Current electricity in which the electrons flow in only one direction. *p. 204*

dome mountain   A mountain that forms when magma pushes the crust up and then hardens under the crust. *p. 278*

dominant gene   A gene that, when present, determines a trait of an offspring. *p. 371*

Doppler effect   The relationship between pitch and motion that causes sounds given off by moving objects to change pitch as the objects move toward, then away, from you. *p. 189*

downdraft (doun'draft)   A falling air current. *p. 299*

earthquake   A movement of the earth's crust. *p. 266*

egg cell   The female reproductive cell. *p. 363*

electromagnetic spectrum (i lek trō magnet'ik spek'trəm)   All the forms of radiant energy. *p. 154*

electrons (i lek'tronz)   Particles that move around the nucleus of an atom. *p. 116*

element (el'ə mənt)   A substance made up of only one kind of atom. *p. 117*

embryo (em'brē ō)   An organism during the early stages of its development. *p. 365*

endocrine (en'dō krin) **system**   A system that helps control the rate of many body activities by releasing chemicals called hormones. *p. 350*

environment (en vī'rən mənt)   The conditions that are found where an organism lives. The environment includes all the living and nonliving things in an area. *p. 32*

estuary (es'chü er ē)   An aquatic habitat where a freshwater river flows into the ocean. *p. 101*

fault-block mountains   Mountains that form when blocks of crust on one side of a fault move up while blocks of crust on the other side move down. *p. 277*

faults   Cracks in the earth's crust where blocks of rock have moved. *p. 267*

feedstock A raw material from which other materials are made. *p. 245*

fertile Condition in which soil is rich in the minerals that plants need to grow. *p. 237*

fertilization (fėr tə lə zā'shən) The process by which a sperm cell and an egg cell join. *p. 364*

fission (fish'ən) A type of reproduction in which a cell splits into two. *p. 361*

focus The place where blocks of rock slip during an earthquake. *p. 267*

folded mountains Mountains that form as a result of collisions between plates. *p. 277*

forecast A statement of what the weather will probably be like in the next few days. *p. 284*

fossil fuels Fuels that have formed from the bodies of dead plants and animals. *p. 245*

frequency (frē'kwən sē) The number of waves that pass a point in a certain period of time. *pp. 155, 187*

freshwater habitat An aquatic habitat such as a pond, lake, or stream. *p. 98*

front The border between two air masses. *p. 292*

genes The units that control a cell's activities. Genes control the growth and development of an organism. *p. 7*

genetics (jə net'iks) The study of inherited traits. *p. 372*

glands Special organs or tissues in the body that make chemical substances. *p. 350*

grassland A biome in which grasses are prominent and trees are scarce. *p. 92*

growth regions The areas within a plant where growth takes place. Such areas contain growth tissue. *p. 28*

hibernation (hī bər nā'shən) The very deep sleep in which some animals spend the winter. *p. 67*

hormones (hôr'mōnz) Chemicals produced by the endocrine glands. *p. 351*

hurricane (hėr'ə kān) A large storm involving strong winds and heavy rain that develops over the ocean in a tropical area. *p. 302*

imprinting Learning that occurs when newly-hatched birds identify the first moving thing they see as being their mother. *p. 13*

incisors (in sī'zərz) Sharp front teeth used by meat-eating animals to tear off chunks of flesh. *p. 51*

indicator (in'də kā tər) A substance that changes color when it is added to an acid or a base. *p. 126*

infancy Stage of human life occurring after birth and lasting for several months. *p. 374*

infrared (in frə red') **waves** Waves of radiant energy with lower frequencies than visible light waves. *p. 158*

inherited traits Traits or features that are passed on from parents to offspring. *p. 368*

instinct (in'stingkt) Any behavior pattern that an animal is born with. *p. 62*

integrated (in'tə grā tid) **circuit** A circuit in which all parts and connections are contained on a chip. *p. 217*

isobar (ī'sə bär) A line on a weather map connecting places that have the same air pressure. *p. 296*

isotherm (ī'sə therm) A line on a weather map connecting areas that have the same temperature. *p. 296*

isotope (ī'sə tōp) An atom of the same element that has a different number of neutrons. *p. 119*

jet streams   High-speed "ribbons" of air high above the earth. *p. 293*

kinetic (ki net'ik) **energy**   The energy of motion. *p. 203*

landfill   A place where wastes are dumped and then covered with soil. *p. 243*

laser (lā'zər)   A device that strengthens light. *p. 173*

lava   Magma that reaches the earth's surface. *p. 272*

law of conservation of energy   The law that states that energy is neither created nor destroyed during a chemical reaction. *p. 141*

law of conservation of matter   The law that states that matter is neither created nor destroyed during a chemical reaction. *p. 141*

life cycle   The stages that a living thing goes through during its life. *p. 374*

longitudinal wave   A wave in which particles of matter vibrate along the same path in which the wave travels. *p. 181*

Mach (mäk) **number**   A scale that compares the speed of objects to the speed of sound. *p. 194*

magma (mag'mə)   Melted rock that forms below the earth's crust. *p. 271*

magma pool   An underground chamber in which magma collects. *p. 274*

mantle   The layer of the earth under the crust. *p. 263*

mariculture   Farming of the oceans for food. *p. 253*

marine habitat   An aquatic habitat in which the water is salt water. *p. 99*

mass   A measure of the amount of matter in an object. *p. 112*

mass number   The total number of particles in the nucleus of an atom. *p. 118*

matter   Anything that has mass and takes up space. *p. 112*

memory circuits   Circuits in a computer that store information. *p. 218*

meteorologist (mē tē ə rol'ə jist)   A scientist who studies weather. *p. 284*

meteorology (mē tē ə rol'ə jē)   The study of weather. *p. 284*

microprocessor (mī krō pros'es ər)   A chip, found in many kinds of computers and other devices, that contains problem-solving circuits. *p. 219*

migration (mī grā'shən)   The movement of an animal or a group of animals over a long distance. *p. 63*

mimicry (mim'ik rē)   An adaption in which an animal looks like a dangerous or poisonous animal. *p. 61*

mineral (min'ər əl)   Any pure, hard material that is found in the earth's crust. *p. 239*

mitosis (mī tō'sis)   The process by which a cell divides to form two cells. *p. 14*

molars (mō'lərz)   The flat teeth found along the sides of the mouth. Such teeth are large in grazing animals. *p. 51*

molecule (mol'ə kyül)   A chemical unit made up of two or more atoms. *p. 122*

motor nerve cells   Nerve cells that carry messages from the central nervous system to parts of the body such as muscles. *p. 341*

native metals   Metals that are not chemically combined with other materials. *p. 241*

natural resource (ri sôrs')   A valuable material that is found in nature and used by people to meet their needs. *p. 234*

nerve cells Cells that carry messages in the nervous system. *p. 340*

nervous system A system that helps control body activities. It includes the brain, spinal cord, and a network of nerve cells. *p. 338*

neutral (nü′trəl) The condition of a substance that is neither an acid nor a base. *p. 126*

neutron (nü′tron) A particle found in the nucleus of an atom. *p. 116*

nodules (noj′ülz) Round lumps found on the ocean floor that contain certain metals. *p. 252*

noise Unpleasant sound. *p. 192*

nonrenewable (non ri nü′ə bəl) **resource** A resource that exists in a limited amount. *p. 238*

nuclear energy Energy that is stored in the nucleus of an atom. *p. 145*

nuclear fission (fish′ən) The splitting of a nucleus into smaller parts. *p. 146*

nuclear fusion (fyü′zhən) The joining, or combining, of nuclei. *p. 147*

nuclear (nü′klē ər) **reaction** A reaction involving the nuclei of atoms. *p. 145*

nucleus (nü′klē əs) A round body inside the cell. It contains the genes. *p. 7* The central part of an atom. *p. 116*

observatory (əb zėr′və tôr ē) A building that is set up for the study of outer space. *p. 310*

ohm (ōm) The unit of electric resistance. *p. 208*

opaque (ō pāk′) Condition of matter through which light cannot pass. *p. 162*

orbits The paths that electrons move in. *p. 116*

ore Rock or mineral from which useful metal can be obtained. *p. 239*

organ (ôr′gən) A group of tissues working together to carry out a body activity. *p. 22*

organism (ôr′gə niz əm) A living thing. *p. 6*

oxides (ok′ sīdz) Compounds formed when oxygen combines with another element. *p. 128*

pancreas (pan′krē əs) An organ that produces substances that help digest food and that also produces a hormone which controls how the cells use sugar. *p. 352*

parallel circuit A circuit in which there is more than one path for the electrons. *p. 216*

parathyroid (par ə thī′roid) **glands** Four small endocrine glands that produce hormones which control the amount of calcium and other minerals found in the blood. *p. 352*

periodic table A chart containing many facts about elements and their atoms. *p. 120*

peripheral (pə rif′ər əl) **nervous system** The nerves that extend from the central nervous system to the edges of the body. *p. 339*

phototropism (fō tō trō′piz əm) The response of a plant to light. *p. 33*

physical change A change in the size, shape, or state of matter. *p. 134*

physical property A property that can be identified without causing a chemical change in the matter. *p. 134*

pitch How high or low a sound seems. *p. 188*

pituitary (pi tü′ə ter ē) **gland** An endocrine gland that controls other glands and is important to normal growth. *p. 351*

419

plankton (plangk'tən) Microscopic plants that float on the surface of the ocean. *p. 99*

plate tectonic (tek ton'ik) **theory** The theory that the crust of the earth is made up of sections, called plates, that are in motion. *p. 263*

printed circuit Circuit in which the transistors and all other parts are connected with flat wires. *p. 217*

prism (priz'əm) A specially shaped transparent object that is used to separate light. *p. 164*

program A set of instructions that tells a computer what to do. *p. 219*

protective coloration (prə tek'tiv kul ə-rā'shən) The structural adaptation in which an animal has a color similar to the color of its environment. *p. 59*

protective resemblance (ri zem'bləns) The adaptation in which an animal looks similar to something in its environment. *p. 60*

protist (prō'tist) A single-celled organism. *p. 17*

proton (prō'ton) A particle found in the nucleus of an atom. *p. 116*

protozoans (prō tə zō'ənz) Animallike protists. *p. 17*

puberty (pyü'bər tē) The beginning of adolescence. *p. 375*

radio telescope A telescope that collects radio waves given off by objects in space. *p. 310*

radioactive (rā dē ō ak'tiv) **elements** Elements that break down into other elements. *p. 149*

rarefaction A region of few air particles. *p. 182*

reaction time The time it takes for a person to react when messages travel to and from the brain. *p. 342*

real image An image that can be focused on a screen or film. *p. 168*

recessive gene A gene that does not determine a trait when paired with a dominant gene. *p. 371*

recycling (rē sī'kling) The collecting and retreating of materials so that they can be reused. *p. 242*

reflected Action in which light waves are bounced off matter. *pp. 161, 187*

reflecting telescope A telescope that uses a curved mirror to gather light. *p. 309*

reflex A response in which messages travel over sensory nerve cells to the spinal cord and directly back to motor nerve cells. *p. 342*

refracting telescope A telescope that uses a lens to gather light. *p. 309*

refraction (ri frak'shən) The bending of light. *p. 170*

relative humidity The amount of water vapor in the air compared with the most the air can hold at that temperature. *p. 286*

renewable (ri nü'ə bəl) **resource** A resource that is replaced naturally. *p. 234*

reproduction The process by which living things produce other living things of the same kind. *p. 360*

response (ri spons') A reaction of an organism to something in its environment. *p. 33*

rocket A vehicle that is used to send objects into space. *p. 313*

salt A compound made from an acid and a base. *p. 126*

satellite (sat'ə līt) An object that orbits a larger object. Satellites are used to study space and also to study conditions on earth, such as weather. *pp. 290, 314*

sea-floor spreading   Process by which hot liquid rock flows up through cracks in the ocean floor, hardens to new ocean floor, and pushes older floor material outward. *p. 262*

seismograph (sīz′mə graf)   An instrument that can measure and record earthquake waves. *p. 268*

sensory nerve cells   Nerve cells that respond to an internal or external stimulus. *p. 341*

series circuit   A circuit in which there is only one path for the electrons. *p. 216*

solar still   A device that uses energy from the sun to separate salt from sea water. *p. 250*

sonar (sō′när)   The use of high-frequency sound waves to locate schools of fish and other underwater objects. *p. 195*

space probe   A spacecraft sent out to gather data about the moon or the planets. *p. 318*

sperm cell   The male reproductive cell. *p. 363*

stimulus (stim′yə ləs)   A condition in the environment that can cause a response. *p. 33*

structural adaptation   An adaptation that involves some part of an organism's body. *p. 50*

supersonic   Speed greater than the speed of sound. *p. 194*

system   A group of organs that work together to do a major job that keeps an organism alive. *p. 22*

taiga (tī′gə)   A large biome south of the tundra. Conifers are abundant in the taiga. *p. 84*

theory (thē′ər ē)   An idea that is used to explain observed facts. *p. 260*

thunderstorm (thun′dər stôrm)   A storm in which violent air currents, rain or hail, and lightning are produced. *p. 298*

thyroid (thī′roid) **gland**   An endocrine gland located in the neck. It produces a hormone that controls how fast cells obtain energy from food. *p. 352*

tissue (tish′ü)   A team of cells in a plant or animal that does a special job. *p. 21*

tornado   A very violent, short-lived windstorm. *p. 300*

translucent (trans lü′sənt)   Condition of matter in which light is scattered as it passes through. *p. 162*

transmitted   Action in which waves are passed through matter. *pp. 161, 183*

transparent   Condition of matter in which light can pass through without being scattered. *p. 162*

tropical forest   A biome that has a warm, rainy climate and that contains a rich variety of plant and animal life. *p. 89*

tropisms (trō′piz əmz)   Plant responses that involve growth. *p. 33*

tundra (tun′drə)   A large biome of the far north. It is the coldest biome. *p. 81*

ultrasonic   Sounds with a frequency above 20,000 cycles per second. *p. 195*

ultraviolet (ul trə vī′ə lit) **waves**   Waves of radiant energy with higher frequencies than light waves have. *p. 157*

updraft (up′draft)   A rising air current. *p. 276*

upwelling   Action in which ocean water from the bottom rises to the surface. *p. 100*

vacuum (vak′yum)   Any space that contains little or no matter. *p. 154*

virtual image   An image that appears behind a mirror. *p. 168*

visible light spectrum   All the bands of visible light. *p. 164*

viruses (vī′rəs es)   Complex chemical links between living and nonliving things that cause disease and must use the energy of a living cell to reproduce. *p. 6*

volcano   An opening in the earth's crust through which magma, ash, and steam erupt. *p. 270*

volt   A unit of measurement used to indicate the force that moves electrons through a circuit. *p. 209*

warm-blooded animal   An animal that has a fairly constant body temperature. *p. 68*

wavelength   The distance between the crest of one wave and the crest of the next wave. *pp. 155, 187*

weather map   A map on which the weather conditions over a large area are recorded. *p. 296*

weight   A measure of the force of gravity on an object. *p. 113*

wet-and-dry-bulb thermometer   An instrument that is used to measure relative humidity. *p. 286*

wind sock   An instrument that can show both wind speed and wind direction. *p. 285*

wind vane   An instrument that is used to determine wind direction. *p. 285*

zygote (zī′gōt)   Cell formed when a sperm cell and an egg cell join. *p. 364*

Index

Credits

Cover: Michael Adams   **Back Cover Photo:** Manfred Kage/Peter Arnold, Inc.

Other art: Richard Amundsen, Ralph Brillhardt, Suzanne Clee, Rick Cooley, Floyd Cooper, Ric Del Rossi, Gail Eisnitz, Terry Foreman, Seward Hung, Robert Jackson, Susan Johnston, Phillip Jones, George Kelvin, Peter Krempasky III, Joseph LeMonnier, John Lind, Rebecca Merrilees, Alan Neider, Taylor Oughton, Heidi Palmer, Tom Powers, Albert Pucci, Sally Schaedler

Map, p. 264, adapted from *Discover* magazine, © 1982, Mark Kaplan.

The Adventure of Science A–B: *bkgd,* © Thomas J. Styczynski/Click, Chicago; *m.* E.R. Degginger. A: *l.* Historical Pictures Service, Chicago; *r.* Camera Hawaii. B: © Manfred Kage/Peter Arnold, Inc. C: Dan De Wilde for Silver Burdett & Ginn. D: NASA; *t. inset* © Grace Moore; *b. inset* © Phil Degginger/Bruce Coleman. E: Silver Burdett & Ginn. F–H: Jane Burton/Bruce Coleman. I: U.S. Geological Survey. J: E.R. Degginger.

Unit One vi: *t.* David Scharf/Peter Arnold, Inc.; *b.* Grant Heilman Photography. 1: *t.l., t.r., b.r.* Runk/Schoenberger/ Grant Heilman Photography; *b.l.* Jeff Rotman.

Chapter 1 Opener: © Lennart Nilsson, *Close to Nature,* Pantheon Books, Inc. N.Y.; © CNRI/Science Photo Library/Photo Researchers, Inc.; © B. Heggeler/Biozentrum, University of Basel/Science Photo Library/Photo Researchers, Inc.; © Lee Simon/Stammers/Science Photo Library/Photo Researchers, Inc.; Silver Burdett & Ginn. 4: *t.* Z. Leszczynski/Peter Arnold, Inc.; *m.* © Gilbert Giant/Photo Researchers, Inc.; *b.* Stephen J. Krasemann/Photo Researchers, Inc. 5: *t.* E.R. Degginger; *m.* Animals, Animals/L.L.T. Rhodes; *b.* © Cosmos Blank/National Audubon Society Collection, Photo Researchers, Inc. 6: © Charles Lightdale/Photo Researchers, Inc. 9: Silver Burdett & Ginn. 11: Alfred Owczarzak/Taurus Photos. 12: *t.l.* Terry Kirk/ Tom Stack & Associates; *b.l.* © Manfred Kage/Peter Arnold, Inc.; *m.r.* Roland Birke/Peter Arnold, Inc.; *b.r.* Alfred Owczarzak/ Taurus Photos. 13: Silver Burdett & Ginn. 16: *t.* E.R. Degginger; *b.* Runk/Schoenberger/Grant Heilman Photography. 17: © Biophoto Associates/Photo Researchers, Inc. 18: © Manfred Kage/Peter Arnold, Inc. 19: E.R. Degginger; *t.l., m.l., m.r. insets* © Manfred Kage/Peter Arnold, Inc.; *t.r. inset* © Eric V. Grave/Photo Researchers, Inc. 20: *l.* © Brain/Parker/Science Source/ Photo Researchers, Inc.; *m.* © Dr. Brad Amos/Science Source/Photo Researchers, Inc. 21: © Manfred Kage/Peter Arnold, Inc. 22: Rita Meyers/Tom Stack & Associates. 23: Dave Davidson/Tom Stack & Associates.

Chapter 2 Opener: © Bruno J. Zehuder/Peter Arnold, Inc.; Trees from the U.S. National Bonsai Collection, National Arboretum, Washington, D.C. Photographs from the book Timeless Trees © 1986, Peter L. Bloomer and Mary Holmes Bloomer; Russ Kinne/Comstock; S. Rannels/Grant Heilman Photography. 28: © Manfred Kage/Peter Arnold, Inc. 31: Dr. David Evans. 32: IMAGERY. 33: Grant Heilman Photography. 34: Silver Burdett & Ginn. 35: *t., m.* Adrian Davies/Bruce Coleman; *b.* Hickson-Bender Photography for Silver Burdett & Ginn. 36: *t.* Breck P. Kent; *b.l.* Stephen J. Krasemann/Peter Arnold, Inc.; *b.r.* E.R. Degginger. 37: *t.l.* John Shaw/Tom Stack & Associates; *t.r.* Grant Heilman Photography; *b.* Bob and Clara Calhoun/Bruce Coleman. 38: Dan De Wilde for Silver Burdett & Ginn. 39: *l., b.* E.R. Degginger; *m.* Grant Heilman Photography; *r.* © Calvin Larsen/Photo Researchers, Inc. 40: Stephen J. Krasemann/Peter Arnold, Inc. 41: *l., r.* W.S. Terhume/ United States Department of Agriculture, Forest Service, Nicolet National Forest; *m.* Minnesota Department of Natural Resources. 42: *l.* Grant Heilman Photography; *r.* Breck P. Kent. 43: *t.* IMAGERY; *b.* Grant Heilman Photography; *t. inset, b. inset* Dan Suizo. 45: Grant Heilman Photography. 47: © Kenneth W. Fink/Photo Researchers, Inc.

Chapter 3 Opener: © Merlin D. Tuttle; © Merlin D. Tuttle/Photo Researchers, Inc.; 50: Leonard Lee Rue III. 51: *l.* Isaac Geib/Grant Heilman Photography; *r.* Grant Heilman Photography; *b.* Jen and Des Bartlett/Bruce Coleman. 52: Hans Pfletschinger/Peter Arnold, Inc. 53: Stephen J. Krasemann/Peter Arnold, Inc.; *b.* Jen and Des Bartlett/Bruce Coleman. 54: *t.* © Tom McHugh/Photo Researchers, Inc.; *b.* G. Ziesler/Peter Arnold, Inc. 55: Animals Animals/R.W. and E.A. Schreiber; *b.* John Macgregor/Peter Arnold, Inc. 56: *t.* C. Allan Morgan/Peter Arnold, Inc.; *b.* Jerry L. Hout/Bruce Coleman. 57: *t.* Breck Kent; *b.* A. Blank/Bruce Coleman. 58: Silver Burdett & Ginn. 59: E.R. Degginger/Bruce Coleman. 60: *t.* © Alan Carey/Photo Researchers, Inc.; *m.* © Charlie Ott/Photo Researchers, Inc.; *b.* G. Ziesler/Peter Arnold, Inc. 61: *m.* Lynn M. Stone/Bruce Coleman; *b.* Kevin Byron/Bruce Coleman. 62: E.R. Degginger. 63: *l.* Bob and Clara Calhoun/Bruce Coleman; *t.r.* © Steve Maslowski/Photo Researchers, Inc., *b.r.* M.F. Soper/Bruce Coleman. 64: *l.* © Michael Fogden/Bruce Coleman; *r.* Richard P. Smith/Tom Stack & Associates. 65: *t.* E.R. Degginger; *b.* Stephen J. Krasemann/Peter Arnold, Inc. 66: *t.* Y. Arthus-Bertrand/Peter Arnold, Inc.; *b.l.* Jeff Foott/Bruce Coleman; *b.r.* Peter Menzel/Stock, Boston. 67: E.R.

Madison/Bruce Coleman. 194: © David M. Doody/Tom Stack & Associates. 196: *t.* Stewart M. Green/Tom Stack & Associates; *b.* © Howard Sochurek.

Chapter 9 Opener: Argonne National Laboratory; © Manfred Kage/Peter Arnold, Inc.; AT&T/Bell Laboratories; Courtesy of International Business Machine Corp. 203: Silver Burdett & Ginn. 204: *l.* Silver Burdett & Ginn; *r.* E.R. Degginger. 205: *l.* E.R. Degginger/Bruce Coleman; *m.* IMAGERY; *r.* Silver Burdett & Ginn. 206: Dan De Wilde for Silver Burdett & Ginn. 207: Silver Burdett & Ginn. 210: *t.* E.R. Degginger; *l., r.* Silver Burdett & Ginn. 211: Milton Rand/Tom Stack & Associates. 212, 213: Silver Burdett & Ginn. 214: Dan De Wilde. 215–217: Silver Burdett & Ginn. 217: *m.* Barry L. Runk/Grant Heilman Photography; *r.* © Alfred Pasieka/Taurus Photos. 218: *t.l.* © 1988 Chuck O'Rear/ Woodfin Camp & Associates; *m.l., b.l., t.r., m.r.* Silver Burdett & Ginn. 219: Nederlandese Philips Bedrijuen B.U. 220: Silver Burdett & Ginn. 221: *l., t.r., m., m.r.* Silver Burdett & Ginn; *b.* Dan De Wilde for Silver Burdett & Ginn. 222: Ford Motor Company. 226: *t.* Tom Tracy/The Stock Shop; *b.* Warren D. Colman/Tom Stack & Associates. 227: E.R. Degginger. 229: Silver Burdett & Ginn.

Unit Three 230: *t.* NASA; *b.* © Hans Pfletschinger/Peter Arnold, Inc. 230, 231: *b.* © Daedalus Enterprises/Peter Arnold, Inc. 231: *t.r.* © Steve Ogden/Tom Stack & Associates.

Chapter 10 Opener: Photo courtesy of Robert G. Moores, Jr./Black & Decker; E.R. Degginger; © James Hanley/ Photo Researchers, Inc.; C. Benjamin/Tom Stack & Associates; © M. Timothy O'Keefe/Tom Stack & Associates. 234: *t.l., m.l.* © Porterfield-Chickering/Photo Researchers, Inc.; *b.l.* Jack D. Swenson/Tom Stack & Associates; *b.r.* © Russ Kinne/Photo Researchers, Inc. 235: *l.* Bob McKeever/Tom Stack & Associates; *r.* Robert P. Carr/Bruce Coleman. 237: Lee Foster/Bruce Coleman. 238: *l.* © D.P. Hershkowitz/Bruce Coleman; *r.* E.R. Degginger/Bruce Coleman. 239: Hickson-Bender Photography for Silver Burdett & Ginn. 240: Owen Franken/Stock, Boston; *inset* Rick Smolan/Leo de Wys, Inc. 242: Silver Burdett & Ginn except *b.r.* © Alexander Lowry/Photo Researchers, Inc. 243: Silver Burdett & Ginn. 244: Dan De Wilde for Silver Burdett & Ginn. 245: Silver Burdett & Ginn. 246: Nicholas de Vore III/Bruce Coleman. 247: Bob Evans/Peter Arnold, Inc. 249: A. Rakoczy/Shostal Associates. 251: Silver Burdett & Ginn. 252: Dr. N.L. Zenkevitch; *inset* Christopher Springman. 253: Photo Research Int. 254: W.H. Hodge/Peter Arnold, Inc.

Chapter 11 Opener: Dr. Joseph Devine. 260: Adrian Davies/Bruce Coleman. 261: Courtesy of Dr. Takeo Susuki, UCLA. 266: *t.* Dan De Wilde for Silver Burdett & Ginn; *b.* Norman Tomalin/Bruce Coleman. 268: Hickson-Bender Photography for Silver Burdett & Ginn. 270: *l.* James Balog/Bruce Coleman; *r.* © 1988 Roger Werths/Woodfin Camp & Associates. 272: *l.* Ken Sakamoto/Black Star; *r.* Nicholas de Vore III/Bruce Coleman. 273: Keith Gunnar/Bruce Coleman. 274: U.S. Geological Survey. 275: *l.* Photo Research Int.; *r., inset* © Chuck O'Rear/Woodfin Camp & Associates. 276: C.B. Frith/Bruce Coleman. 277: Breck P. Kent. 278: *t.* Silver Burdett & Ginn; *b.* R.E. Pelham/Bruce Coleman. 279: *l.* Scott Ransom/Taurus Photos; *r.* © J.H. Robinson/Photo Researchers, Inc.

Chapter 12 Opener: © Joe Viesti for Silver Burdett & Ginn. 284: *t.l.* Silver Burdett & Ginn; *b.l.* © 1988 Mike Yamashita/Woodfin Camp & Associates; *r.* © 1988 Sepp Seitz/Woodfin Camp & Associates. 285: *l.* Silver Burdett & Ginn; *r.* E.R. Degginger/Bruce Coleman. 286: *l.* Silver Burdett & Ginn; *m.* Owen Franken/Stock, Boston; *r.* Runk/ Schoenberger/Grant Heilman Photography. 290: *t.l.* © 1988 Jim Brandenburg/Woodfin Camp & Associates; *b.l.* NASA; *r.* © Carleton Ray/Photo Researchers, Inc. 291: *l.* Gerald Davis/Contact Press Images; *r.* © Lawrence Migdale/Photo Researchers, Inc. 292: Jim McNee/Tom Stack & Associates. 294: W.H. Hodge/Peter Arnold, Inc. 299: Runk/Schoenberger/Grant Heilman Photography. 300: Edi Ann Otto. 301: *t.* Robert Screnco/Shostal Associates; *l.* NASA; *r.* © Dr. P. Menzel/Science Photo Library/Photo Researchers, Inc. 302: *t.* Herman J. Kokojan/Black Star; *b.* NASA.

Chapter 13 Opener: © Flip & Debra Schulke/Black Star; © Flip & Debra Schulke. 309: *l.* M. Timothy O'Keefe/Bruce Coleman; *r.* © Townsend P. Dickinson/ Photo Researchers, Inc. 310: *t.* Photo Enterprises, Inc./Bruce Coleman; *m.* Stouffer Enterprises, Inc./Bruce Coleman; *b.l.* Dr. M.R. Kundu, University of Maryland; *b.r.* Robert P. Carr/Bruce Coleman. 311: NASA. 312: Silver Burdett & Ginn. 314: Sovfoto. 315: Silver Burdett & Ginn. 316, 317: NASA. 319: *t.* NASA; *b.* © HSE/Science Source/Photo Researchers, Inc. 320–325: NASA. 326: Silver Burdett & Ginn. 327: Barry L. Runk/Grant Heilman Photography. 330: *t.* Michael Collier/Stock, Boston; *b.* Michal Heron. 331: David Siskind/Liaison.

Unit Four 334: *t.* © Ohio-Nuclear Corporation/Science Photo Library/Photo Researchers, Inc.; *b.* © David Madison. 335: *t.* © Steve Lissau/Rainbow; *b.* Shostal Associates.

Chapter 14 Opener: E.R. Degginger; The New York Times/Steve Miller. 338: © David Madison. 339: Dan De Wilde for Silver Burdett & Ginn. 340: Alfred Owczarzak/Taurus Photos. 342: David Madison/Bruce Coleman. 343: Dan De

Answers to matching exercise on page 49:

1. D, **2.** A, **3.** C, **4.** F, **5.** E, **6.** B

C D E F G H I J—VH—96 95 94 93 92 91 90 89